LIBRARY OF HEBREW BIBLE/ OLD TESTAMENT STUDIES

452

Formerly Journal for the Study of the Old Testament Supplement Series

T&T CLARK • LIBRARY OF BIBLICAL STUDIES •

MISSING PRIESTS

The Zadokites in Tradition and History

Alice Hunt

t&t clark

NEW YORK • LONDON

T & T Clark International, 80 Maiden Lane, New York, NY 10038

T & T Clark International, The Tower Building, 11 York Road, London SE1 7NX

T & T Clark International is a Continuum imprint.

Library of Congress Cataloging-in-Publication Data
Hunt, Alice.
Missing priests : the Zadokites in tradition and history / Alice Hunt.
p. cm. -- (Library of Hebrew Bible/Old Testament studies ; 452)
Includes bibliographical references and index.
ISBN-13: 978-0-567-02852-5 (hardcover)
ISBN-10: 0-567-02852-6 (hardcover)
1. Zadokites--History 2. Zadokites--Historiography. 3. Bible. O.T.--Criticism, interpretation, etc. 4. Judaism--History--Post-exilic period, 586 B.C.-210 A.D. I. Title. II. Series.

BM175.Z3H78 2006
296.4'95--dc21

2006022070

06 07 08 09 10 10 9 8 7 6 5 4 3 2 1

Printed and bound in Great Britain by Biddles Ltd., King's Lynn, Norfolk

To Eric and Carl and their asking of questions

CONTENTS

ACKNOWLEDGMENTS

Always already, I am thankful for the educational environment at Vanderbilt University. I am grateful to my teachers Renita Weems, Douglas Knight, Peter Haas, Karen Campbell, and James Barr. A special thanks to Victor Anderson who continually encourages better questions and to Dean James Hudnut-Beumler for wisdom and encouragement. And I am thankful for friends and colleagues who teach me and learn with me, Herbert Marbury, Annalisa Azzoni, Jack Sasson, Bill Hook, Paul DeHart, Forrest Harris, Monya Stubbs, Jon Berquist, Israel Finkelstein, Norma Franklin, Philip Davies, Magen Broshi, John Halligan, Kristin Swanson, Teresa Hornsby, Jennifer Koosed, Greg Carey, and Cheryl Kirk-Dugan. Thanks to Linzie Treadway and Kaye Nickell for their editing eyes. And thanks to my parents, Rosalie and Bob Hunt for feeding my love for the Bible and heritage and to my sons Carl and Eric Hudiburg, who continually inspire me. Finally, I am thankful for my learning colleagues at Vanderbilt University, students, staff, and faculty, for sustained and rigorous conversation.

ABBREVIATIONS

AB	Anchor Bible
ABD	*The Anchor Bible Dictionary*. Edited by D. N. Freedman. 6 vols. New York: Doubleday, 1992
ABRL	Anchor Bible Reference Library
AJSL	*American Journal of Semitic Languages and Literature*
AnBib	Analecta biblica
ANET	*Ancient Near Eastern Texts Relating to the Old Testament*. Edited by J. B. Pritchard. Princeton, 1954
APOT	*The Apocrypha and Pseudepigrapha of the Old Testament*. Edited by R. H. Charles. 2 vols. Chicago, 1926–1927
BA	*Biblical Archaeologist*
BAR	*Biblical Archaeology Review*
BDB	Brown, F., S. R. Driver, and C. A. Briggs. *A Hebrew and English Lexicon of the Old Testament*. Oxford, 1907
BHT	Beiträge zur historischen Theologie
BibInt	*Biblical Interpretation*
BibInt	Biblical Interpretation Series
BJRL	*Bulletin of the John Rylands University Library of Manchester*
BJS	Brown Judaic Studies
BR	*Bible Review*
BW	*The Biblical World: A Dictionary of Biblical Archaeology*. Edited by C. F. Pfeiffer. Grand Rapids, 1966
BZAW	Beihefte zur Zeitschrift für die alttestamentliche Wissenschaft
CANE	*Civilizations of the Ancient Near East*. Edited by J. Sasson. 4 vols. New York, 1995
CAT	Commentaire de l'Ancien Testament
CBC	Cambridge Bible Commentary
CBQ	*Catholic Biblical Quarterly*
CD	Damascus Document
CHJ	*Cambridge History of Judaism*. Edited by W. D. Davies and Louis Finkelstein. Cambridge: Cambridge University Press, 1989
ConBOT	Coniectanea biblica: Old Testament
DJD	Discoveries in the Judaean Desert
DSD	*Dead Sea Discoveries*
Enc	*Encounter*
EncJud	*Encyclopaedia Judaica*. Jerusalem: The Macmillan Company, 1971
ESHM	European Seminar in Historical Methodology
ET	English translation
ExpTim	*Expository Times*
FOTL	The Forms of the Old Testament Literature

FRLANT	Forschungen zur Religion und Literatur des Alten und Neuen Testaments
HAT	Handbuch zum Alten Testament
HeyJ	*Heythrop Journal*
HSM	Harvard Semitic Monographs
HTR	*Harvard Theological Review*
HUCA	*Hebrew Union College Annual*
ICC	International Critical Commentary
IDB	*The Interpreter's Dictionary of the Bible: An Illustrated Encyclopedia.* Edited by George Arthur Buttrick. Nashville, 1962
IEJ	*Israel Exploration Journal*
Int	*Interpretation*
ITC	International Theological Commentary
JAOS	*Journal of the American Oriental Society*
JBL	*Journal of Biblical Literature*
JCS	*Journal of Cuneiform Studies*
JE	*The Jewish Encyclopedia.* Edited by Isidore Singer. 12 vols. New York, 1905
JJS	*Journal of Jewish Studies*
JNES	*Journal of Near Eastern Studies*
JPOS	*Journal of Palestine Oriental Society*
JSJ	*Journal for the Study of Judaism in the Persian, Hellenistic and Roman Period*
JSJSup	Journal for the Study of Judaism in the Persian, Hellenistic and Roman Period: Supplement Series
JSOT	*Journal for the Study of the Old Testament*
JSOTSup	Journal for the Study of the Old Testament: Supplement Series
JSP	*Journal for the Study of the Pseudepigrapha*
JSS	*Journal of Semitic Studies*
JTS	*Journal of Theological Studies*
LHBOTS	Library of Hebrew Bible/Old Testament Studies
NCB	New Century Bible
OBT	Overtures to Biblical Theology
OTG	Old Testament Guides
OTL	Old Testament Library
OtSt	Oudtestamentische Studiën
RevQ	*Revue de Qumran*
SBLDS	Society of Biblical Literature Dissertation Series
SBLSymS	Society of Biblical Literature Symposium Series
SJLA	Studies in Judaism in Late Antiquity
STDJ	Studies on the Texts of the Deserts of Judah
TBC	Torch Bible Commentaries
TynBul	*Tyndale Bulletin*
VT	*Vetus Testamentum*
VTSup	Vetus Testamentum Supplements
ZAW	*Zeitschrift für die alttestamentliche Wissenschaft*

Chapter 1

PRESUPPOSITIONS SET THE PARADIGM: ZADOKITES AS THE DOMINANT PRIESTHOOD

The Issue

The extent to which modern scholarship has magnified the prominence of Zadokites as the dominant priestly institution from the monarchy through much of the Second Temple period cannot be substantiated. No extant evidence attests their existence in monarchic Israel. Rather, the Second Temple period serves as the *terminus a quo* for all literary references to the Zadokites and provides a socio-historical context which allows for the development of a plausible reconstruction explaining their appearance in the ancient texts.

As early as the turn of the twentieth century, biblical scholars began to articulate concerns about the ambiguous nature of any study of (the) priesthood in ancient Israel. In 1902, W. R. Smith and A. Bertholet, discussing priests as seen in P, note, "How these stand related to the sons of Zadok...is an excessively puzzling question to which a conclusive answer is, in the silence of the sources, perhaps impossible."[1] For G. B. Gray, in 1925, "The difficulty attaching to most questions of Jewish history is perhaps at its greatest in relation to the priesthood."[2] Eighty years later,

1. W. R. Smith and A. Bertholet, "Priests," in *Encyclopaedia Biblical: A Critical Dictionary of the Literary Political and Religious History the Archaeology Geography and Natural History of the Bible* (ed. R. K. Cheyne and J. Sutherland Black; New York: Macmillan, 1902), 3844.

2. George Buchanan Gray, *Sacrifice in the Old Testament: Its Theory and Practice* (Oxford: Clarendon, 1925), 211. Gray further reflects on the paradoxical conundrum found in the elusive nature of this crucial aspect in the history of ancient Israel: "It may at once be said that some of these questions are far more readily raised than answered, and that for precise and complete answers, the data simply do not exist. Yet it is important to determine, if not the extent of our knowledge, the depth of our ignorance, that what knowledge is possible may be the more clearly and vividly apprehended" (ibid.).

the challenges remain; Gary Knoppers states, "The early history of the priesthood is one of the most intractable problems in the reconstruction of Israelite religion."[3]

Unquestionably the priests of ancient Israel are pivotal figures for understanding both biblical texts and historical contexts of related periods; yet we know little about these priests or their priesthoods. Understanding these axial figures is critical for understanding biblical texts and historical contexts of related periods. Frequently biblical scholars and historians of ancient Israel base their histories of ancient Israel on assumptions about priests and priesthoods, likely as a consequence of previous work or historiographic method and yet, without plentiful data, historical conclusions have been difficult to substantiate. Broad issues as well as specifics about the priesthood remain obscure for contemporary scholarship.[4] Who were priests in ancient Israel? How did the priesthood or priesthoods form? What role did the priests play? Was there linear development of a single priesthood in ancient Israel? Was there a lineage system within priesthoods of ancient Israel and was the priestly position passed patrilineally? How did the priesthood fit into the social structure of ancient Israel? Were there high priests in ancient Israel and, if there were, when did the institution of high-priesthood come into being? Of the priestly groups named in biblical material—the Mushites, the Aaronites, the house of Dan, the house of Bethel, the house of Jerusalem, the sons of Zadok, the sons of Eli, the Levites, and the priests of Shiloh—what do we know about their origins, roles, and interactions? Was there competition between priestly groups? How and when did priests contribute to the formation of the biblical material? How and when did priests come to be mentioned in the biblical material? How does our understanding of priesthood in ancient Israel contribute to our vision of the history of ancient Israel?

3. Gary N. Knoppers, *I Chronicles 10–29: A New Translation with Introduction and Commentary* (AB 12A; New York: Doubleday, 2004), 707.

4. For example, see Joseph Blenkinsopp, *Ezekiel* (Interpretation; Louisville, Ky.: John Knox, 1990), and Lester L. Grabbe, *Priests, Prophets, Diviners and Sages: A Socio-Historical Study of Religious Specialists in Ancient Israel* (Valley Forge, Pa.: Trinity, 1995). Both acknowledge the elusive nature of understanding ancient Israelite priesthoods. Disclaimers are frequent. Heinrich Ewald, regarding biblical material as providing historical accounts, uses phrases such as "as far as we can conclude." Regarding 1 Chr 5:34–41 (ET 6:8–15), Ewald (*The History of Israel.* Vol. 3, *The Rise and Splendour of the Hebrew Monarchy* [8 vols.; 2d ed.; London: Longmans, Green & Co., 1878], 268), comments on the misfortunes of being supplied with only one "passage in the O.T. where the line of these High Priests is recorded."

While some studies raise questions about various aspects of priesthood and priestly groups among the priesthoods of ancient Israel, few make direct inquiries about the Zadokites. And yet this particular priestly group, בני צדוק, the sons of Zadok, generally are thought to have gained the high-priesthood under the reign of David and retained this dominance until the time of the Hasmoneans.[5] Assumptions about the Zadokites are wide reaching; data are scarce.

Placing the Zadokites

Among scholars writing histories, introductory texts, and commentaries, some do not mention the Zadokites and many assume the prominence of a Zadokite priesthood during the monarchic period. Those not mentioning the Zadokites include Iain Provan, V. Philips Long, and Tremper Longman III in their 2003 *A Biblical History of Israel*, Alberto Soggins in his 1984 *A History of Ancient Israel*, Bernard Anderson in his *Understanding the Old Testament*,[6] Ronald Clements in his 1996 commentary on Ezekiel,[7] Henry McKeating in his 1993 commentary on Ezekiel,[8] and Gösta Ahlström in his 1993 *The History of Ancient Palestine*.[9] Several scholars raise questions about priestly identity but do not delve deeply in Zadokite issues.[10]

5. While some scholarship assumes dominance only until the exile, examples are not cited here since they are discussed throughout this chapter.

6. Iain Provan, V. Philips Long, and Tremper Longman III, *A Biblical History of Israel* (Louisville, Ky.: Westminster John Knox, 2003) (these authors mention Zadok as David's priest at pp. 236, 248); J. Alberto Soggin, *A History of Ancient Israel* (Philadelphia: Westminster, 1984); Bernard Anderson, *Understanding the Old Testament* (4th ed.; Englewood Cliffs: Prentice–Hall, 1986).

7. Ronald Clements, *Ezekiel* (Westminster Bible Companion; Louisville, Ky.: Westminster John Knox, 1996).

8. Henry McKeating, *Ezekiel* (OTG; Sheffield: Sheffield Academic Press, 1993.)

9. Gösta Ahlström (with a contribution by Gary O. Rollefson), *The History of Ancient Palestine* (ed. D. V. Edelman; Sheffield: Sheffield Academic Press; Minneapolis: Fortress, 1993). He mentions "Zadoq" in his discussion on David.

10. Morton Smith, *Palestinian Parties and Politics that Shaped the Old Testament* (New York: Columbia University Press, 1971), seems to assume the traditional dominant Zadokite interpretation but makes plain his questions: "The priests of the Jerusalem temple had been instrumental in introducing the deuteronomic reform under Josiah which prohibited sacrifice outside Jerusalem, but they had refused to implement the deuteronomic law that Levites from other holy places might serve in the Jerusalem temple. They had cooperated in syncretistic worship of Yahweh with the rulers before and after Josiah, but they had also, during or after the exile, claimed that only they, the *soi-disant* descendants of Zadok, had remained faithful to Yahweh alone, and that, in consequence, only they should be permitted to serve at the

Many follow a traditional interpretation placing the Zadokites in control of a centralized Jerusalem priesthood. In their *A History of Ancient Israel and Judah*, J. Maxwell Miller and John J. Hayes assume a "Zadokite line established under David and Solomon" that was dismantled by

altar of the restored temple" (pp. 170–71). We might also read Smith as doubting a Zadokite dominance.

Marc Z. Brettler, *The Creation of History in Ancient Israel* (London: Routledge, 1995), states, "The Chronicler, however, in an effort to legitimate the Zadokites' role as priests, has made them linear descendants of Aaron, the first high priest (1 Chr 5:29–34). Though it does not reflect historical reality, this genealogy is indistinguishable in form from genealogies which are thought to accurately reflect family relationships" (p. 137). Brettler questions but still seems to assume the existence of a Zadokite priesthood.

Lester Grabbe, in *Priests, Prophets, Diviners, Sages*, is alert to the questionable aspects of a dominant Zadokite priesthood: "Even though the text attempts to give a smooth synthetic picture, it cannot disguise the fact that there are various priestly groups and that a certain tension exists among them. The dominant picture is probably a priesty one, which divides the clergy into Aaronites, who preside at the altar, and Levites, who form the inferior clergy with more menial tasks though Levitical duties could include positions of power in the areas of security (e.g. gatekeepers) and the fabric of the building. Deuteronomy clearly sees no such division, however, suggesting a historical development in which some viewed all priests as Levites and equal, but this view did not ultimately prevail. Stories about the sin of the Levites and about their punishment by being deprived of service at the altar were no doubt circulated to support the main priestly position (cf. Ezek 44:10–14). Yet even among the priests, there are hints at diverse groups: Ezekiel considers Zadokites alone as worthy to preside at the altar, apparently lumping the other Aaronites in with the Levites. There is also a hint at a group descended from Moses, though someone has tampered with the text at this point to disguise the fact (Judges 18:30; 3.1.3). The text thus seems to bear discrete witness to serious rivalries, which developed and were fought out in the history of the priesthood. Eventually some sort of compromise was apparently reached by the Second Temple period, since we hear nothing further of major disputes in the literature of this period. The final result of the various struggles for position was basically a twofold division of the priesthood. All 'Aaronites' were priests and could carry out the duties relating to the altar. The 'Zadokites' may have become a specific family of these from whom the high priests were traditionally drawn, but otherwise there is little to suggest a special position for them (but cf. Ezek 44:15). Apart from the sacrificial system, the priests had to make decisions about cultic practices, judge whether a leper could be declared clean or not (Lev 14–15), and declare on other matters of ritual purity (Hag 2). The 'Levites' were responsible for the more menial functions of cleaning, carrying, provisioning, and running the temple in general. The only major change was at the time of the Maccabean revolt, when the high priesthood was taken out of the traditional ('Zadokite'?) line, an act apparently not accepted by some groups (cf. *Damascus Document* 3.21–4.4, etc.)" (p. 195).

the Babylonian exile.[11] Gerhard von Rad places the pre-exilic priesthood in the hands of the Zadokites.[12] John Van Seters follows suite: "It also parallels the promise to David of a 'sure house' and clearly refers to the Zadokite priesthood established by David for the service of the Jerusalem Temple. A new era is marked not only by the election of David and the building of the Temple but also by the beginning of a new priestly line."[13] In the second edition of *A Theological Introduction to the Old Testament*, Bruce Birch, Walter Brueggemann, Terrence E. Fretheim, and David L. Peterson make two references to the Zadokites. While reviewing the history of Eli's sons, they state, "God will raise up a new faithful priest (Zadok, made the priestly family of Solomon's temple, 1 Kgs 2:35)" and when discussing the temple, they note "...Solomon's appointment of Zadok and his descendants as the permanent priesthood of the temple in Jerusalem."[14] Norman Gottwald, in *The Hebrew Bible: A Socio-Literary Introduction*, likewise assumes a dominant Zadokite priesthood in Jerusalem during the monarchy, noting simply, "The Samuel birth and 'call' stories (1 Samuel 1–3) were recognized to justify the replacement of the Elide priests of Shiloh with the line of Zadok of Jerusalem later installed by David (1 Sam. 2:27–36; cf. 2 Sam. 15:24–37; 20:25; 1 Kings 1:22–39; 2:26–27)."[15] Robert Wilson assumes Zadokite dominance as well: "If Abiathar was indeed a descendant of Eli, then some form of the oracle now contained in 1 Sam 2:22–36 may have been used either by the Zadokites to explain how they came to be the sole

11. J. Maxwell Miller and John H. Hayes, *A History of Ancient Israel and Judah* (Philadelphia: Westminster, 1986), 426. They name the "...family of Zadok, the ruling priestly family in Jerusalem" (p. 457; cf. also p. 173) but note the caveats they provide about Zadokite lineage (pp. 114–15).

12. Gerhard von Rad, *Old Testament Theology*. Vol. 1, *The Theology of Israel's Historical Traditions* (trans. D.M.G. Stalker; New York: HarperCollins, 1962), 248–49; trans. of *Theologie des Alten Testaments*. Vol. 1, *Die Theologie der geschichtlichen Überlieferungen Israels* (Munich: Kaiser, 1957), and including revisions for 2d German ed., 1962. Von Rad also notes uncertainties about timing, "We do not know from what date the Zadokites regarded themselves the legitimate descendants of Aaron. Ezekiel still designates the priesthood at Jerusalem as Zadokite (Ezek. XLIV.15) but P knows only of the Aaronites" (p. 1:249). Also, "There is a secret surrounding the priest Zadok which it is now pretty well impossible to unveil..." (p. 1:249 n. 144).

13. John Van Seters, *In Search of History: Historiography in the Ancient World and the Origins of Biblical History* (New Haven: Yale University Press, 1983), 351.

14. Bruce C. Birch et al., *A Theological Introduction to the Old Testament* (2d ed.; Nashville: Abingdon, 2005), 225, 252.

15. Norman K. Gottwald, *The Hebrew Bible: A Socio-Literary Introduction* (Philadelphia: Fortress, 1985), 312–13.

priestly house in the Jerusalem temple or by the descendants of Abiathar to explain why they lost their priestly office."[16] In *The Old Testament: Text and Context*, Victor Matthews and James Moyer place the monarchic and the Hasmonean priesthood in the hands of the Zadokites; in speaking of high priesthood,

> According to tradition, the office was to be held by a member of the Zadokite priestly family (Ezra 7:1–6). The connection that this family had to the temple worship during the preexilic period provided legitimacy for the position of high priest. It also reassured the people that, at least in matters of religion, nothing had changed.[17]

John J. Collin's *Introduction to the Hebrew Bible* names the Zadokites "Priests descended from Zadok (priest under David and Solomon)" and "High Priests in the Second Temple period…down to the Maccabean revolt."[18] Martin Noth states,

> For it is through this Eleazar that the postexilic high priests traced their lineage from Aaron (I Chron. 5:30–41) by way of the Zadokites, who officiated as priests in the state sanctuary at Jerusalem during the period of the Davidic kings. The question may be raised as to whether for some unknown reason these Zadokites at one time usurped the tradition of the Eliezer group—concerning whose historical position we know absolutely nothing—and traced their line back to Moses, only to exchange Moses later with Aaron, as did the Gersonite.[19]

In his commentary on Ezekiel, Walther Eichrodt states "…Zadok evidently became the sole high priest of the Jerusalem sanctuary and his successors naturally tried to presume this privileged position in the sanctuary when its importance continued to increase after the fall of

16. Robert R. Wilson, *Prophecy and Society in Ancient Israel* (Philadelphia: Fortress, 1980), 171. Also see his note on Ezekiel, "He was thus a Zadokite, with deep roots in the priestly traditions of the Jerusalemite establishment" (p. 282).

17. Victor H. Matthews and James C. Moyer, *The Old Testament: Text and Context* (Peabody, Mass.: Hendrickson, 1997), 108, 215, 253.

18. John J. Collins, *Introduction to the Hebrew Bible with CD-Rom* (Minneapolis: Fortress, 2004), 613. He also names Ezekiel a Zadokite priest (p. 358; cf. p. 373).

19. Martin Noth, *A History of Pentateuchal Traditions* (trans. with an Introduction by Bernhard W. Anderson; Scholars Press Reprints and Translations Series; Atlanta: Scholars Press, 1981; repr. from Englewood Cliffs, N. J.: Prentice–Hall, 1972), 185–86. Noth suggests it was the Zadokites who formed the new sanctuary in the Persian period (*The Deuteronomistic History* [JSOTSup 15; Sheffield: Sheffield Academic Press, 1981], 316; trans. of *Überlieferungsgeschichtliche Studien* [2d. ed.; Tübingen: Niemeyer, 1957; 3d ed., 1967], pp. 1–110; first appeared as "Schriften der Königsberger Gelehrten Gesellschaft," *Geisteswissenschaftliche Klasse* 18 [1943]: 43–266).

northern Israel."[20] Johannes Pederson attributes the monarchic priesthood to the Zadokites: "The priesthood at the royal temple of Jerusalem was organized under a leader even in the monarchical period. The first in Solomon's time was Zadok, from whom the whole of the ruling priesthood traced its descent."[21] Likewise, Max Weber sets the Zadokites in a primary position: "The Zadokites, since Solomon, were the leading priest sib of the king of Jerusalem"[22] and this struggle of the priesthood

> necessarily grew in intensity when the Jerusalemite priesthood, then the Zadokite, drew the final conclusions after the destruction of the Northern Kingdom and raised the quite unheard claim, in the face of the clear old tradition, that from now on there should exist a Temple and ritualistically fully-qualified place of sacrifice only in Jerusalem.[23]

In his *Kingdom of Priests: A History of Old Testament Israel*, Eugene Merrill states: "This mistake on Abiathar's part cost him the priesthood, for Solomon, once he had become king, deposed him and replaced him with Zadok alone. Thus the priesthood of Eli came to an end and the Zadokite began in a formal manner."[24] Likewise we find in *A People of the Covenant: An Introduction to the Old Testament*,

> David's successor Solomon made Zadok the chief priest and, from then until the beginning of the Babylonian exile in 587 B.C.E., Zadok's line was responsible for worship in the Jerusalem Temple, the most important Israelite sanctuary. After the exile, the Aaronic family of priests again claimed authority and for all practical purposes the two lines of priests were united.[25]

20. Walther Eichrodt, *Ezekiel* (trans. Cosslett Quinn; OTL; London: SCM Press, 1970), 565. Eichrodt also sees the Zadokites as Levitical priests as distinct from the country Levites and identifies them as the priests who did not stray.

21. Johannes Pedersen, *Israel: Its Life and Culture* (trans. Aslaug Møller; 2 vols.; South Florida Studies in the History of Judaism 29; Atlanta: Scholars, 1991), 2:165. Also he notes the "transference of the priesthood from the house of Eli to that of Zadok" (p. 2:154), and that "at Jerusalem the descendants of Zadok survived down through the ages as the leading priesthood..." (p. 2:174). Also see pp. 2:184–97.

22. Max Weber, *Ancient Judaism* (ed. and trans. Hans H. Gerth and Don Martindale; New York: Free Press, 1982), 181.

23. Weber, *Ancient Judaism*, 183. Also according to Weber, the Zadokites, in pre-Deuteronomic times, "were treated as part of the Aaronites" (p. 182), and "Ezekiel still advocated the monopoly of the Jerusalemite Zadokites..." (p. 185).

24. Eugene H. Merrill, *Kingdom of Priests: A History of Old Testament Israel* (Grand Rapids: Baker, 1996), 283. Also, he states that the priesthood was taken "from Eli's line and given to Zadok, a descendant of Eleazar (1 Kings 2:35; cf. Num. 3; 1 Chron. 6:8)" (pp. 175–76).

25. Henry J. Flanders, Robert W. Crapps, and David A. Smith, *People of the Covenant: An Introduction to the Old* Testament (3d ed.; New York: Oxford University Press, 1988), 188.

Rainer Albertz, in both *A History of Israelite Religion in the Old Testament Period* and *Israel in Exile: The History and Literature of the Sixth Century* B.C.E., recognizes the Zadokites as the dominant priesthood in the monarchic period and in the postexilic vision of Ezekiel's followers: "Ministry at the altar and in the temple building itself was to be taken over exclusively by the old Zadokite priesthood of Jerusalem."[26] Richard Nelson assumes Zadokite dominance throughout his *Raising Up a Faithful Priest: Community and Priesthood in Biblical Theology*, as do Risto Nurmela in *The Levites: Their Emergence as a Second-Class Priesthood* and Kyung-jin Min in *The Levitical Authorship of Ezra–Nehemiah*.[27] Martin S. Jaffee joins the traditional viewpoint: "Reputed to be a descendant of Aaron, Zadok had been appointed High Priest by King Solomon (I Ki. 2:35). His descendants dominated the Jerusalem Temple throughout much of the history of ancient Yehudah and, it appears, were installed in the High Priesthood during the Persian and Hellenistic periods as well."[28] Robert B. Coote and Mary P. Coote, in *Power, Politics, and the Making of the Bible*, follow suit,

> For the temple cult David's veteran priest Zadok, now also Solomon's national security adviser, whose family claimed Aaron as its forebear, established a state priesthood of cult specialists, a caste that, like the top echelons of the military, became hereditary. (Zadok's name continued powerful in Judah through subsequent centuries and appears in the New Testament in the name of the Sadducees.)[29]

Michael D. Coogan raises critical issues concerning priestly rivalries and identity throughout his new introductory text, *The Old Testament:*

26. Rainer Albertz, *Israel in Exile: The History and Literature of the Sixth Century* B.C.E. (trans. David Green; Studies in Biblical Literature 3; Atlanta: Society of Biblical Literature, 2003), 371, and *A History of Israelite Religion in the Old Testament Period.* Vol. 1, *From the Beginnings to the End of the Monarchy* (trans. John Bowden; OTL; Louisville, Ky.: Westminster John Knox, 1992).

27. Richard D. Nelson, *Raising Up a Faithful Priest: Community and Priesthood in Biblical Theology* (Louisville, Ky.: Westminster John Knox, 1993). See especially pp. 6–15 and p. 12 Fig. 1. Nelson discusses lineage issues as well. See too Risto Nurmela, *The Levites: Their Emergence as a Second-Class Priesthood* (South Florida Studies in the History of Judaism 193; Atlanta: Scholars Press, 1998), 73–81, 101–6; Kyung-jin Min, *The Levitical Authorship of Ezra–Nehemiah* (JSOTSup 409; London: T. & T. Clark International, 2004), passim, and note his references to the Zadokites in his discussion of the Levites in P (pp. 62–65).

28. Martin S. Jaffee, *Early Judaism* (Upper Saddle River, N. J.: Prentice–Hall, 1997), 139.

29. Robert B. Coote and Mary P. Coote, *Power, Politics, and the Making of the Bible: An Introduction* (Minneapolis: Fortress, 1990), 36. Also see p. 28 and their reference to "Zadokite Aaronids," 78.

A Historical and Literary Introduction to the Hebrew Scriptures. In the end, he acquiesces to a traditional view of the Zadokites in his discussion of the Hellenistic period, stating: "One of the precipitating factors in the Maccabean revolt was that the high priesthood, a hereditary office passed from father to son that since the time of David had belonged to the descendants of Zadok...was first corrupted and then transferred by the Seleucid rulers to non-Zadokites."[30] In his *A Journey Through the Hebrew Scriptures*, Frank Frick provides a concise summary of the traditional viewpoint concerning the Zadokites:

> Before the destruction of the Temple by the Babylonians, the Zadokite priesthood (believed to be descendants of Zadok, a priest in the time of David—2 Sam 8:15–17) had dominated the Temple and the cult at Jerusalem. Because they belonged to the upper levels of the society, however, they were taken away into exile. While in exile, they made plans for the restoration of the temple cult and priesthood, some of which are reflected in the book of Ezekiel. In the absence of the Zadokites, the Levites, with others who remained in Judah, exercised control of the cult and developed their own plans concerning the restoration of the Temple cult and priesthood. When the Zadokites returned to Jerusalem, conflict arose between them and the Levites. The Levites gradually lost ground in this struggle and had to endure much suffering. In the struggle with the Zadokites, the Levites were excluded from the principal religious and social institutions of the postexilic community, becoming a marginalized group.[31]

Lawrence H. Schiffman connects the Zadokites with the Sadducees: "The Sadducees derived their name from that of Zadok, the high priest of the Jerusalem Temple in the time of Solomon. The Zadokite family of high priests had served as the head of the priesthood throughout First Temple times, except when foreign worship was brought into the temple,

30. Michael D. Coogan, *The Old Testament: A Historical and Literary Introduction to the Hebrew Scriptures* (New York: Oxford University Press, 2006), 506, but also see 133, 140–42, 146–48, 156–58, 164, 178–79, 260–61, 420, 504. Other scholars, including Jon Berquist, while not naming the Zadokites directly, note the crucial evidence of conflict between priestly factions throughout his book *Judaism in Persia's Shadow* (Minneapolis: Fortress, 1995). Note, for example, his comment that "The Yehudite priesthood of Jerusalem's Second Temple was not the first manifestation of a religious hierarchy. Monarchic Jerusalem had produced an elaborate temple cult that had endured in Jerusalem for over three centuries. The earlier priesthood maintained a conscientious existence in the midst of conflict between two powerful priestly families, this difficulty continued through the monarchy" (p. 150).

31. Frank S. Frick, *A Journey through the Hebrew Scriptures* (A Completely Revised and Expanded Edition; 2d ed.; Belmont, Calif.: Wadsworth/Thomson, 2003; 1st ed., New York: Harcourt Brace, 1995), 527.

and during Second Temple times until the Hasmoneans took control of the high priesthood.[32]

Clyde E. Fant, Donald W. Musser, and Mitchell Reddish add to that traditional interpretation in their *An Introduction to the Bible: Revised Edition*: "The traditional view of the Sadducees understands them as being composed mainly of aristocratic and priestly families in Palestine. Their name is likely derived from Zadok who as an important priest during the reigns of David and Solomon and whose descendants provided the majority of High Priests in Judaism."[33]

Joseph Blenkinsopp consistently questions details of priestly history and raises specific and crucial issues about the Zadokites in 1995 in *Sage, Priest, Prophet*:

> It is generally assumed that the Zadok line continued to occupy the office of chief priest during the Judean monarchy. This may be correct, but the name never occurs again in Dtr after the reign of Solomon, and there is no hard evidence even that the preexilic priestly leadership in Jerusalem was hereditary. The next mention of Zadok and Zadokites occurs in Ezekiel's 'law of the temple' in chapters 40–48, or, more probably, in contentious additions made to it (Ezek. 40:46; 43:19; 44:15; 48:11). From these we gather that some time in the late exilic or early postexilic period, a priestly faction claiming descent from a real or putative Zadok, priest of David and Solomon, arrogated to itself exclusive rights to the office, privileges, and perquisites of the Jerusalem priesthood.[34]

32. Lawrence H. Schiffman, *From Text to Tradition: A History of Second Temple and Rabbinic Judaism* (Hoboken: Ktav, 1991), 108. He also mentions the Zadokites when discussing Chronicles: "The centrality of the Zadokite priesthood, descended from Zadok, who served as high priest during the reign of David, is also stressed throughout the book" (p. 52).

Likewise, Helmut Koester, in his *Introduction to the New Testament*, Vol. 1, *History, Culture and Religion of the Hellenistic Age* (New York: de Gruyter, 1982); trans. of Chapters 1–6 of *Einführung in das Neue Testament* (Berlin: de Gruyter, 1980), discussing the Sadducee derivation from the Zadokites, states, "Ezekiel and Ezra had demanded that the descendants of Zadok the high priest of David, should always provide the high priest…" (p. 229). Scholars such as Jacob Z. Lauterbach, "Sadducees and Pharisees: A Study of Their Respective Attitudes Towards the Law," in *Studies in Jewish Literature Issues in Honor of Professor Kaufmann Kohler, Ph.D., on the Occasion of His Seventieth Birthday* (Berlin: Reimer, 1913), 176–98; Yehezkel Kaufmann, *History of the Religion of Israel*. Vol. 4, *From the Babylonian Captivity to the End of Prophecy* (New York: Ktav, 1977); and Hugo Mantel, "The Dichotomy of Judaism During the Second Temple," *HUCA* 44 (1974): 55–87, associate the Zadokites with the Sadducees.

33. Clyde E. Fant, Donald W. Musser, and Mitchell G. Reddish, *An Introduction to the Bible* (rev. ed.; Nashville: Abingdon, 2001), 262.

34. Joseph Blenkinsopp, *Sage, Priest, Prophet* (Louisville, Ky.: Westminster John Knox, 1995), 76–77. Also see p. 89.

And again, Blenkinsopp notes, "While there is nothing inherently improbable about a Zadokite dynasty of priests in control of the Temple under the monarchy, it is poorly supported and may be another example of the tendency to construct the past in the light of contemporary realities."[35]

Summary

What do we really know? What evidence do we have and how should we interpret that evidence? The priest Zadok plays an important role in the narratives about the early monarchy; the sons of Zadok are the preeminent priestly family in Ezekiel's temple vision; and the sons of Zadok appear as the righteous ones in the Dead Sea Scrolls. In fact, substantial textual evidence regarding Zadok or a Zadokite priesthood remains scarce. The Hebrew Bible contains few references to the Zadokites.[36] In fact, all four references to the בני צדוק, "sons of Zadok," occur in one small section of the book of Ezekiel (Ezek 40:45–46; 43:18–19; 44:6–16; 48:9–11.). Second Chronicles 31:10 makes reference to בית צדוק, "house of Zadok." In an oft-debated portion of the writings of Ben Sira (51:13–30), the "sons of Zadok" are mentioned. Later works such as the *Damascus Document* of Khirbet Qumran and the *Zadokite Fragments* of the Cairo genizah refer to the "sons of Zadok." These extrabiblical references are discussed in Chapter 6.

Recognized concurrently as critical figures for historical understanding and as historically elusive, the Zadokites present an opportunity for

35. Ibid., 84. He continues, "We cannot, in other words, exclude the possibility that a branch of the priesthood named for Zadok, priest of David and Solomon, created the genealogical link as a way of claiming continuity with the past, thereby establishing its own legitimacy."

Lester Grabbe, *Judaic Religion in the Second Temple Period: Belief and Practice from the Exile to Yavneh* (London: Routledge, 2000), raises similar questions concerning the postexilic period: "One question is what family held the high priesthood, since it is often asserted that the high priest had to be a Zadokite in pre-Maccabean times. Although Ezekiel (e.g. 43:15–16) confines the priesthood to the Zadokites, most of our sources say nothing on this question (though compare the expression 'sons of Zadok' for priests in some of the Qumran scrolls), and it is not at all clear that the Oniad family claimed to be of Zadokite descent" (p. 145).

36. צדוק is mentioned fifty-three times. At least twenty-two of the twenty-six occurrences in Samuel–Kings refer to a priest named Zadok. The other four refer to Ahimaaz son of Zadok (three times) or Jerusha daughter of Zadok. Chronicles has seventeen references to someone named "Zadok" (of these, eight seem to refer to a priest). Ezra–Nehemiah contains six references to persons named "Zadok," and a "Zadok" is cited in both First Esdras and Second Esdras. In Josephus' work, the name "Zadok" occurs in material about the monarchy, but there is no reference at all to Zadokites (sons of Zadok).

today's scholars both to examine how we function as historiographers and to attend to the Zadokites as a major focal point. The present study makes an assessment of the Zadokites by locating them historiographically in biblical scholarship, by analyzing historiographic methods used in this scholarship, and then by offering a portrait of the Zadokites through historiographic, literary, and social-scientific analysis.

This comprehensive treatment of the Zadokites and their place in the Hebrew Bible requires the integration of three methodological approaches. First, a study of historiography traces the growth of scholarly notions concerning the Zadokites (Chapters 1 and 2). In addition to providing a thorough history and analysis of previous research on the Zadokites, the present project examines historiographic issues related to the development of these conceptualizations. The investigation includes an examination of theoretical approaches, historical starting points, underlying historical assumptions, consideration given to source material, and incorporation of external and comparative data.

Second, literary analysis indicates the role and status of the Zadokites in the available textual evidence (Chapters 4 and 5, and 6). Although an examination of the extant texts involves the review of previous literary scholarship, this study primarily pursues an understanding of the development of the Zadokites within the respective texts.

A socio-historical portrait completes the study. Gerhard Lenski's macro-sociological theory, which incorporates components of functional and conflict theories, forms the theoretical basis for the presentation of a socio-historical reconstruction and will attempt to answer questions such as: Who placed the Zadokites in these texts? Why were the Zadokites included in these texts? In particular, Lenski's work makes possible an inquiry into the results of group interactions as various segments of society respond to internal power struggles and external pressure from the imperial overlords, situating the Zadokites in relation to the Dead Sea Scrolls.

Chapter 2

HISTORIOGRAPHY AND THE ZADOKITES

Historiography: The Importance of Pre-judgments

> The relation between a historian and his facts is one of equality, of give-and-take. As any working historian knows, the historian is engaged in a continuous process of moulding his facts to his interpretation and his interpretation to his facts.[1]

This chapter seeks to examine conceptualizations of the Zadokites as they have been taken for granted and have consequently led to certain presuppositions used to construct the historical context of the Zadokites. This study ultimately seeks to demystify the historical and hermeneutical positions of the Zadokites while concurrently appreciating and engaging the tradition out of which these positions arose. It seeks to disclose the pre-judgments co-present with presuppositions in order to open discourse about the Zadokites.

Early Tradition and Scholarship

Built upon the tradition and scholarship of earlier periods, the nineteenth century provides a clear starting point for discussing the relationship between Zadokites and biblical scholarship. Thus this study takes up the trajectory of biblical historiography as it relates to Zadokites in the nineteenth century. When the Renaissance methods of textual criticism were applied to biblical texts, new interpretations challenged traditional historiography which subsequently served as an outlet for ideological and political tensions of the day. Questions facing biblical historiography included applications of scientific developments to the verification of previous interpretations of events, increasing application of literary and documentary criticism to biblical texts, and application of comparative

1. Edward H. Carr, *What Is History?* (New York: Knopf, 1962), 29.

analysis to biblical texts using other ancient material. While some questions prompted a developing critical inspection, others remained taken for granted as part of a foundational historiographic schema. In particular, those questions interested in biblical history retained the presumption of a direct relationship between the order of the biblical books and their presumed historicity as generated by early historiographers.[2]

As early as mid-eighteenth century, these historiographic issues inform conclusions about Zadok and Zadokites. For example, in 1735 Augustin Calmet notes that Saul bestowed the high-priesthood upon Zadok, who was "son of Ahitub, high-priest of the Jews, of the race of Eleazar... It is not known when he died; but his successor was his son Ahimaash, who enjoyed the high-priesthood under Rehoboam."[3] Conflation of historiographic presuppositions was necessary to formulate conclusions about Zadok. Taken for granted are historicity, linearality, unified intention of unified material, and a presumption the existence of a high-priesthood.[4]

Nineteenth-Century Tradition and Scholarship

Although history and historiography received much attention in the nineteenth century, that attention did not filter through comprehensive studies far enough to reach presuppositions about the Zadokites. Still, in many ways, nineteenth-century inquiry into issues of historiography set the stage for contemporary studies. In 1875, Abraham Kuenen wrote

2. A brief summary of the impact of earlier tradition and scholarship will suffice to provide a context for understanding the presuppositions of subsequent scholarship. Early historiographers writing Jewish histories such as Alexander Polyhistor, Nicolaus of Damascus, Justus of Tiberias, and Josephus, arranged historical events according to the order and presumed historicity of the biblical books, synchronizing them with known world events. Such histories likely established this same order as presumptive for historical discussions. Later Christian writers, like Eusebius and Augustine, followed the same historical scheme.

3. Augustin Calmet, *Calmet's Dictionary of the Holy Bible as Published by the Late Mr. Charles Taylor* (8th ed.; Boston: Crocker & Brewster, 1837), 758, 938. Notice also how Calmet conflates various texts, enabling him to conclude that Zadok was the son of Ahitub and that Ahimaash was Zadok's son.

4. By saying that Calmet presumed linearality, I mean that Calmet, and numerous readers and scholars after him, presumed in the order of the biblical books a chronological reflection of historical events moving in a single trajectory. While this may seem obvious, this assumption continues to inform the development of histories. Concurrently, Calmet anachronistically projects high-priesthood, mentioned only in late literature, on early periods, even when said high-priesthood received no mention in the texts he sees as originating in early periods. Historiographically, Calmet begins the investigation with questions about Zadok and Zadok's descendants.

an analysis of religion in ancient Israel, setting it as one among many religions, non-unique except in the eyes of the writers of "their holy records."[5] Kuenen deliberately establishes his operating assumptions and addresses the issue of his sources: "The entire literature of Israel, so far as it originated within the period of which we have to treat, or bears witness of that period, is the source of our knowledge of Israel's religion and its history."[6] He focuses on historiographic methodology, particularly as it relates to the dating of biblical material, and concludes, "No one will deny that our conception of Israel's religious history entirely depends upon our verdict on the Old Testament."[7] He acknowledges his own historiographic dependence on the biblical material. He states emphatically, "[T]his testimony must be simply accepted," but then immediately continues,

> [W]e have to investigate how far it reaches and what can be legitimately deduced from it. But further we cannot and may not go... [F]or this very reason it is of the highest importance to trace out and determine first of all the age of the various books... [T]he historian cannot pay too much attention to this. If there exists a tradition with regard to the authors of the books and the times at which they lived...he [*sic*] of course takes notice of, but does not rely upon, it. On the contrary, he [*sic*] considers himself [*sic*] called upon to test such traditions.[8]

Much of Kuenen's analysis of historiography remains pertinent and even helpful for contemporary discussions. Still, Kuenen, like scholars today, frequently relied on unchallenged presuppositions allowing him to draw certain conclusions about Zadok and Zadokites. Zadok was David's priest along with Abiathar.[9] Ezekiel, in exile, declared the sons of Zadok as the legitimate priests.[10] The sons of Zadok were "the families of priests who had served in the temple of Solomon from the very first...the descendants of the priestly families of Jerusalem."[11] While Kuenen raised helpful historiographic questions, his work did not extend to the point of asking such questions about the Zadokites.

5. Abraham Kuenen, *The Religion of Israel to the Fall of the Jewish State* (trans. Alfred Heath May; 2 vols.; London: Williams & Norgate, 1874–5), 1:5–30.

6. Ibid., 1:12.

7. Ibid., 1:13, 15–30, especially 19–27. This is basically where we, as biblical scholars and historians of ancient Israel, find ourselves today. His historiographic methodology points are still pertinent.

8. Ibid., 14.

9. Ibid., 1:320–21.

10. Ibid., 2:115.

11. Ibid., 2:168, 203.

In 1877, Samuel Ives Curtiss dedicated an entire volume to ancient Israelite priesthood, although the work is primarily an engagement with Kuenen and Graf regarding Pentateuchal criticism.[12] Curtiss was disturbed that "the natural consequence of these purely microscopic and anatomical investigations is a growing irreverence towards the Holy Scriptures among the critics." He defended Christianity in Great Britain and the United States as "greatly in advance of that in Germany." Evaluating Kuenen's work, he said, "...while Dr. Kuenen's views, judged from a purely critical standpoint, solve many difficulties, they occasion, when subjected to a rigid analysis, still greater ones—to say nothing of their degrading the Scriptures from their high position of authority to the level of other books."[13] He criticized Kuenen for his reliance on science, particularly as it related to Kuenen's confidence that the religion of Israel developed naturally. Of Kuenen he said, "He is to all intents and purposes a theological Darwin."[14]

Curtiss laudably named his own position and methodological starting point—his operating assumptions:

> We regard the religion of Israel as something more than one of the principal religions. We believe in its supernatural origin, in its vital importance in the scheme of redemption and that God has given a revelation of Himself in the book of the Old Testament... Nevertheless, while we start with these presuppositions, we shall try to employ the scientific method, and give the objections which arise their full force.[15]

Even though Curtiss argued with Kuenen's conclusions about priestly lineage and hence the veracity of biblical texts and their interpretation, he shared similarities with Kuenen.[16] Thus Curtiss's understanding of the Zadokites was established by his dating of Deuteronomy, Ezekiel, and P, as well as by his assumption of a dominant Zadokite priesthood from the time of David.[17]

12. Samuel Ives Curtiss, *The Levitical Priests: A Contribution to the Criticism of the Pentateuch* (Edinburgh: T. & T. Clark, 1877).

13. Ibid., ii–iii.

14. Ibid., 2.

15. Ibid., 6.

16. Like Kuenen, Curtiss acknowledged that interpretation of the biblical material depends on the dating of the material (ibid., 7). Like Kuenen, Curtiss took for granted that the sons of Zadok were the high priests of the temple from the time of David onward. Accepting Keunen's 572 B.C.E. date for Ezekiel, he saw the prophet Ezekiel as confirming the division of the priesthood into two branches, the faithful Zadokites and the faithless Ithmaarites. In his view, genealogies in Chronicles substantiate this division which is merely reflective of Abiathar's demotion by Solomon.

17. Ibid., 68–76.

Heinrich Ewald, in his multi-volume *The History of Israel*,[18] focused attention on issues surrounding the historiography of ancient Israel, particularly issues concerning sources, both tradition and memory, available for writing histories of ancient Israel. He sought "to describe this history, therefore, as far as it can be known in all its discoverable remains and traces."[19] He described the challenges he faced:

> Like every history which reaches back into remote antiquity, this especially lies before us only in scattered notices and monuments—here in faint hardly discernable traces, there in simple lofty ruins, which stand out amidst the desolation, and strike every eye; and the farther back its beginnings ascend into the primitive times, the more does every sure trace seem to vanish... It is only when the investigator indefatigably pursues with equal zeal everything that has been preserved and can be understood; and cheerfully follows out the faint and hidden traces also, that what is dead is recalled to life, and what is isolated enters into its necessary coherence.[20]

Ewald declared, "Our ultimate aim is the knowledge of what really happened—not what was only related and handed down by tradition, but what was actual fact."[21]

Ewald addressed Zadok and Zadokites in his third volume. He assumed a hereditary priesthood affiliated with an increasingly consolidated monarchy during the time of David.[22] Zadok was a Levite from the branch of Eleazar who came to David at Hebron where David appointed him high priest of the new sanctuary in Jerusalem alongside Abiathar, thus adjacently positioning two priestly houses. Because Zadok was "honoured chief of Priests of the house of Eleazar" who supported Solomon, Abiathar was eventually deposed, so that

> the High-Priesthood which had been administered under David by Zadok from the one house and Abiathar from the other (the latter, however, with a slightly higher rank) was transferred solely to the former (citing I Kings ii.35, cf iv.2; 1 Chron. v.34-41 [vi.8-15]. The remark in 1 Chron. v.36 [vi. 10] belongs properly to ver. 35 [vi.9]), and all subsequent High-Priests to the time of the Maccabees belong to his house.[23]

18. Heinrich Ewald, *The History of Israel* (8 vols.; trans. Russell Martineau; London: Longman, Green & Co., 1874).
19. Ibid., 1:6.
20. Ibid., 1:8.
21. Ibid., 1:13.
22. Ibid., 3:133–35, 180.
23. Ibid., 3:213.

Later, Ewald confirmed that the house of Zadok retained the priesthood: "The family of Zadok, as far as we can conclude from later accounts, retained from this time [Davidic monarchy] onwards without break the High-Priestly dignity in Jerusalem."[24] He noted that 1 Chr 5:34–41 (ET 6:8–15) is "unfortunately the only passage in the O.T. where the line of these high priests is recorded. According to this, from Zadok under David to the Hilkiah known to us from 2 Kings xxii, there were only ten high priests, perhaps nothing but a round number."[25]

Even though Ewald is tentative and notes the tenuous nature of making assumptions about high-priesthood, he proceeds to make his own assumptions. Ewald, along with Kuenen, Curtiss, Milman, and Graetz, establishes a historiographic baseline, a conclusion about Zadok and the Zadokites—that a high-priesthood existed even prior to monarchy, that priesthood was hereditary and belonged to houses or families, and, most pertinent for this study, that the house of Zadok ascended to and functionally retained control of a centralized high-priesthood in Jerusalem from the time of (the Levites or) David until the Hasmonean period.[26] These conclusions continued to be taken for granted in subsequent scholarship.

24. Ibid., 3:268.

25. Ibid., 1:268 n. 5.

26. Also see Milman and Graetz. Henry Hart Milman likewise wrote a critical history of Israel, *History of the Jews of the Jews from the Earliest Period Down to Modern Times* (3 vols.; New York: Crowell, 1881), evaluating contradictions, noting that "discrepancies become more embarrassing and irreconcilable," and engaging the work of other scholars, particularly Ewald. While attempting a critical commentary, Milman relied heavily on prior presuppositions, particularly on the order and context of biblical material, allowing the continuation of previous assumptions and conclusions. He designated Chronicles as "the books of the High Priests, more especially those of the House of Zadok, the line of Eleazar" (p. 1:26). In his second volume, when discussing the accession of the high priesthood to the "Asmoneans, the Maccabees," Milman assumed that the priesthood was Zadokite, that the high priests were and had been "descendants of the High Priest Zadok" (p. 1:375).

Writing in 1891, Heinrich Graetz (*History of the Jews*. Vol. 1, *From the Earliest Period to the Death of Simon the Maccabee [135 B.C.E.]* [Philadelphia: The Jewish Publication Society of America, 1891], and *History of the Jews*. Vol. 2, *From the Reign of Hyrcanus [135 B.C.E.] to the Completion of the Babylonian Talmud [500 C.E.]* [Philadelphia: The Jewish Publication Society of America, 1893]) based his work primarily on he narratives of the biblical text. While not engaging contemporary scholars and their histories, Graetz nonetheless drew similar conclusions about Zadok and the Zadokites. Zadok, set in place by Saul after the demise of the sons of Eli at Nob, served as high priest at Gibeon where he was later confirmed and affirmed by David, who also maintained Abiathar as high priest at Zion. Zadok and Abiathar served David faithfully. At some point, Abiathar assumed an inferior position and, after Abiathar's support of Adonijah, Zadok was given singular prominence

Wellhausenian Historiography

In the assessment of many, the work of Julius Wellhausen made the most significant impact on historiography of ancient Israel in the late nineteenth century. Scholars today both assume and continue to respond to the conclusions of his work. Wellhausen, who systematized, schematized, and synthesized to produce a reconstruction of the history of ancient Israel in his *Prolegomena*,[27] was clearly influenced by contemporary conclusions of literary studies. He offered the synthesizing culmination of source-critical work. While deviating on certain points, scholarly consensus still retains the general conceptualization as seen in the JEDP sequence (particularly his dating of P), his notion of cultic centralization, his generally negative view of postexilic life, his *Tendenzkritik*, his confidence that biblical material serves as a historical source even as it does not give a direct historical account, his tripartite division of the history of the priesthood, and his notion about covenant.

Some scholars perhaps think of Wellhausen as simply a voice from the past. Some might read the following comments of Douglas A. Knight as an acknowledgment that Wellhausen was a *once* prominent historical scholar:

> The discipline of biblical studies has moved well beyond the milestone of Wellhausen's *Prolegomena*. Exegesis is now unthinkable without form criticism, tradition criticism, and "new" literary criticism. Discourse analysis, narratology, and structuralism are now partners in the discussion. Attention to social location, feminist and liberationist hermeneutics, and ideological criticism have altered the very way in which we approach texts and historical phenomena. The history-of-religions approach, canonical criticism, and new issues in theology have expanded the discussion of Israel's religious ideas. Sociology, anthropology, archaeology, folklore studies, and other comparative fields have enhanced the examination of life in ancient Israel... Such is the nature of scholarship.[28]

as high priest, "Zadok was made the sole head of the priesthood, and his descendants, invested with that dignity, maintained it for over a thousand years" (p. 1:160). Subsequently, "his descendents, invested with that [sole head of the high priesthood] dignity, maintained it over a thousand years." The sons of Zadok (Graetz sometimes calls them Aaronites, e.g., 1:284) suffered temporary demise as high priests under the rule of Manasseh (1:120, 141, 152, 160, 284).

27. Julius Wellhausen, *Prolegomena to the History of Ancient Israel* (Edinburgh: A. & C. Black, 1885).

28. Douglas A. Knight, Foreword to Julius Wellhausen, *Prolegomena to the History of Israel* (Atlanta: Scholars Press, 1994), xv–xvi.

Knight's analysis is probably more properly read as a recognition that Wellhausen was instrumental in laying the foundation for many of these developments. Certainly his work continues to inform many of these methodologies. In fact, one of Wellhausen's own underlying principles assists in examining his actual impact on those who use the product of Wellhausen's work. Wellhausen saw the identification of the biblical writer's presuppositions as critical in both literary analysis and historical reconstruction. Using his principle, we can see Wellhausen in almost every facet of biblical scholarship today: even the segments of biblical criticism that purport to be at the opposite polarity from historical criticism make historical assumptions.[29]

Julius Wellhausen continues to form, inform, and reform biblical research. Joseph Blenkinsopp, in the foreword to his work, *The Pentateuch*,[30] notes that Pentateuchal studies are on the precipice of a shift from the Wellhausen paradigm but readily admits that no new paradigm is apparent. Over one hundred years after Wellhausen, scholars attempting to begin a new direction often start their work with Wellhausen.[31] The underlying historiographic principles of his work continue to prove valuable.[32] Even for Wellhausen, though, the Zadokites were a peripheral issue. Wellhausen's primary priestly concern was with establishing the various genealogies of the numerous priestly families as they fit within

29. Some scholars may do this contextually if not factually. While distinctions can certainly be drawn, a perusal of underlying assumptions once again demonstrates the prominence of Wellhausen's work. For example, several narrative critics use the work of Robert Alter as an underlying basis for their own work; Robert Alter, in turn, deals with and eventually assumes the product of Wellhausen's work, in his *The Art of Biblical Narrative* (New York: Basic Books, 1981), 132–3; 140–45. Alter, in fact, believes that new criticism provides new avenues for discovering meaning (p. 166). For Alter, Wellhausen's work maintains a useful tension.

30. Joseph Blenkinsopp, *The Pentateuch: An Introduction to the First Five Books of the Bible* (ABRL; New York: Doubleday, 1992).

31. See, e.g., Thomas L. Thompson, *Early History of the Israelite People: From the Written and Archaeological Sources* (SHANE 4; Leiden: Brill, 1992).

32. Certainly, some questions raised against Wellhausen deserve an answer. For example, Yehezkel Kaufmann, *The Religion of Israel: From Its Beginnings to the Babylonian Exile* (trans. Moshe Greenberg; Chicago: University of Chicago Press, 1960), challenges Wellhausen's dating of P with specific and relevant questions (see pp. 153–57, 188–89, 193–94). On the other hand, some points raised by Wellhausen deserve to be brought, once again, into view. For example, his emphasis on the biblical texts as historical sources for the period in which they were written. Rudolf Smend, in "Julius Wellhausen and His *Prolegomena to the History of Israel*," *Semeia* 25 (1983): 1–20, reminds us that Wellhausen would "mercilessly mock colleagues who followed him blindly" (p. 8), and would expect no less today; he would certainly applaud persistent questioning of the *status quo*.

his tripartite scheme. The House of Eli represents for Wellhausen the priesthood of his first period, the premonarchic Israel. For Wellhausen, there was no doubt that the originally illegitimate sons of Zadok obtained power and presided over the temple of Solomon during the monarchy, Wellhausen's second period in Israel's history—rising to exclusive power with the fall of the high places during Josiah's reform.[33] Assuming Ezekiel as representative of a transition time between the monarchy and his third period, which reflected the legalistic control of the priests, Wellhausen placed the Zadokites in priestly power at Jerusalem, although still with a need to justify themselves, hence the rhetoric of Ezek 40–48.[34] Wellhausen in fact presumed the dominance of a Zadokite priesthood in Jerusalem from the time of David through at least the time of the writing of the book of Chronicles.[35] The Zadokites were the priesthood of choice, "who were at first parvenus and afterwards became the most legitimate of the legitimate"[36] so that "other priests also by degrees attached themselves to the family of Zadok, and ultimately came even to call themselves his sons."[37]

The peripheral nature of Wellhausen's references to the Zadokites was and is no exception. His conclusions about them appear to have come as a by-product of his major foci—particularly of his tripartite division and dating. Thus, while Wellhausen made groundbreaking progress in historiographical studies, the developments did not have an impact on conceptualizations of the Zadokites.

Studies subsequent to Wellhausen continued along a similar vein, thus comprising what became and remains the traditional view—the default consensus—the notions about the Zadokites that remain taken for granted: Zadok became David's high priest and subsequently Solomon's high priest.[38] Zadok and his descendants served in the Jerusalem temple as the dominant high priests. Zadokites remained faithful even when other priestly groups faltered. Zadokites were among the elites removed to exile after the Babylonian conquest. With the permission and support of Cyrus, Zadokites returned from exile to (re-)establish the proper and appropriate priesthood in Jerusalem. Zadokites maintained the temple and significant political power until the Maccabean revolt, at which time the Hasmoneans usurped the priesthood.

33. Wellhausen, *Prolegomena to the History of Ancient Israel*, 124–25.
34. Ibid., 123.
35. Ibid., 126 n. 1.
36. Ibid., 142.
37. Ibid., 132.
38. "Tradition" will be referenced throughout the present study and refers to this traditional view, the default consensus.

Post-Wellhausen Historiography and the Zadokites

James Henry Breasted's 1893 comparison of the development of priesthoods in Israel and Egypt assumes a linear and progressive[39] development of priesthood from general to specific and broad to specialized, culminating in the refined and powerful family of Zadok.[40] B. Pick presumes a unilateral and likewise linear biblical portrait of a single ancient Israelite priesthood that began with Aaron. The first patrilineal line began with Aaron, shifted with the entrance of Eli, and ended with the ousting of Abiathar at which time the high priesthood was assumed by another Aaronite line, that of Zadok, whose heirs continued to function until the time of Jonathan (152–143 B.C.E.) when there

> was a break in the succession of the high priests, such as had only taken place twice before, once when Eli, from some unexplained cause, superseded the elder house of Eleazar; again, when Zadok was placed by Solomon in the place of Abiathar.[41]

Around the turn of the century, studies specifically related to priestly lineage begin to appear. Albin van Hoonacker offered a dissident and largely unheard voice as he departed from typical treatments in that he saw the Zadokites as a "symbolic creation" of Ezekiel. For Hoonacker, there were no Zadokites after the monarchy: "No one after the Exile knows the 'sons of Zadok,' etc."[42] Hoonacker's conclusions came as a product of his conversation with König concerning the appropriate interpretation of Ezek 40–48 as pertaining to the Levites and the Zadokites. König took what is now considered the traditional view although he labels Hoonacker as having "failed, like others, to vindicate the old conception of the history of the legal relations of priests and Levites."[43]

Wolf Baudissin, using the conclusions of Pentateuchal source criticism, sees the Zadokites as *the* continuous priestly line, in control of the sanctuary and the priesthood not only from the time of David through the

39. By this I mean scholars sometimes make certain linear assumptions about the biblical material by presuming that the order of the biblical books presented a record of historical events in linear, chronological order.

40. James Henry Breasted, "The Development of the Priesthood in Israel and Egypt—A Comparison," *The Biblical World* (July–December 1893): 19–28.

41. B. Pick, "The Jewish High Priests Subsequent to the Return from Babylon," *The Lutheran Church Review* 17 (1898): 127–42.

42. Albin van Hoonacker, "Ezekiel's Priests and Levites," *ExpTim* 12 (1900–1901): 494–98.

43. Eduard König, "The Priests and the Levites in Ezekiel XLIV. 7–15," *ExpTim* 12 (1900–1901): 300–303 (303).

exile but continuing beyond the Hellenistic period so that the Zadokite influence extended to the formation of the powerful Sadducees.[44] Working in the same general time period and engaging the work of both Baudissin and Kuenen concerning priestly lineage, William Robertson Smith and A. Bertholet likewise situate the Zadokites as the dominant priesthood of Jerusalem through the monarchical periods.[45]

R. H. Kennett, in his 1905 study of the Aaronite priesthood, followed similar lines regarding the Zadokites: they achieved the supreme position in the Temple in Jerusalem and maintained that position until they were exiled to Babylon where they produced P. A "new" Aaronite priesthood took their place in Jerusalem in their absence so that, upon return from exile with a late group of returnees, the Zadokites were forced to affect a compromise with these Aaronites. Ultimately Zadokites became equated with Aaronites, thus explaining the confusion in biblical studies concerning the "sons of Aaron."[46] The story does not change with Samuel Krauss's 1905 article in *The Jewish Encyclopedia* as he states, "Reliable historical data show that the high-priesthood remained in the hands of the Zadokites from this time [Solomon] until the rise of the Maccabees."[47]

Kaufmann Kohler, in studying the Sadducees, names the Zadokites as the group that "formed the Temple hierarchy all through the time of the First and Second Temples down to the days of Ben Sira" and were eventually claimed by a group known as the Sadducees.[48] In his study on the origins of the synagogue, Kohler holds the dominant priesthood, the Zadokites, responsible for reforming inherited traditions after the demolition of the Northern Kingdom in an effort to rid the nation of idolatrous practices. As the only legitimate priests, the Zadokites were transformed into Aaronites during the restoration. Although Kohler's analysis relies on traditional assumptions, he raises a critical issue, commenting on the oddity that the Zadokites appear only rarely in biblical material:

> Strange to say, the Zadokite priesthood, with the exception of Ezek. 43:19, 44:15 and 2 Chron. 31:10, is nowhere mentioned in our Biblical and post-Biblical records, and only Solomon Schechter's fortunate discovery of a Temple hymn in the Hebrew Ben Sira, 51, 12f., in which God is praised

44. Wolf Wilhelm Grafen Baudissen, *Die Geschichte des alttestamentlichen Priesterthums* (Leipzig: Hirzel, 1889).

45. Smith and Bertholet, "Priests," passim. Ewald is an exception since he, as mentioned earlier, sees the beginnings of the Zadokites with the Levitical tribe.

46. R. H. Kennett, "The Origin of the Aaronite Priesthood," *JTS* 6 (1905): 161–86.

47. Samuel Krauss, "Zadok," *JE* 12:628–29 (628).

48. Kaufmann Kohler, "Sadducees," *JE* 10:630–33 (630).

> for having 'chosen the sons of Zadok to be priests,' has evidenced the fact that the ruling priests before the Maccabean era belonged to the house of Zadok.[49]

Theophile James Meek, writing on the rival priesthoods in "Hebrew history" and following Kennett's basic tenets, assumes the prominence of the Zadokites in the centralized cult. He concludes: "By the end of the Greek period the cause of the Zadokites had so far advanced that they and their supporters constituted a distinct party in Judaism and came to be known as the Sadducees."[50] W. O. E. Oesterley and Theodore Robinson, in their *A History of Israel*, likewise maintain the underlying assumption that the Zadokites were the dominant priesthood from the time of David until the time of Antiochus Epiphanes.[51] Julius Morgenstern and H. H. Rowley after him assume the traditional stance in seeing the Zadokites as controlling the sanctuary with the exception of the exilic period.[52]

In his general work on life in ancient Israel based primarily on biblical material, Johannes Pedersen notes the long-standing nature of the Zadokite priesthood in the political face of both declines and reforms.[53] He further recognizes as remarkable the postexilic claim on the foundational

49. Kaufmann Kohler, *The Origins of the Synagogue and the Church* (ed. and with a bibliography by H. G. Enelow; New York: MacMillan, 1929), 11–12. Kohler completes the sentence: "; thus confirming the opinion long ago expressed by Abraham Geiger that they were identical with the Sadducees spoken of by Josephus and the New Testament, as the ruling priestly aristocracy."

50. Theophile James Meek, "Aaronites and Zadokites," *AJSL* 45 (1929): 149–66.

51. W. O. E. Oesterley and Theodore H. Robinson, *A History of Israel: From the Fall of Jerusalem, 586 B.C. to the Bar-Kokhba Revolt, A.D. 135* (2 vols.; Oxford: Clarendon, 1932). See, for example, p. 2:422. Oesterly further sees no connection between Zadokites and Sadducees. Also, for George H. Box and William O. E. Oesterley, "The Book of Sirach," *APOT* 1:268–517, the Zadokites were the priests prior to the Hasmoneans (p. 1:277). Similarly Frederick C. Forrester in *First and Second Kings in Old Testament Commentary: A General Introduction to and a Commentary on the Books of the Old Testament* (ed. Herbert C. Alleman and Elmer E. Flaer; Philadelphia: Muhlenburg, 1948), 416: "though we know nothing of his family, he established a priesthood which continued long after the Exile."

52. Julian Morgenstern, "A Chapter in the History of the High Priesthood," *AJSL* 55 (1938): 1–24, 183–97, 360–77; H. H. Rowley, "Zadok and Nehushtan," *JBL* 58 (1939): 113–41. Also see idem, *The Growth of the Old Testament* (London: Hutchinson University Library, 1950), and *The Zadokite Fragments and the Dead Sea Scrolls* (New York: Macmillan, 1952). Rowley continues the same line of reasoning in his 1967 work, *Worship in Ancient Israel: Its Forms and Meanings* (London: SPCK, 1967). He is an excellent example, along with de Vaux, of the following of the Documentary Hypothesis to form assumptions and historical ideas.

53. Pedersen, *Israel: Its Life and Culture*, 2:153–56, 164–70, 170, 174–97, 232. "Zadokide" for Pedersen.

Jerusalemite Zadokite priesthood. He chooses not to take a stand on whether the Zadokites were actually Levites or only claimed Levitical descent. He sees Ezekiel's distinction between Zadokites and non-Zadokites as a carryover from the monarchical period that was maintained through the exile. Furthermore, struggles throughout the historical periods of ancient Israel produced a fluctuating priesthood that sometimes admitted and sometimes excluded a variety of priestly families, though the Zadokites maintained their prominence. So, although scholars discuss aspects of priesthood, the general presupposition remained that the Zadokites obtained and maintained control of a centralized temple in Jerusalem with few interruptions from the time of David until the Hasmonean period.

H. H. Rowley, in a 1939 work that triggered years of scholarly discussion, examined the biblical figure Zadok, raising questions about existing ideas concerning his genealogy.[54] Rowley bases his arguments almost entirely on the historical accuracy and order of the biblical texts, except where he chooses to declare certain biblical texts as "unhistorical." In discussion with Kennett, Graf, Wellhausen, Kittel, Calmet, Budde, and Sellin, he claims that David appointed Zadok as priest over the Jerusalemite shrine where he housed the ark in an effort at reconciliation with the conquered Jerusalemites. To support his case, he posits the existence of an ancient Jerusalem shrine, as evidenced by the etiology in Gen 14 and the reference to Melchizedek in Ps 110.[55] The priesthood of this shrine needed legitimization, hence these biblical references. As further proof of his thesis, he uses negative evidence to justify his conclusion: David did not destroy Jerusalem's (and Zadok's) shrine as shown by the lack of textual evidence that David built a replacement shrine.[56] Thus, David needed to legitimize the existing shrine. Rowley continued that David chose not to remove Zadok because he wanted to cultivate favor with his new, Jebusite subjects. When Rowley encounters any biblical contradictions to his thesis, he dismisses the biblical references as unhistorical. His thesis, then, explains Zadok's lack of previous biblical genealogy. Rowley also mentions a possible association between Zadok and Zedek, the name of a Semitic deity, drawing further connections with Jerusalem.[57] Rowley grants the priesthood a wider circle dating

54. Rowley, "Zadok and Nehushtan."

55. He dates Gen 14 early based on his previous dating of the Samaritan Pentateuch and Chronicles.

56. A few pages later, Rowley cautions against making arguments from silence.

57. In closing his article, he turned to Nehushtan, suggesting, while without any "direct evidence," that it was the "principal sacred object" of Zadok's Jerusalem shrine until the Ark entered the shrine.

from the time of P, when the priesthood was expanded to include all descendants of Aaron.[58]

Post-1940s Historiography and the Zadokites

Beginning in the 1950s, studies concerning priesthood and the Zadokites became more specific and therefore more intricate, with scholars examining particular details about Zadokites and priesthood in ancient Israel. While they made modifications to certain portions of the general conceptualization of priesthood, they did not pursue questions about the underlying presupposition that Zadokites obtained and maintained control of a centralized Jerusalem priesthood. As in the past, numerous scholars commented on the elusive nature of studying priesthood in ancient Israel.

In 1954, Francis Sparling North expanded the discussion by detecting the presence of an Aaronite priesthood at Bethel/Mizpah, which served as the religious center during the exilic period. He concludes, however, that although they maintained a presence, they never gained prominence in the Jerusalem temple. He continues to operate on the presupposition that the Zadokites were taken into and later returned from exile, at which time they reclaimed the centrality of the Jerusalem temple and created a Levitical ancestry for themselves.[59]

H. G. Judge focused on uncertainties about reconstructing a history of the Jerusalem priesthood.[60] He raises problems with attempts to view Aaronites as inclusive of Zadokites when the Zadokites held the priesthood in monopoly during the exile, and likely prior to the exile. For Judge, the priesthood broadened during the postexilic reconstruction period and the Zadokites should be described as one part of the Aaronites. Judge, agreeing with A. C. Welch, who wrote *The Work of the Chronicler*, rightly posits that no Aaronite lineage claim was made by Zadokites prior to the exile, considering the Zadokite acquisition of an Aaronite lineage a postexilic necessity developed from Aaronite prominence in Jerusalem upon Zadokite return from exile.[61] In claiming Aaronite lineage in postexilic Jerusalem, the Zadokites could claim seniority by power and by ancestry.

Martin Noth, in *The History of Israel*, places the beginning of an institutional priesthood during Josiah's reign, whose deuteronomic reforms

58. Rowley, *The Growth of the Old Testament*. See, e.g., p. 33.

59. Francis Sparling North, "Aaron's Rise in Prestige," *ZAW* 66 (1954): 191–99.

60. H. G. Judge, "Aaron, Zadok, and Abiathar," *JTS* n.s. 7(1956): 70–74.

61. A. C. Welch, *The Work of the Chronicler* (London: Oxford University Press, 1939).

established the high priesthood from the family of the Zadokites, who had served as priests since the time of David and Solomon. While some Zadokites were sent into exile, Noth suggests that others may have remained in Jerusalem and participated in the recovery process. These priests, along with Zadokites among the returnees, assumed the reconstruction priesthood with more power and status than before.[62] For Noth, it was during the Persian period that this Zadokite priesthood found it necessary to extend their point of origin beyond the beginning of the monarchy. As the significance of their role increased along with their need to maintain their position, they added to their prominence by claiming ancestry from Aaron.[63]

John Bright's history likewise assumes the dominance of a Zadokite priesthood from the pre-exilic temple until the Hasmoneans.[64] In his *A History of Israel*, Bright allows the question of Zadok's origin to remain open while acknowledging Zadok as David's priest. He gives little direct attention to Zadokites other than noting that, when Zerubabbel was governor, "Direction of spiritual affairs was assumed by the high priest Joshua ben Jehozadak (Hag 1:1; Ezra 3:2, etc.), a man of Zadokite lineage born in exile (1 Chr 6:15), who had apparently returned at the same time."[65] He also claims that during this period,

> Presiding over the cult was the high priest, who was the spiritual head of the community and, progressively, its secular prince as well. The high-priestly office was hereditary with the house of Zadok, the priestly line of the preexilic Temple, which claimed direct descent form Aaron through Eleazar and Phinehas (1 Chron. 6:15).[66]

His only other mention of Zadokites connects them to the Essenes who promoted the ideals of the Hasidim and who "seem to have drawn their strength from members of the Zadokite priesthood."[67] Clearly, from his two references to the Zadokites, and his references to Zadok, Bright assumes the establishment of a Zadokite priesthood in Jerusalem from the time of David until the Hasmoneans.

Yehezkel Kaufmann's long and comprehensive works on the religion of Israel follow Wellhausen in focusing more on the Levites that the

62. Martin Noth, *Geschichte Israels* (Göttingen: Vandenhoeck & Ruprecht, 1956), and *The History of Israel* (2d ed.; New York: Harper, 1960).

63. Noth, *The History of Israel*, 339.

64. John Bright, *A History of Israel* (Westminster Aids to the Study of the Scriptures; Philadelphia: Westminster, 1960).

65. Ibid., 384.

66. Ibid., 421.

67. Ibid., 451.

Zadokites.[68] While he sees the Zadokites as Levitical, he notes their consecration along with the monarchy, in contrast with the Elides who already served as priests in Egypt. During the monarchy, the Zadokites were obscured by the monarchy and the prophets. Nevertheless, Kaufmann operates under the assumption that there existed a large Zadokite priesthood which was taken into exile. He allows his placement of Ezek 55 in the exilic period to designate Zadokites as the exclusive exilic priests whereas the economic conditions of post-exilic life make the priesthood more inclusive during that period. He sees them as being of the Levitical family which served during the monarchy with the originally pagan(?) Aaronites who were connected with the Elides. He acknowledges the exclusive nature of Ezekiel's Zadokites and comments on the sheer numeric impossibility of the Zadokites completing the ranks of the priests returning from exile.

De Vaux's study of institutions specifies the difficulties in trying to understand priesthood in ancient Israel.[69] The information scholars seek either is not available or scanty at best. Roland de Vaux uses textual material to present the priestly institution. He carefully reminds his readers that the work of the Chronicler must be viewed through the lens of "the situation of his own day" making the information pertinent to the postexilic period. He, like many others before and after, assumes that 1 Chr 5 serves as a list of Zadok's ancestors and descendants. He further presumes the dominance of Zadok's heirs from the time of David until the exile when he posits that most Zadokites were taken into exile, leaving Levites from the family of Abiathar to assume the priestly role in deserted Palestine. Ezra's return brought about the formal establishment of the priestly institution when the returning Zadokites joined forces with those who served in their absence, thus marking the time when priests were no longer called "sons of Zadok" but were instead called "sons of Aaron." Still, for de Vaux, the Zadokites retained some special distinction until the time of the Hasmoneans.

R. Abba, along with Hans-Joachim Kraus, R. W. Corney, D. S. Russell, Nigel Allan, and G. B. Gray, follows similar lines. Zadokites replaced

68. Yehezkel Kaufmann, *The Religion of Israel: From Its Beginnings to the Babylonian Exile* (trans. and abridged Moshe Greenberg; Chicago: University of Chicago Press, 1960); trans. of קולדות האמוצה הישראלית: מימי קדם עד סוף בית שני יחזקאל (Tel Aviv: Bialik Institute-Dvir, 1937–56); idem, *History of the Religion of Israel*. Vol. 4, *From the Babylonian Captivity to the End of Prophecy* (New York: Ktav, 1977); trans of תולדות האמוצה הישראלית (Bialik Institute-Dvir, 1966).

69. Roland de Vaux, *Les institutions de l'ancien testament* (Paris: Cerf, 1958); *Ancient Israel: Its Life and Institutions* (trans. John McHugh; London: Darton, Longman & Todd, 1961).

the house of Eli and remained the dominant Jerusalemite priesthood until they were taken into exile.[70] The Zadokites remained faithful during the apostasy of the Israelites and were rewarded by continued prominence, although not exclusive control, during the postexilic period. Reasons for a postexilic emphasis on Aaronites as opposed to Zadokites puzzled Abba. Nevertheless, he saw the Zadokites as eventually regaining their exclusive control. Abba remained cognizant of the difficulties in reconstructing this idea of the priesthood, at one point stating, "Any reconstruction of the situation can only be tentative."[71]

H. J. Katzenstein raises important questions in 1962 with his article on הרוש הכהן, the chief priests in Solomon's temple.[72] Following the biblical tradition, he traced the Zadokite line to Zadok's "(grand)son" Azariah. The priestly genealogical lists frustrate Katzenstein; he puzzles over repetitions and omissions. He concludes that 1 Chr 5 provides a list of Zadokite priests who served as high priest so that the gaps in the list come through omissions of names of high priests who were not Zadokite.[73] Presuming that Zadokites controlled the temple at the time of the Maccabean takeover, he wonders when the Zadokites lost and then regained control of the Jerusalem temple. He suggested that the Zadokites lost prominence some time during the divided monarchy, regaining it when Manasseh finally repented.[74]

With the discovery of the Dead Sea Scrolls and their references to "sons of Zadok," new questions could be raised about Zadokites.[75] Many scholars assumed that the Dead Sea Scroll sect was founded by disenfranchised Zadokites. Only recently, as will be discussed in the section on the Dead Sea Scrolls, has new evidence come to light that the role of the sons of Zadok came later in the history of the sectarian community.

70. R. Abba, "Priests and Levites," *IDB* 876–89; R. W. Corney, "Zadok the Priest," *IDB* 928–29; Hans-Joachim Kraus, *Worship in Israel: A Cultic History of the Old Testament* (trans. Geoffrey Buswell; Richmond: John Knox, 1962); D. S. Russell, *The Jews from Alexander to Herod* (The New Clarendon Bible: Old Testament 5; London: Oxford University Press, 1967); Nigel Allan, "The Identity of the Jerusalem Priesthood During the Exile," *HeyJ* 23 (1982): 259–69; and Gray, *Sacrifice in the Old Testament*, 266, follow similar reasoning.

71. Abba, "Priests and Levites," 884.

72. H. J. Katzenstein, "Some Remarks on the Lists of the Chief Priests of the Temple of Solomon," *JBL* 81 (1962): 377–84.

73. Ibid., 379.

74. His major difficulty is the prominence he gives to the historicity of the list.

75. While the Dead Sea Scrolls and their impact deserve discussion on their own—that will take place in a later chapter—they are included here with the general post-'40s discussion because the underlying assumptions remain similar.

Still, early in the study of the scrolls, Jacob Liver asked pointed questions concerning the Zadokites:

> Precisely who are these sons of Zadok, and what is their status within the sectarian grouping? What relationship do they bear to priests in general, whose mention is interspersed throughout the writings? Wherein lies the point of historico-literary contact between the sons of Zadok of the sect and those encountered in Ezekiel's cult regulations, and the song of thanksgiving toward the end of the Book of Ben-Sira? And lastly, what motivated the bestowal of the honorary appellation "the sons of Zadok the priests" or similar titles specifically in these works, whereas they make virtually no appearance in all the vast biblical and post-biblical literature dealing with the priesthood, its status and varied functions?[76]

While Liver sees the designation "sons of Zadok" in the scrolls as an honorary appellation, other opinions existed. As Dead Sea Scroll references to Zadokites are found primarily in the sectarian documents, note that Schechter, Charles, and Rowley posit Zadokites as a "general sectarian" appellation—Schechter and Charles basing this on the *Fragments of a Zadokite Work* discovered by Schechter in a Cairo genizah around the turn of the century.[77] Disagreeing with Schechter, Charles, and Rowley, Liver sees their designation as an honorary recognition of priestly hierarchy, hearkening back to golden days. Despite his challenging questions, Liver follows the general traditional presuppositions about the Zadokites as a priesthood: "The meaning of the term is merely genealogical, with Zadok as reference to the ancient 'Father' of these priests to wit their *pater eponimos*, the high priest Zadok of the Davidic era, and the ancestor of the high priestly family from the early post-exilic days down to the Hasmonean revolt."[78]

Based on Chronicles, Ezra–Nehemiah, the writings of Josephus, and his own presuppositions, Liver concludes, as do many others, that the genealogical lists in Chronicles established the Zadokites as the priestly power until the time of the Hasmoneans. He justly notes both the meager data available for ascribing the Oniad priesthood to Zadokite lineage and the "non-appearance" of Zadokites in Talmudic literature. Still he presumes they were Zadokite. Liver suggested that the appellation, "sons of

76. Jacob Liver, "The 'Sons of Zadok the Priest' in the Dead Sea Sect," *RevQ* 21 (1967): 3–30 (3).

77. R. H. Charles, "Fragments of a Zadokite Work," *APOT*, 785–837; Rowley, *The Zadokite Fragments and the Dead Sea Scrolls*; Simon Schechter, *Documents of Jewish Sectaries: Fragments of a Zadokite Work: Two Volumes in One* (The Library of Biblical Studies; New York: Ktav, 1910).

78. Liver, "The 'Sons of Zadok the Priest' in the Dead Sea Sect," 7.

Zadok," went through several transformations from the time of the exile until the end of the Persian period.[79] For Liver, the Oniads were called Zadokites so that, when the Oniads lost their power, the title became used less frequently. Thus, for Liver, "Zadokite" simply refers to the family of high priests.

Cody's major work in 1969, *A History of Old Testament Priesthood*, sought to move study of ancient Israelite priesthood into its ancient Near Eastern context.[80] Building upon the work of predecessors such as Baudissin, Hoonacker, Smith and Bertholet, Gray, and Gunneweg, he seeks to incorporate archaeology, philology, and comparative studies into his study. Cody attempts to reconstruct a chronological history of the priesthood of ancient Israel, apparently aware that even the beginning question can direct the subsequent answers in an investigation. He acknowledges the shifting meanings for the term "Levite" and notes the existence of many priestly groups including the Elides of Shiloh, the Zadokites of Jerusalem, and the Aaronites. He casts doubt on the existence of a priesthood in early Israel. As for Zadok, he cautiously follows the traditional notion of Zadok as a Jebusite from Jerusalem and worries over the idea of kings as priests. Cody suggests that the idea of the Aaronites as priests was a product of a compromise between Levites and Zadokites, whereas "Levite" referred at first to a tribe and was only later associated with the priests. As for the Zadokite–Levite conflicts, they began as a result of Josiah's reforms and climaxed in the postexilic period when the Zadokites closed their ranks, offering a small consolation to the Levites who, afterward, were not considered priests.

Cody notes the dependence of studies preceding his on the dating of biblical material yet finds himself likewise dependent on the dating and content of such material. For example, his entire thesis concerning the unfolding of the Zadokite–Levite relationship appears to stem from an effort to explain the Zadokite rhetoric in Ezek 40–48 which culminates during postexilic times in a compromise between Zadokites and Levites so that all priests would be called Levites but Zadokites would retain ultimate authority. He acknowledges the difficulties facing historians of ancient Israelite priesthood and chooses to base his work on divisions of ancient Israelite history—tribes, monarchy, divided monarchy, exile, and postexilic Judaism. Cody is further bound by his concern for seeing a

79. Ibid., 23.

80. Aelred Cody, *A History of the Old Testament Priesthood* (AnBib 35; Rome: Pontifical Biblical Institute, 1969). Also see his *Ezekiel with an Excursus on Old Testament Priesthood* (Old Testament Message: A Biblical–Theological Commentary 2; Wilmington: Glazier, 1984).

linear and evolutionary development of priesthood. He carefully reviews available evidence, offering comparative data and models, but is still bound in almost every interpretation by a presupposition that Zadokites stood in prominence in the temple of Jerusalem for centuries, from the early monarchy through the exile and on.[81]

Morton Smith presents a comprehensive though occasionally self-contradicting portrait of political parties in Judea during the Persian period by describing tensions between loosely defined parties.[82] His driving thesis seeks to demonstrate that the biblical material is a product created over a long period of time and engendered through compromises between political groups. He posits three groups that compromised to form the biblical corpora. The first was "the local party" composed primarily of those who remained in Judea after the Babylonian invasions. Smith identifies this group as generally syncretistic and standing in opposition to the second group. The second "party" was a majority segment of the group returning to Jerusalem from exile and is distinguished by Smith as being a group dedicated to YHWH alone. In addition to this returning party came "priests of the Jerusalem temple, who had an economic interest in its restoration."[83] Certain factions of those returning might also have included members of the Davidic line as well as those families who had been among the elite of Jerusalem at the time of the fall. According to Smith, these various parties in postexilic Judea engaged in struggles for power. Under Nehemiah, opposing coalitions formed so that the Levites joined with the common people's stand against the elite Zadokite priesthood and the local gentry. Nehemiah's coalition gained control for only a short time but still long enough for the party to have a sizable impact on the final formation of the Hebrew Scriptures. This coalition, called the "separatist's party" by Smith, took on the mantle of "sole Deuteronomistic reform." Smith sees the Levites as "the backbone of the separatist's party, the ones who obtained the support of the common people for Nehemiah's ideology."[84] Their work included an emphasis on "absolution of interest, release of land and other property already seized in debt and remission of debts," as well as an emphasis on the impurity of the local gentry.[85] Smith attributes the compilation of Chronicles, Ezra–Nehemiah, and Psalms to the separatists. He further attributes the

81. See, for example, his conclusion that the "faithful priest" must be Zadok (Smith, *Palestinian Parties and Politics*, 170), who else could it be?

82. Ibid.

83. Ibid., 108.

84. Ibid., 163.

85. Ibid., 131.

cessation of the collection of prophetic works to Nehemiah's party during this time. He closes his analysis with the opposing group, that of the Zadokite priesthood and the local gentry, regaining power early in the fourth century. Circumstances had changed for this group and, due to the popular support that still resided with the Levitical/Nehemiah/separatist group, these elite Zadokites and gentry were forced to adopt a conciliatory attitude in their decision-making processes. It was this conciliatory attitude that explained the production of "the great document of this compromise," the Pentateuch.

Menachem Haran, writing about priesthoods along with Menachem Stern, Leopold Sabourin, and Baruch Halpern, acknowledges the pervasive influence of Wellhausen in forming histories of ancient Israelite priesthoods.[86] Haran, like many others, develops his history based on dating of biblical material as a form of the documentary hypothesis. He also assumes that the Zadokites constituted the Jerusalem priestly dynasty.

Frank Moore Cross not only examines religious life but also looks at how the development of royal ideology affected the priesthood.[87] He brings fresh ideas to scholarship long dominated by Wellhausen by suggesting two major priestly houses: the Mushite house of Eli of Shiloh in the northern kingdom led by Abiathar and the Aaronite house of Hebron led by Zadok. He uses both P and Chronicles to find Zadok an Aaronite. This Aaronite faction increased in stature and strength until it was unrivaled and the Zadokites "became the dominant Aaronite family."[88]

86. Menachem Haran, "Priests and Priesthood," *EncJud* 1071–87. The same position is held by Menachem Stern, "Priests and Priesthood: From the Beginning of the Hellenistic Era until the Destruction of the Temple," *EncJud* 1087–88. Also see Leopold Sabourin, *Priesthood: A Comparative Study* (Studies in the History of Religions 25; Leiden: Brill, 1973), and Baruch Halpern, "Sectionalism and the Schism," *JBL* 4 (1974): 519–32.

87. Frank Moore Cross, "Aspects of Samaritan and Jewish History in Late Persian and Hellenistic Times," *HTR* 59 (1966): 201–11; *Canaanite Myth and Hebrew Epic: Essays in the History of Israel's Priesthood* (Cambridge, Mass.: Harvard University Press, 1973); "The Discovery of the Samaria Papyri," *BA* 26 (1963): 110–39; "The Early History of the Qumran Community," in *New Directions in Biblical Archaeology* (ed. David Noel Freedman and Jonas C. Greenfield; Garden City, N.Y.: Doubleday, 1969), 63–80; *From Epic to Canon: History and Literature in Ancient Israel* (Baltimore: The Johns Hopkins University Press, 1998); "Papyri of the Fourth Century B.C. From Daliyeh: A Preliminary Report on Their Discovery and Significance," in Freedman, ed., *New Directions in Biblical Archaeology*, 41–62; "A Reconstruction of the Judean Restoration," *JBL* 94 (1975): 4–18; see also Frank Moore Cross and Shemaryahu Talmon, eds., *Qumran and the History of the Biblical Text* (Cambridge, Mass.: Harvard University Press, 1975).

88. Cross, *Canaanite Myth and Hebrew Epic*, 208.

Cross then questions how Wellhausen could possibly deny Zadok's Aaronite lineage.[89] Cross' ingenious theory brought priestly studies to a concrete level by focusing on papponymy and textual issues. Geo Widengren and Lester Grabbe rightly criticize Cross' reconstruction of the high priestly lineage for its dependence on an abstract notion of papponymy, its selective use of haplographic explanations, its establishment of twenty-five years as a statistically accurate length of time for one generation, its sometimes arbitrary designation of ancient characters as sons, fathers, or brothers, and its dependence on Josephus for reliable historical information.[90] To these criticisms may be added another. Throughout his works, Cross operates under the assumption that the Zadokites obtained and retained priestly prominence in the Jerusalem priesthood until the time of the Maccabees.

Work on priesthood during the 1970s continued along the same vein. J. Gordon McCullough, Jon Levenson, Ephraim Stern, Samuel Sandmel, and Elias Bickerman are among those scholars who presume the traditional notions that the Zadokites served as high priests in Jerusalem from the time of David until they were exiled to Babylon and then continued to serve after their return until the time of the Maccabees.[91] Raymond Abba's article on "Priests and Levites in Ezekiel" refers to his previous

89. He briefly mentions that the Essenes were guided by an orderly succession of Zadokite lineage that was eventually broken up under the Hasmoneans.

90. Geo Widengren, "The Persian Period," in *Israelite and Judaean History* (ed. J. H. Hayes and J. M. Miller; Philadelphia: Westminster, 1977), 489–538; Lester L. Grabbe, *Judaism from Cyrus to Hadrian: The Persian and Greek Periods* (2 vols.; Minneapolis: Fortress, 1992), 1:112–13.

91. W. Stewart McCullough, *The History and Literature of the Palestinian Jews from Cyrus to Herod: 550 BC to 4 BC* (Toronto: University of Toronto Press, 1975); see, e.g., pp. 10, 56, 132. See also Jon D. Levenson, *Theology of the Program of Restoration of Ezekiel 40–48* (HSM 10; Missoula, Mont.: Scholars Press, 1976), 131–63. For a further analysis of Levenson, see the discussion in the section on Ezek 40–48. Although Levenson raises important questions, he remains bound by assumptions about the history of ancient Israelite priesthood as (in)formed by a traditional dating of the biblical material, particularly Ezekiel, D, and P; Ephraim Stern, "Aspects of Jewish Society: The Priesthood and Other Classes," in *The Jewish People in the First Century: Historical Geography, Political History, Social, Cultural and Religious Life and Institutions* (ed. S. Safrai and M. Stern; 2 vols.; CRINT; Amsterdam: Van Gorcum, 1976), 2:561–630; see, e.g., pp. 561, 565, and 567. Also see idem, "The Persian Empire and the Political and Social History of Palestine in the Persian Period," *CHJ* 70–87; Samuel Sandmel, *Judaism and Christian Beginnings* (New York: Oxford University Press, 1978); see, e.g., pp. 41, 80, 95, 97–98, 102, 156, 207, 429, and 431. Also Elias Bickerman, *The God of the Maccabees: Studies on the Meaning and Origin of the Maccabean Revolt* (SJLA 32; Leiden: Brill, 1979); see, e.g., p. 43.

work, where he sees all pre-exilic priests as Levites (though not necessarily all pre-exilic Levites as priests) and the postexilic priesthood as narrowing to Levites of Aaronite lineage.[92] He tries to draw a picture of the priesthood during the exilic period by examining the book of Ezekiel, agreeing with H. H. Rowley against Gese and Cody that the cultic material in chs. 40–48 is not composite and noting the distinct division between Zadokite and non-Zadokite Levites.[93] He disagrees with conventional identification of the priests who served "before the idols" in Ezekiel with the rural priests of Josiah's reign by reasoning that the Zadokites would not condemn the non-Zadokite priests for a "national apostasy" in which they, themselves, had played a part. Abba suggests the calf-worship mentioned in 1 Kgs 12:28–32 as a possible referent for Ezekiel's condemnation. He argues, somewhat from a position of silence, that his analysis invites a re-examination of the traditional late date for the Priestly Code so that Ezekiel writes based on his understanding of the Priestly material. Still, he, like those before him, assumes the prominence of a Zadokite priesthood.

In his study of ancient Israelite temples, *Temples and Temple-Service in Ancient Israel*, Haran sets forth the thesis that P laid the foundations for Hezekiah's reform and is therefore pre-exilic instead of postexilic as is commonly held.[94] He acquiesces somewhat by noting that the Priestly material remained in secret until the time of Ezra. He sees P as a comprehensive plan dictating cultic life and finds that P has no connection to Deuteronomy except that they both advocate centralization in some form (although Deuteronomy does not mention Jerusalem). He follows his mentor, Yehezkel Kaufmann, in the pre-exilic dating of P but differs with him on the exact dating and on P's sharing of some characteristics with D. He supports this pre-exilic theory by analyzing the relationship of P to Ezekiel as they present the sons of Aaron and the sons of Zadok. Ezekiel is an "epigonic growth" of P. As Haran sees the situation, P presents the sons of Aaron as including the sons of Zadok while the sons of Zadok alone do not account for the whole of the sons of Aaron. With a pre-exilic P, Ezekiel's Zadokite exclusivity is a natural offshoot of Josiah's reform when the only acceptable priesthood was the centralized,

92. Raymond Abba, "Priests and Levites in Ezekiel," *VT* 28 (1978): 1–9.

93. H. H. Rowley, "The Book of Ezekiel in Modern Study," *BJRL* 36 (1953): 146–90; Harmut Gese, *Der Verfassungsentwurf des Ezechiel (Kap. 40–48) traditionsgeschichtlich untersucht* (BHT 25; Tübingen: J. C. B. Mohr, 1957).

94. Menahem Haran, *Temples and Temple-Service in Ancient Israel: An Inquiry into the Character of Cult Phenomena and the Historical Setting of the Priestly School* (Oxford: Clarendon, 1978). See also his "The Law-Code of Ezekiel XL–XLVIII and Its Relation to the Priestly School," *HUCA* 50 (1979): 45–71.

Jerusalem priesthood. He, like Abba (while they both published in 1978, Haran's book is a reprint of earlier articles), finds it wrong-headed to associate Ezekiel's idolatrous priests with the rural priests of Josiah's reign. For Haran, the idolatrous priests were non-Zadokite Levites.

Haran bases his acceptance of Zadok as a member of the tribe of Levi on Ezekiel's association of the sons of Zadok with the sons of Levi. He challenges the notion that P presupposes Ezekiel's work and identifies Ezekiel's non-Zadokites as priests from the North who served in Manasseh's religious structures. But, if these non-Zadokites defiled worship, how would they have survived Josiah's reform and still been around for Ezekiel to condemn? Haran notes that the ark was central to worship in the monarchy and is not even mentioned in Ezekiel's temple material. As for the Second Temple period, Haran finds the notion of "sons of Zadok" a figment of Ezekiel's imagination and in no way a reality. Once again, conceptualizations of Zadokites depend on the dating of the biblical material.

Paul Hanson represents the next major discussion of the Zadokites in his work, *The Dawn of the Apocalyptic: The Historical and Sociological Roots of Jewish Apocalyptic Eschatology*.[95] In an attempt to examine the nature of the apocalyptic, Hanson starts with prophecy and suggests that, from the time of the exile, a certain group, "the visionaries," developed the apocalyptic. He examines carefully both Isa 56–66 and Zech 9–14, which he understands to be the product of intense power struggles in postexilic Judea. Those returning from exile, including the Zadokites, formed the hierocracy with the support of the Persians and developed Ezek 40–48, Zechariah, Haggai, and Chronicles. The visionaries, mostly Levites (Mushite for Hanson), developed out of prophetic (particularly Deuteronomic) traditions in opposition to the hierocracy and are responsible for Trito-Isaiah, Malachi, and Nehemiah. Hanson sees the populace as generally drawn to the work of the visionaries until the prophets Haggai and Zechariah appeal for popular support of and legitimization for the hierocratic agenda. Because of their eventual achievement of dominance, the hierocrats demonstrate an attitude of conciliation, which is demonstrated by the more lenient designation of "sons of Aaron" in P as contrasted to the earlier (so Hanson) designation of "sons of Zadok" in Ezekiel. In the end, Hanson's hierocratic party, the Zadokites, controlled the priesthood from the time of Solomon through the third century B.C.E. and cooperated with the ruling class, whether Davidic or Persian.

95. Paul D. Hanson, *The Dawn of Apocalyptic: The Historical and Sociological Roots of Jewish Apocalyptic Eschatology* (rev. ed.; Minneapolis: Fortress, 1979). Also see his "The Matrix of Apocalyptic," *CHJ* 524–33.

Seven years later, in *The People Called: The Growth of Community in the Bible,* Hanson looks at the socio-political context of the postexilic period. To establish the setting, he recalls the prominence of the Zadokites in the period between 722 and 587 B.C.E.[96] He sees the Zadokites gradually edging out their competition until they achieved full exclusivity in Josiah's reform (thus accepting the traditional notion of Ezekiel's idolatrous priests as Josiah's rural Levitical priests). The Zadokites advocated centralization of power in the temple and sought to diminish the monarchy. This ideology set the Zadokites in good stead in their efforts to retain power through the exilic and postexilic periods. Hanson sees the prophetic material as a clear demonstration of the tension between varying traditions. For example, Zechariah shows how the Zadokites tried to exert their influence and consolidate power. He then posits his main thesis that these tensions gave birth to the "roots of apocalypticism." Hanson questions his own thesis by calling attention to the inclusion of "opposition" material within the Zadokite material. He basically reads his idea back into the book of Zechariah and claims that its "growth and transmission" give a picture of historical developments. He suggests that the final version of the book of Ezekiel included insertions from both the pro- and anti-Zadokite traditions. Finally, he reminds the reader that the Zadokites moved from service to the Israelite monarchy through hierocracy to service of foreign overlords. Hanson continues with traditional presuppositions about the Zadokites in developing their innovative theses.

Robert R. Wilson uses a socio-historical approach to examine prophecy in ancient Israel and, in so doing, briefly examines the Zadokites.[97] He sees Zadok as representing the "Aaronid priests from the southern Judahite shrine at Hebron" and speculates that some ancient form of oracle might have been employed to explain the Zadokites' ascendancy to sole proprietorship of the Jerusalem priesthood, at least until the exile.[98] Wilson accepts the traditional understanding that the Zadokites maintained exclusive control of the priesthood at least through the exile and thus assumes that Ezekiel was a Zadokite. He posits that Ezekiel was "a peripheral prophet whose views were largely rejected by the orthodox Zadokite community" because of his (Ezekiel's) tendency to combine Zadokite and Deuteronomistic ideology.[99]

96. Paul D. Hanson, *The People Called: The Growth of Community in the Bible* (San Francisco: Harper & Row, 1986; repr. with a new introduction, Louisville, Ky.: Westminster John Knox, 2001).

97. Wilson, *Prophecy and Society in Ancient Israel.*

98. Ibid., 18.

99. Ibid., 282–86, 299.

In his two-volume commentary on Ezekiel, Walther Zimmerli uses a number of exegetical methods to demonstrate that the mention of the Zadokites in Ezek 40–48 is the work of a postexilic redactor.[100] The Zadokites were an elite group of Levites who performed a particular service in the centralized temple. He tends to agree with Rowley that Zadok was Jebusite and eventually became so much a part of the Israelite tradition that his lineage overtook the Aaronite lineage and eventually the entire priesthood of Jerusalem. Ezekiel 40–48, then, served to clarify "the rules of a pure priesthood" and to guarantee the privileges of the exclusive Zadokites.

In discussing the compilation of Genesis–2 Kings, Maxwell Miller and John Hayes make an attempt to create a priestly genealogy from biblical texts.[101] They comprehensively cite numerous priestly lines, which the compilers tried to combine under the tribe of Levi. As for Zadok, they associate him with "the indigenous Jerusalem priesthood" and further follow Rowley's line by mentioning Melchizedek of Salem and Adonizedek of Jerusalem. At the end of their book, Miller and Hayes mention a vexing question of how non-Aaronite Zadokites would be responsible for the final editing of biblical materials that seem to promote the Aaronites. Even their question is fraught with presuppositions: that the Zadokites were non-Aaronite; that the Zadokites were responsible for the final editing of biblical materials; that the biblical materials promote the Aaronites.

The standard presuppositions, then, permeating traditional scholarship are as follows: Zadok was established as high priest in the time of the united monarchy; the priesthood was hereditary and became instantiated in the Zadokite family which dominated the priesthood from the time of Solomon through the divided monarchy. The Zadokites remained faithful even when other priestly families strayed. The Zadokite priests were taken into exile. Here the traditional scholarship picture offers several scenarios: some say the Zadokites returned to an empty Jerusalem and re-established their power; others say they came back to Jerusalem only to find the priesthood occupied by those who developed their priestly power while the governing class of former Judah was in exile. In this case, then, the Zadokites had to compromise with those who remained in the land and eventually gained supremacy. For those holding this view, these conflicts are borne out in the biblical material.

100. Walther Zimmerli, *Ezekiel 2: A Commentary on the Book of the Prophet Ezekiel Chapters 25–48* (trans. James D. Martin, Hermeneia—A Critical and Historical Commentary on the Bible; Philadelphia: Fortress, 1983).

101. Miller and Hayes, *A History of Ancient Israel and Judah*.

Completing the summary of the consensus view, the Zadokites eventually held complete power over the priesthood in some sort of theocracy. These Zadokites honed their institutional power by finessing their relationship with the empire, the colonial overlords. This priestly family, the Oniads, remained in the priesthood throughout numerous political struggles until the Hasmoneans bought their office from the empire.

The 1980s: New Questions and the Zadokites

Throughout the history of scholarship but particularly starting in the 1980s, new questions began to be raised due to particularized studies on literature from the Hellenistic period, including Ben Sira and the Dead Sea Scrolls. Saul Olyan wrote in 1982 on Zadok's origins.[102] Olyan raises again the issue of Zadok's (lack of) genealogy in the biblical material. He reviews several prominent theories before offering his own conclusions. "The most flamboyant theory," says Olyan, "is the association of Zadok with Jebusite/Jerusalemite origins. He calls on de Vaux and Cross to note several problems with that theory: it depends on weak, circumstantial evidence; it assumes (as do many scholars) an ancient shrine in Jerusalem that was appropriated by David upon entrance to the city even though there is no evidence for a shrine, only evidence for a "tent of YHWH"; it relies on the notion that Gen 14 legitimates the Jebusite priesthood as accepted by David. Olyan suggests that Gen 14 as easily could be an attempt to establish connections with the patriarch, Abraham. Furthermore, Olyan remarks that Zadok is not alone among officials without genealogy in biblical records and that the scant information about Zadok during Solomon's reign and death in a biblical text that contains sparse material about Solomon's life is no justification for the Jebusite theory.

Olyan examines Cross' (and Haran's) agreement concerning Zadok's membership in the lineage of Aaron. In addition to Cross' evidence, Olyan speculates about the relationship between Jehoiada and Zadok. He criticizes the Cross/Haran theory on several counts, finding no early "concrete evidence" for an Aaronite Hebron or a Hebronite Zadok. The sociological context of Absalom's revolt also raises issues for Cross; Olyan asks how an Aaronite center could serve as the focal point for the rebellion.

Finally, Olyan presents his own thesis about Zadok's origins, placing him in the Aaronite line of Jehoiada. Agreeing in part with Hauer, Olyan

102. Saul Olyan, "Zadok's Origins and the Tribal Politics of David," *JBL* 101 (1982): 177–93.

sees Zadok as a "secondary figure" in the Chronicler's passage about Jehoiada.[103] Unlike Hauer, who posits Zadok as non-Aaronite and therefore Jebusite, Olyan finds a young Zadok of southern-Judahite origins, as an Aaronite who is "not yet the leader of his house." He suggests Jehoiada as the possible father of Zadok and Benaiah. After Solomon came into power, Zadok became chief priest and Benaiah became chief general. As for Hebron, Olyan places the Kenite clans in the Hebronite priesthood.

Olyan turned his attention in 1987 to Ben Sira and Ben Sira's perceived interest in the priesthood. Olyan reviews scholarship regarding Ben Sira's sometimes ambiguous relationship with temple and priesthood. Olyan effectively establishes "the priority of the priesthood" in Ben Sira and seeks to locate the priesthood exalted by Ben Sira.[104] Olyan raises interesting questions relevant to previous interpretations of priesthood, particularly as they pertain to the Zadokites. He wonders if the rhetoric of the Phinehas covenant (Num 25 and/or Ben Sira 45:24) really refers to the Zadokites. Ben Sira was concerned with uplifting the Pinhasid priesthood. For Olyan, if Ben Sira had wanted to exalt the Zadokites, he would have done so when he praised Simon ben Onias.[105] Olyon wonders why, if the Zadokites were so prominent, they remain largely unmentioned in Ben Sira—he uses the term "ignored consistently." I would add, if P is priestly and presents the priestly view, should not the Zadokites maintain a presence? The next logical question asks if they ever were prominent. It seems as if Aaronites were the prominent ones in P. Furthermore, why would Ben Sira not call the Oniads Zadokite if the Zadokites were indeed dominant?[106]

Olyan compares Ben Sira's priestly ideology with that of the deuteronomistic writer, the Chronicler, the Priestly writing, and additions to Ezek 40–48. The deuteronomistic writer is "pan-Levitic," never referring to the Aaronites or the Zadokites. Olyan rightly concludes that Ben Sira's

103. Christian E. Hauer, Jr., "Who Was Zadok?" *JBL* 82 (1963): 89–94.

104. Olyan is also bound, perhaps correctly, by the documentary hypothesis; see his "Ben Sira's Relationship to the Priesthood," *HTR* 80 (1987): 261–86, for a discussion of P.

105. This argument of course depends on equating the Oniads with the Zadokites, which is much in question today.

106. Olyan too falls prey to the Zadokite/Oniad assumption. He says "A wish for the continuity of the Zadokite (specifically Oniad) high priesthood forever fits best into the period after Menalaus has taken over the office. There was likely much resistance to a non-Zadokite high priest (see Josephus, *Ant.* 13.62 on Onias IV). The accretions must have come from Zadokite–Oniad circles" ("Ben Sira's Relationship to the Priesthood," 271 n. 31).

commitment lies with the everlasting Aaronite priesthood and is thus more closely aligned with the Chronicler and P, which respectively represent two versions of Aaronite claims. Ben Sira basically ignores the Levites and the Zadokites, even going so far as not to mention Zadok in his recitation of great Israelites. The Zadokite stratum of Ezek 40–48 is overtly anti-non-Zadokite-Levites. Olyan, along with many scholars, recognizes the hymn praising the Zadokites as a late addition to the book, and as evidence for the exertion of Zadokite control over the priesthood at some later date. Olyan rightly then asks how Ben Sira, ignoring the Zadokites, would expend over twenty verses to praising Simon in ch. 50. What Olyan fails to recognize is that there is no direct or primary evidence that the Oniads were Zadokites or that the Zadokites were the dominant priests in Jerusalem.

In his commentary on Ezekiel, Joseph Blenkinsopp has little to say about the Zadokites.[107] He does concur with traditional scholarship about the multiple layers of Ezek 40–48 that at least one of the layers reflects a pro-Zadokite revision. He acknowledges the elusiveness of any study of the priesthood and simply concludes that the group finally gaining control identified themselves as descendants of Zadok. He finds the Babylonian exile as the referent of the criticism of idolatrous priests. He ends his discussion of the Zadokites by noting their long tenure of power that lasted until the time of the Maccabees and notes the importance for the Qumran community.

Peter Haas focuses on the socio-political events surrounding the Maccabean revolt in an effort to understand the consequences of ideological conflict.[108] He correctly cautions against the common tendency to distinguish Judaism from Hellenism and then moves to a close examination of "three major types of authority" that dominated the period: the colonial overlords, the local institution, and the local constitution. The colonial overlords, the Seleucids, allowed the local institution, the priesthood, to govern local affairs according to the local constitution, "the laws of the fathers," the Torah. This symbiotic governance between these three authorities disintegrated when the balance between them shifted. Each of the four available sources, the books of Daniel, First Maccabees, Second Maccabees, and the works of Josephus, lays blame for the conflict at the feet of different combinations of power shifts at various points of time. Pertinent to any interest in Zadokites is the recognition that the

107. Blenkinsopp, *Ezekiel*.

108. Peter J. Haas, "The Maccabean Struggle to Define Judaism," in *New Perspectives on Ancient Judaism: Religion, Literature and Society in Ancient Israel, Formative Christianity and Judaism* (ed. J. Neusner; BJS 206; Atlanta: Scholars Press, 1990), 49–65.

Zadokites lost their control over the office of the High Priest during this period when a shift occurred in the balance between guarantors and holders of authority.

Albertz agrees with Rowley in positing that Zadok's Jebusite origins are supported by "the unbroken continuity in the Jerusalem priesthood from pre-Israelite times."[109] He further agrees with the associations made between Zadok and the deity Zedek and criticizes the Hebronite interpretation of Cross as followed by Olyan. Albertz notes the Deuteronomistic compliance with the view that Zadokites as well as rural priests were Levitical, seeing this compliance as an attempt to create ideological unity. He characterizes the reality of the monarchic priesthood as a standing competition between a number of local priestly families including the sons of Eli in Shiloh, the sons of Zadok in Jerusalem, and the sons of Aaron in Bethel in which the Zadokites usually maintained the upper hand and occasionally operated in coalition. For Albertz, the early tensions within the priesthood help to clarify postexilic priestly history. He finds the initiative of such a *status quo*-prone group to discuss reform as seen in Ezek 40–48 remarkable and speculates on the dissatisfaction of an extreme faction with the notion of "royal service." In discussing Ezekiel's delineation of priests, Albertz agrees with traditional scholarship that the Zadokites were trying to exclude the rural priests ousted in Josiah's reform. Albertz picks up discussion of the Zadokites again as the Maccabean period approaches. The displacement of the Zadokite line contributed to a chain of political events that eventuates in the revolt of the Maccabees. He agrees with many others that this may also have prompted the development of the community at Khirbet Qumran.

Steven Tuell presents a conceptualization of Ezek 40–48 that offers a new view of Zadokite ideology by placing the Persian exclusive installation of the Zadokites on a par with their (the Persians') installation of Marduk priests in Babylonia.[110] He sees Ezek 40–48 as a primarily legislative and practical restoration plan. He considers the shifting of geographical boundaries to be a conciliatory effort on the part of the Zadokites and falls somewhere between the composite-oriented Zimmerli (following Gese) and the unitary-oriented Haran (and Greenberg) in finding only one level of redaction in the book of Ezekiel. He questions any outright identification of the Aaronites solely with the Zadokites and associates the Zadokite priesthood with the priestly house of Jerusalem. He also notes the anomaly of Ezekiel's Zadokite exclusivity.

109. Albertz, *A History of Israelite Religion in the Old Testament Period*, 1:295.

110. Steven Tuell, *The Law of the Temple in Ezekiel 40–48* (HSM 49; Atlanta: Scholars Press, 1992).

John W. Miller approaches canonization processes for the Hebrew Bible by examining theological conflicts between priestly groups which he sees as finally resolved during the time of Ezra/Nehemiah.[111] He questions Zadok's Hebronite/Aaronite origins and states his position that Ezekiel precedes P. As he traces the developmental history of the priesthood through his text-based analysis, Miller posits the creation of various biblical material. He characterizes the Zadokites as "a small stream that swelled into a great river."[112] He describes Zadokite ideology as

> belief in the greatness, goodness and wisdom of God made manifest through his creation of the universe, his promises to Abraham of progeny and land, his deliverance of Israel from Egypt, and the fulfillment of these promises in and through the Davidic kingdom and dynasty and the Jerusalem shrine where Yahweh chose to be at home forever.[113]

Miller associates the Zadokites with an eternal, Davidic-like covenant while associating the Levites with a more casuistic, deuteronomistic theology. He views Deuteronomy as a response to the Zadokites and their promulgation of the *status quo*. He maintains the theological legitimacy of both the Zadokites and the Levites throughout the biblical material. As for Ezekiel, Miller says that the "Zadokite priest has joined the ranks of the Levite prophets in declaring that he no longer regards Jerusalem or its temple as indestructible," causing Ezekiel to re-evaluate his Zadokite ideology.[114] Miller (re)reads Ezekiel's exclusive "sons of Zadok" statements through his universal theology lens. Haggai is the representative of the Zadokite theological vision for the future. In the end, the Levites controlled the compilation of the scriptures and, though respectful of the Zadokite tradition and ideology, made certain that the theology they deemed appropriate found its way into the final corpus.

In his 1995 study, Stephen L. Cook characterizes Wellhausen's *Prolegomena* as misdirecting the picture of the history of Israelite religion and sets about to clarify the confusing relationship of Zadokites and Levites found in Ezek 40–48 (and particularly in ch. 44).[115] After reviewing Wellhausen's position, he casts doubt on the traditional understanding that Ezek 44 chastises the rural priests of Josiah's reform as well as the

111. John W. Miller, *The Origins of the Bible: Rethinking Canon History* (Theological Inquiries: Studies in Contemporary Biblical and Theological Problems; New York: Paulist, 1994).

112. Ibid., 49.

113. Ibid., 55.

114. Ibid., 78–79.

115. Stephen L. Cook, "Innerbiblical Interpretation in Ezekiel 44 and the History of Israel's Priesthood," *JBL* 114 (1995): 193–208.

notion that Ezekiel is a stepping-stone between early traditions and P. The purpose of his article is to demonstrate that Ezekiel serves as an interpretation of Pentateuchal priestly material for the purpose of supporting a radical Zadokite vision for restoration. He argues against reading the text strictly as a political move. Instead, he advocates a recognition of the group's respect for its tradition, its religious heritage.

As J. Gordon McConville aptly points out in "Priests and Levites in Ezekiel: A Crux in the Interpretation of Israel's History," Ezek 40–48 serves as a crux of biblical interpretation.[116] McConville questions the traditional interpretation dating Ezek 44 to an earlier period than does the Priestly material of the Pentateuch. In summarizing the history of the Israelite priesthood, he challenges two assumptions: "(i) that the only meaningful distinction within the priesthood is that between Jerusalemite (Zadokite) and non-Jerusalemite priests; and (ii) that the non-Jerusalemite priests are to be equated with the priests of the "high-places" which Josiah destroyed."[117] By studying the relationship between Deut 18:6–8 and 2 Kgs 23:8–9, he finds fault in the equating of "the priests of the high-places" with Deuteronomy's Levites. He relies on Haran's analysis of the pre-exilic Levitical cities as solely places of residence. In light of his reassessment of Deut 18:6–8 as a text indicating the relationship of rural priests to the centralized temple, McConville calls for a reassessment of Ezek 44. Since the Zadokites controlled the priesthood of Jerusalem, and since both P and Ezekiel are assumed to stem from that priesthood, how could P broaden the structure that Ezekiel narrowed? His answer, of course, lies in his assumptions. He reviews both Zimmerli's and Gese's attempts to deal with the issue; they both posit Zadokite layers in the pericope in opposition to Haran who sees Ezek 40–48 as a single unit created by Ezekiel. While Zimmerli, Gese, and Haran all seem to agree that this part of Ezekiel post-dates P, McConville stresses his point that the whole of chs. 40–48 depends on the entire Pentateuch. He concludes that, while chs. 40–48 might have been written long after "those parts of P to which it particularly relates," the part about the Zadokites firmly establishing their relationship to the non-Zadokite Levites, was written by Ezekiel himself.

For Daniel Falk in his article on "High Priests" in the 2000 *Encyclopedia of the Dead Sea Scrolls*, the priests in the Seleucid period were Zadokites.[118] William R. Millar takes a postmodern approach to studying

116. J. Gordon McConville, "Priests and Levites in Ezekiel: A Crux in the Interpretation of Israel's History," *TynBul* 34 (1983): 3–32.

117. Ibid., 5.

118. Daniel K. Falk, "High Priests," in *Encyclopedia of the Dead Sea Scrolls* (ed. Lawrence H. Schiffman and James C. VanderKam. 2 vols. New York: Oxford University Press, 2000), 1:361–64.

the priesthood in his 2001 *Priesthood in Ancient Israel*. Privileging multivocal narrative, he attempts to focus on alternate spatial and temporal levels in examining story as indicative of a way of thinking. His thesis, that "blocks of literary tradition reflect the social-political experience of the various priestly families. The formation and combination of the literary strata also reflect the politics of the priestly families,"[119] allows him to examine the spirituality of priesthood. Millar designates two strands of priestly spirituality, that of the Mushite Levites and that of the Aaronid (also Levite) Zadokites. The narrative of Chronicles reveals Zadokite ideology while the narrative of Samuel/Kings represents Mushite Levite ideology. Millar assumes a Zadokite dominance of the centralized priesthood throughout the monarchy and into the postexilic period stating, "Thus within Judaism Aaronid Zadokite priests stood at the highest level one could aspire to as a Jew in the Persian empire."[120]

Mario Liverani, seeking to write a history in terms of contemporary historiographic practices and knowledge in *Israel's History and the History of Israel*, continues in traditional lines of thought concerning the Zadokites. Liverani sees the priests of the monarchic, exilic, and postexilic periods as Zadokites.[121] Iain M. Duguid likewise considers the Zadokites dominant: "...the Zadokites seem to have held effective sway in the priesthood in Jerusalem, although this never seems to have been elevated into an exclusive claim to priestly office... Since the deportation would likely have focused on the capital, it would certainly have been natural for Zadokites to form the dominant party among the exilic priests."[122]

119. William R. Millar, *Priesthood in Ancient Israel* (Understanding Biblical Themes; St. Louis, Miss.: Chalice, 2001), 7.

120. Millar, *Priesthood in Ancient Israel*, 34–35. This raises a lingering question for postmodern approaches in that they are so often dismissive of modern interest in linear history while concurrently utilizing "modernist," linear history. Millar's study only works because he assumes Zadokite dominance. It seems to me that he also assumes a traditionalist interpretation of Ezek 40–48—that the Zadokites governed the centralized priesthood and that the Levites were apostates, straying from pure spirituality and thus eventually marginalized.

121. Mario Liverani, *Israel's History and the History of Israel* (trans. Chiara Peri and Philip R. Davies; BibleWorld; London: Equinox, 2005), 94, 326, 337–39; originally published as *Oltre la Bibbia: Storia Antica di Israele* (Roma-Bari: Gius, Laterza & Figli Spa, 2003).

122. Iain M. Duguid, "Putting Priests in their Place: Ezekiel's Contribution to the History of the Old Testament Priesthood," in *Ezekiel's Hierarchical World: Wrestling with a Tiered Reality* (ed. Stephen L. Cook and Corrine L. Patton; SBLSymS 31; Leiden: Brill, 2004), 43–60 (46–47).

Lester Grabbe summarizes the traditional notions concerning Zadokites in the Hellenistic period well in his article "Were the Pre-Maccabean High Priests 'Zadokites'?," stating:

> It is conventionally argued, therefore, that a crisis developed at the time of the Maccabean revolt when the office of high priest passed out of the Zadokite family. Thus, when Jason replaced his brother Onias (2 Macc. 4.7–10), this might have been an illegitimate usurpation of power, but at least the office was kept in the family, so the story goes. With Menelaus, however, the high priesthood left the traditional Zadokite family and went to another priestly family (2 Macc. 4.23–25). After Menelaus was executed, Alcimus was appointed as high priest but, although of the tribe of Aaron, he was not of the Zadokite line (1 Macc. 7.11–14; 2 Macc. 14.3, 13; cf. Josephus, *Ant* 12.9.7 §387; 20.10.3 §235). After his death, the office of high priest was probably vacant for a period of time. Then Jonathan Maccabee took the office (1 Macc. 10.17–21), and it remained in the Hasmonean family until the reign of Herod, at which time it became the practice for Herodean rulers and the Romans to set up individuals in the office from a number of priestly families—and to depose them quite frequently.[123]

In 2004, James VanderKam took up the study of high priesthood from the Persian period into the Roman period in his *From Joshua to Caiaphas: High Priests after the Exile*. He states explicitly, "It is worth emphasizing what this book is and is not. It is a history of the Second-Temple *high* priests; it is not a history of the *priesthood*. As a result, there is no discussion of thorny issues such as the origin of the Aaronides."[124] Even so, his work gives evidence that he follows traditional assumptions about a dominant Zadokite priesthood through the monarchies. For example, in his section on Joiakim, he states, "It is not only in 1 Esdras and Josephus, however, that he has the rank of a leading priest: his genealogy in Ezra 7:1–5 (1 Esd 8:1–2) could hardly be improved, as it traces his descent through the Zadokite line during the First Temple back to Zadok himself and eventually to Aaron (none of the postexilic high priests is named in this list.)"[125]

123. Lester L. Grabbe, "Were the Pre-Maccabean High Priests 'Zadokites'?," in *Reading from Right to Left: Essays on the Hebrew Bible in Honour of David J. A. Clines* (ed. J. Cheryl Exum and H. G. M. Williamson; JSOTSup 373; Sheffield: Sheffield Academic Press, 2003), 205–15 (205–6).

124. James C. VanderKam, *From Joshua to Caiaphas: High Priests After the Exile* (Minneapolis: Fortress, 2004), xi.

125. Ibid., 45. Also see p. 18 n. 56, 37, 40, 270 n. 90 (which provides an interesting twist on traditional assumptions about Oniads, Zadokites, and Hasmoneans), 397.

Summary

I suggest that the development of historiography as it relates to Zadokites (and priesthood in ancient Israel) has been heavily dependent on the dating of the biblical material, particularly in terms of the documentary hypothesis.[126] Scholars typically take JE to provide the earliest material about priesthood—and usually date this information to the tribal system. D begins in the monarchy and so gives information about the centralized priesthood. Typically, P pulls it all together with the Wellhausenian religious stage of institutionalized priesthood of the exilic and postexilic periods. In the end, final interpretation is formed by the need to explain the references to Levites, priests, and sons of Zadok in Ezek 40–48.

The history of priesthood has been explained traditionally as follows: priests functioned in the "tribal" period, serving the people at shrines and in villages. Priesthood was already hereditary at that time. There were probably several priestly families and, as social stratification increased, so did the conflict between these families. With the emergence of the state, David appointed the obscure Zadok, and priesthood achieved a primary role in the centralized administration. Zadok's family, the Zadokites, gained and maintained their power as part of the governing class, serving the monarchy. These same Zadokites were taken off into exile with the monarchy when the Babylonians destroyed Jerusalem. This priesthood flourished in the exile, ruminating over the demise of the monarchy, developing explanations and plans for the future, and compiling the Torah. As this priesthood consolidated their power within the Diaspora community, they became more and more exclusive so that, as evidenced in Ezek 40–48, they set themselves apart over and against other priestly families, in final triumph over centuries-long conflicts between families. When Cyrus conquered Babylon, he called on this priesthood to help him establish the empire in Yehud. They returned and began the restoration, at some point establishing Judaism with Ezra's Torah. They created lineages and genealogies further to establish and distinguish themselves. Although there are some variations on these ideas, the presentation is basically the same.

126. This, of course, is precisely what Wellhausen intended, to first date the sources and then utilize them for information about religion and socio-historical context. For a summary of the lasting effects of the dominance of the much disputed documentary hypothesis, see Rolf Rendtorff, "What Happened to the Yahwist: Reflections After Thirty Years," and D. J. A. Clines, "Response to Rolf Rendtorff's 'What Happened to the Yahwist: Reflections After Thirty Years,'" *The SBL Forum* (August 2006), n.p. Online: http://www.sbl-site.org/Article.aspx? ArticleId=553 (Rendtorff) and http://www.sbl-site.org/Article.aspx?ArticleId=551 (Clines).

Baruch Halpern discusses the historiographic ramifications of writing history based on dating of sources.[127] He attributes this type of historiography to Burckhardtian methods: "In *Prolegomena*, Wellhausen applied to the Bible the principles pioneered by Burckhardt. First, he interrogated his sources chiefly about the times that had produced them—the sources were his events. Second, he used his sources as sketches of single stages in the history of Israelite society."[128] For Halpern, Wellhausen was a biblicist. Wellhausen's work "encouraged scholars to pursue the history of theology while only semiconscious of political history."[129] Halpern's ultimate and most salient critique focuses on the ramifications of this type of work on the history of ancient Israel:

> The tendency to approach Israelite history as the history of books fostered the delusion that historical battles could be fought at the level of compositional analysis. More substantive historiographic issues—how the historians came to believe what they wrote, what they thought writing history demanded—were neglected by scholars obsessed with isolating the sources verbatim, even in the Former Prophets and Chronicles.[130]

The historiographic trajectory launched by Wellhausen, while productive for many aspects of biblical and historical studies, neglects issues related to the philosophy of history, limiting the kinds of history that may be produced. This study suggests that current biblical studies, history of ancient Israel, and philosophy of history milieu invite a (re-)examination of the history of priesthood as it relates to the Zadokites.[131] The following chapter (Chapter 3) analyzes these milieux, reflecting on how they

127. Baruch Halpern, *The First Historians: The Hebrew Bible and History* (San Francisco: Harper & Row, 1988).

128. Ibid., 21.

129. Ibid., 26.

130. Ibid., 26–27.

131. As with other traditional interpretations that have been sustained for long periods of time and for good reasons and then have dissolved due to additional evidence or new scholarship developed from changed methodology, this traditional interpretation seems ripe for further development. See, for example, Douglas A. Knight, "The Pentateuch," in *The Hebrew Bible and Its Modern Interpreters* (ed. Douglas A. Knight and Gene M. Tucker; Atlanta: Scholars Press, 1985), 263–96, as he discusses "A Synthesis and its Dissolution" regarding the consensus formed around the work of Gerhard von Rad and Martin Noth. "The synthesis that explained so much about the formative history and meaning of the literature has met with such formidable opposition at individual points that only with multiple reservations can one defend it any longer. Heuristically, it still continues to prompt productive debate—not the least with regard to the determination of the right questions to ask of the text. However, there is no other grand plan, at the present, which promises to take the place of this influential proposal" (pp. 271–72).

impact a study of the Zadokites. The remainder of the study focuses on the Zadokites in view of the conclusions of Chapters 1 through 3 by examining available biblical data in Chapter 4, by examining available extra-biblical data in Chapter 5, and by providing a socio-historical context for the Zadokites in Chapter 6.

Chapter 3

A Time for Cacophony, a Time for Polyphony: Historiography

If one does not seek the unexpected, it will not be found, for it is hard to be sought out, and difficult to compass.

—Heraclitus, *Fragments*

Trajectories of Historiography

Chapters 1 and 2 demonstrated some of the ways historiographic practices have affected conceptualizations of the Zadokites. In particular, Chapter 2 contemplated the role of presuppositions in the formation of historical conclusions about the Zadokites. This chapter seeks to join with other voices in suggesting ways biblical historiography can and should engage the broader discipline of philosophy of history, as it relates to a study of the Zadokites.[1]

Pre-judgments—Presuppositions

The Possibility of Presuppositionless History

In 1960, Rudolf Bultmann asked, "Is Exegesis Without Presuppositions Possible?"[2] He answered his own question in a both/and fashion—he answered with "Yes" and with "No," making his ultimate answer dependent on the understood meaning of "without presuppositions." Exegesis is without presupposition if the exegete does not presuppose the result. Exegesis cannot be presuppositionless because the exegete brings knowledge, experience, and pre-judgment to the exegetical task. Bultmann concludes without qualification that interpreters bring pre-judgments to

1. The list of voices includes those of Baruch Halpern, V. Philips Long, William G. Dever, Niels P. Lemche, Philip R. Davies, and Abraham Kuenen.

2. Rudolph Bultmann, "Is Exegesis Without Presuppositions Possible?," *Enc* 21 (1960): 194–200.

their work. He endorses the fore-grounding of these pre-judgments. He recognizes that pre-judgments are value-laden. For Bultmann, "Every exegesis that is guided by dogmatic prejudices does not hear what the text says, but only lets the latter say what it wants to hear."[3] He calls for open-ended understandings of text and history, an engagement with text and with previous scholarship on the text that is open to developing meanings.[4] As analyzed in Chapter 2, various presuppositions continue to guide our study of the Zadokites.

The Discipline of History and Philosophy of History

Rolf Rendtorff proclaimed in 1992 that "Old Testament scholarship at present is in crisis" and that "any consensus is gone."[5] Today the resultant cacophony seems to have intensified. In his recent article, "The Future of Biblical Studies," Marc Zvi Brettler writes of our current situation:

> One observation about the present seems certain: biblical studies is now a field without paradigms. This development has really snuck up on us quite quickly—when I was a Ph.D. student two decades ago, I knew that JEP and D existed, what their order was, how the archaeology of Israel helped us recreate the ideal Solomonic age, etc. I feel less certain about all of these, as a result of the research of my colleagues in biblical studies. It is quite ironic that we now know much less than we did twenty or thirty years ago. It would be an interesting exercise to try to find ten significant points that ninety percent of scholars of Hebrew Bible could agree on. As a result, even when biblical scholars are talking about the same passage, their presuppositions are so different, they can hardly talk to each other. In addition, scholars spend so much time explaining and defending their suppositions that much scholarship is deadly boring, as it takes too long to get to the point.[6]

Our understanding of the Zadokites is trapped in the dissonance of these historiographic issues. In fact, historiography of ancient Israel struggles alongside historiography in general. Elizabeth Fox-Genovese and

3. Ibid., 195.

4. Much of this discussion on historiography is grounded in the work of Hans Georg Gadamer, *Truth and Method* (trans. Joel Weinsheimer and Donald G. Marshall; New York: Crossroad, 1989), a work I see as foundationally critical for contemporary historiography.

5. Rolf Rendtorff, "The Paradigm Is Changing: Hopes—and Fears," *BibInt* 1 (1992): 34–54, 61. Rendtorff challenges the entrenchment of consensus again in his recent article, "What Happened to the Yahwist."

6. Marc Zvi Brettler, "The Future of Biblical Studies," *The SBL Forum* (October 2004), n.p. Online: http://www.sbl-site.org/Article.aspx?ArticleId=320.

Elisabeth Lasch-Quinn edited a volume intending to turn the tide of a general malaise in historical studies. In 1998, they gathered notable historians[7] to begin a new organization, The Historical Society, in an effort to "foster the intellectual and ideological openness that alone nurture rich and challenging historical work of every variety—from social history to economic and diplomatic history."[8] Their meeting resulted in the publication of a volume intended as a protest to the academic inroads gained by "postmodernist relativism and indeterminacy" found in now-institutionalized historical studies focusing on critical theory, race, class, and gender.[9] Their motivating frustration stemmed from a perceived lack of attention to philosophy and methodology of history. With a desire to enter into conversation with multiple ideological and political ideals, they suggest that historians move beyond the acrimony of polarization and villainization of polarities that turn out to be mirror images of themselves. The contributors to the volume, while bemoaning the shift from modernism to postmodernism, eventuate in ratifying a commitment to the inclusive value of multiple historical approaches, advocating an "'ecumenical' standard for the study of history" and believing that "Our only prospects for intellectual and educational reconstruction lie in a renewed commitment to civilized and engaged argument with those who differ from us."[10] Useful as a descriptor of the current historiographic debates within the field of biblical studies, the volume bemoans the consequential methodological crisis facing a new generation of historians.[11] Yet, even in their collective despair over the loss of their historical ideals, they recognize the value of new ideas: "If postmodern philosophy and literary criticism were necessary to remind American historians that evidence does not speak for itself and that we need to think about what we are doing when we claim to speak for it, then we should be grateful

7. The list of participants includes Eugene Genovese, Marc Trachtenberg, Alan Charles Kors, Daniel C. Littlefield, Elizabeth Lasch-Quinn, Elizabeth Fox-Genovese, Roschelle Gurstein, Gertrude Himmelfarb, Russell Jacoby, Phillip M. Richards, Leo P. Ribuffo, Deborah A. Symonds, Bruce Kuklick, Victor Davis Hanson, Paul A. Rahe, Donald Kagan, Edward Berkowitz, Diane Ravitch, John Patrick Diggins, Sean Wilentz, Walter A. McDougall, Martin J. Sklar, Miriam R. Levin, John Womack, Louis Ferleger, and Richard H. Steckel.

8. Eugene D. Genovese, "A New Departure," in *Reconstructing History: The Emergence of a New Historical Society* (ed. Elizabeth Fox-Genovese and Elisabeth Lasch-Quinn; New York: Routledge, 1999), 6–8 (8).

9. Elizabeth Fox-Genovese and Elisabeth Lasch-Quinn, "Introduction," in Fox-Genovese and Lasch-Quinn, eds., xiii–xxii (xiv).

10. Ibid., xx.

11. Gertrude Himmelfarb, "Postmodernist History," in Fox-Genovese and Lasch-Quinn, eds., *Reconstructing History*, 71–93 (87).

for the lesson."[12] These scholars recognize that history has come to a new place; in a way, their work is only deconstructive; they fall prey to their own criticism of postmodernism—for they offer no means to move beyond that which they deconstruct.[13]

Michael Stanford's 1999 work on the philosophy of history attends to issues of history as a form of knowledge.[14] For Stanford, history is both science and art, and yet is not quite either. He argues that for too long, the philosophy of history has been distracted both by efforts to view history as strict science and efforts to view history as pure fiction. Both attempts are in error. Biblical historians and historians of ancient Israel, as will be discussed below, seem to be caught in these traps, insisting that history is either hard science or pure art. Stanford advocates seeing history as an activity, an ongoing action of conversation seeking to understand humanity in relation to time and space.

Stanford champions a kind of historical realism, emphasizing the multivalent nature of historiographic methodology: historiography has "no single methodology either of research or of explanation, no artificial language of its own to give it the precision of scientific terms, lacking the mathematical base of the more advanced sciences, and, above all, with no theoretical structure, no hierarchy of laws of increasing generality."[15]

The task of historiography lies in the relationship between history-as-event, von Ranke's 1824 *wie es eigentlich gewesen*, "as it really was," and history-as-account, history as produced by historians. Stanford calls these "history 1" and "history 2," illustrated respectively by the use and interpretation of the phrase "It's all hunky-dory." "There is no obvious or necessary connection between history 1 and what historians do with it, any more than there is between flour and what bakers do with it."[16]

For Stanford, "Evidence and interpretation are the twin pillars of historical knowledge."[17] As he articulates,

> History as it comes to us in the present seems to consist of memories, relics, monuments, documents, books... But they are solid lumps of lifeless matter... It is only when we bring our own interpretive understanding to them that they reveal their meaning and their values, then history comes

12. Leo P. Ribuffo, "Confession of an Accidental Historian," in Fox-Genovese and Lasch-Quinn, eds., 161.

13. As Berkowitz says—a new turn in the wheel.

14. Michael Stanford, *An Introduction to the Philosophy of History* (Oxford: Blackwell, 1998).

15. Ibid., 7.

16. Ibid., 145.

17. Ibid., 162. And, of course, each pillar has its own biases.

> alive… The study of history, the bringing of our human understanding to the past, transforms these solid lumps, the dead weight of the past, into a flowing, living reality.[18]

Philosophy of history becomes critical in the process at the intersection of evidence and interpretation. Historians ask specific questions and seek to answer those questions by finding, analyzing, and interpreting available evidence. An analogy between historiography and jurisprudence is helpful for considering evidence and interpretation.[19] During a trial, judge and jury are to discern beyond reasonable doubt what happened in a particular circumstance at a particular space and in a particular time. They examine material evidence, primary and secondary, and hear evidence presented from at least two perspectives. Those presenting eyewitness and expert testimony are examined and cross-examined. Formation of questions frames the conceptual picture for each juror. Eventually jurors engage to generate a product. The judge participates in the process by informing the jury's process with history, theories, and principles of jurisprudence. The verdict produced by the engagement of the judge and jury reconstructs events of the past as they specifically pertain to the original questions.

Likewise in the interpretation of evidence, the production of meanings, historians set themselves in dialogue with data. Historians acknowledge the role that pre-judgments play in binding them to their experience and in allowing them to enter into dialogue with tradition. Historians fore-ground and test these pre-judgments in a hermeneutical effort to pursue every avenue of interpretation. Since history rests on interpretation and there are many available interpretations, historians set about to define interpretive horizons.

Historiography and Histories of Ancient Israel

Historians of ancient Israel face similar perspectival and methodological issues as historiography seems to wallow in a state of flux, trapped in webs of polemics. Extreme points of view readily name the methodological faults of the other point of view. Extreme points of view frequently commit the errors they accuse their opponents of committing. While particulars may differ, contemporary polarities bear remarkable similarities to earlier debates over historiography between two historical schools as

18. Ibid., 162–63.

19. V. Philips Long draws this useful analogy in his article, "The Future of Israel's Past: Personal Reflections," in *Israel's Past in Present Research: Essays on Ancient Israelite Historiography* (ed. V. Philips Long; Sources for Biblical and Theological Study 7; Winona Lake, Ind.: Eisenbrauns, 1999), 580–86.

seen in the contrast between Europeans Albrecht Alt and Martin Noth's emphasis on history of tradition and American William F. Albright's qualified substantiation of the historicity of the biblical material.[20] Today's polarities are seen most clearly in the engagements (or lack thereof) between the non-traditionalists Neils Peter Lemche, Thomas L. Thompson, and Philip R. Davies (and perhaps Keith Whitelam and Giovanni Garbini[21]) and the traditionalist American scholars William G. Dever and Frank Moore Cross. While they have not yet moved the discussions past polemics, these scholars raise critical methodological issues that may in fact provide a starting point for future historiography and may be instructive in the study of the Zadokites. The following analysis first examines general historiographic issues raised by these scholars in an effort to recognize common assumptions and methodological approaches and to frame the current methodological setting by mooring it in philosophy and the philosophy of history, then relates these issues to this study of the Zadokites, and finally establishes a historiographic structure in which to develop a history of the Zadokites.[22]

Niels Peter Lemche

Niels Peter Lemche has written prolifically, precisely, and often polemically about biblical historiography. In one of his less strident works on the topic, *The Israelites in History and Tradition*, Lemche rightly acknowledges the vast contributions of previous critical scholarship to our knowledge of the history of ancient Israel while criticizing traditional, "consensus" scholarship for presuming for ancient Israel a unilateral uniqueness bound by common language, common geography, and common nationality as expressed in a biblical meta-narrative that "transposed the essentials of Judaism back in time."[23] He finds this traditional scholarship circumscribed both by the "structure of the biblical narrative"[24]

20. These polarities include: *naturgeschichte–geistsgeschichte*; maximalists–minimalists; modernists–post-modernist; fundamentalists–nihilists; explanation–description/significance; meaning–meaning; universality–particularity.

21. See Keith Whitelam, *The Invention of Ancient Israel: The Silencing of Palestinian History* (London: Routledge, 1994); Giovanni Garbini, *History and Ideology in Ancient Israel* (trans. John Bowden; London: SCM Press); idem, *Myth and History in the Bible* (trans. Chiara Peri; JSOTSup 362; Sheffield: Sheffield Academic Press, 2003).

22. This in the hopes that such recognition will provide a starting point and a means to move beyond polemics.

23. Niels Peter Lemche, *The Israelites in History and Tradition* (Library of Ancient Israel; Louisville, Ky.: Westminster John Knox, 1998), 139.

24. Ibid., 135–37.

and by use of the Hebrew Bible as a primary source. In other words, in some form or another, the biblical narrative serves as the historical basis or starting point for traditional histories.[25] Lemche is helpful here for a study of the Zadokites in fore-grounding frequently present presuppositions. Once fore-grounded they can be historiographically evaluated. For Lemche, the critical mass of available evidence and analysis creates the opportunity for a new approach based on a disinfected set of presuppositions.[26] When we are able to separate the substance of Lemche's scholarship from his engagement in polemic disputation, we can acknowledge the judicious nature of his central, methodological question regarding the status and role of primary sources in writing history. For Lemche, caution precedes progress. Irrespective of the critical nature of documentary evidence, the historian must be cognizant of the crucial role of interpretation. In this, Lemche returns to a recurring theme—every historian brings their own context, circumstance, and set of presuppositions to the act of writing history. Every historian is "a kind of treasure hunter, looking for booty in the form of new knowledge, improved knowledge, a reconfirmation of something we thought we knew in advance or had already guessed or argued in favor of."[27] He accuses traditional scholarship of approaching new material in error—of "using every kind of ingenuity" in asking "how this new textual evidence relates to the Bible."[28] For Lemche, these biblical scholars commit "a transgression against one of the most fundamental rules of historical research."[29]

Lemche's work calls into question the long-held practice of utilizing biblical narrative as the primary source for historical chronology. For study of the Zadokites, the biblical material is used to establish the framework for David's kingship and priestly appointments. From that framework, conclusions are drawn that the priesthood of subsequent monarchs—first in the united monarchy and then in the southern kingdom—must have followed an established pattern that resulted in the sons of Zadok serving as the dominant priesthood until the Hasmonean period. Lemche advocates a different approach. He suggests instead that, when presented with new material, the historian/scholar should investigate ways in which this evidence relates to history.

Lemche deconstructs and then constructs. Based on his understanding of the centrality of ethnicity, Lemche presents his conceptualization of

25. Ibid., 139.

26. Does not Lemche rightly question elsewhere whether a disinfected set of presuppositions is even possible?

27. Lemche, *The Israelites in History and Tradition*, 38.

28. Ibid., 38, 57.

29. Ibid., 115.

the context and ideology which spawned the biblical material. Lemche expands on Herodotus' classical conception of ethnicity—"common blood, common religion, and common language."[30] For Lemche, an ethnic group "consists of the persons who think of themselves as members of this group, in contrast to other individuals who are not reckoned to be members and who do not reckon themselves to belong to this group...ethnic groups are by definition unstable with borders that can be transgressed in every possible way."[31] For Lemche, ethnic groups exist on a continuum with overlapping borders. They have numerous identities; individuals can belong to many and may change frequently. The situation is fluid. These ethnic groups are maintained by founding myths. In keeping with his Wellhausenian methodological proposition that texts provide information about the time in which they were written, Lemche understands history as "written in order to create identity among members of...a...certain...group."[32] He calls on scholars to recognize that the Old Testament "was not written as or intended to be 'past as it was.'"[33] He further suggests that the Old Testament is a history and that the history as found in the Old Testament "was accepted by its audience; otherwise it would not have been preserved."[34] Using as an example Noth's amphictyony concept, Lemche suggests that there are several ways to approach textual material—historically, ideologically, and literarily—but for Lemche any and all of these ultimately produce ethnicity.[35]

30. Ibid., 8.

31. Ibid., 20.

32. Ibid., 96. With this Wellhausen would certainly agree, the difference being the dating of the material.

33. Ibid., 130.

34. Ibid., 96.

35. Ibid., 99–110. Lemche participates in this discussion of ethnicity and "the other," an area of growing concern in biblical studies, with other scholars including Mark G. Brett, ed., *Ethnicity and the Bible* (BibInt Series 19; Leiden: Brill, 1996), and "Israel's Indigenous Origins: Cultural Hybridity and the Formation of Israel's Ethnicity," *BibInt* 11, nos. 3–4 (2003): 400–12; Jon L. Berquist, *Controlling Corporeality: The Body and the Household in Ancient Israel* (New Brunswick: Rutgers University Press, 2002); Claudia V. Camp, *Wise, Strange, and Holy: The Strange Woman and the Making of the Bible* (JSOTSup 320; Gender, Culture, Theory 9; Sheffield: Sheffield Academic Press, 2000); Gale A. Yee, *Poor Banished Children of Eve: Women as Evil in the Hebrew Bible* (Minneapolis: Fortress, 2004); Kenton L. Sparks, *Ethnicity and Identity in Ancient Israel: Prolegomena to the Study of Ethnic Sentiments and their Expression in the Hebrew Bible* (Winona Lake, Ind.: Eisenbrauns, 1998); Elizabeth Bloch-Smith, "Israelite Ethnicity in Iron I: Archaeology Preserves What is Remembered and What is Forgotten in Israel's History," *JBL* 122 (2003): 401–25; Thomas L. Thompson, "Hidden Histories and the Problem of

The ideology that produced the biblical literature—particularly as seen in the foundation myths of the exodus and the exile—needed to create a unique and chosen people, separate from others. It needed to emphasize the centrality of the *land*. The most plausible context for the creation of this Old Testament picture for Lemche, then, is found in the late Persian and Hellenistic periods when issues of common blood decided who held power; when society was so fragmented that people needed ethnic identities in order to survive; when "members" of a certain "society constructed their own origin myth as a program for taking over a country which they had reclaimed for themselves in spite of the inhabitants who already lived there"; when the progenitors of the ideology needed exclusively to distinguish themselves from others.[36] The exodus, like the tale of Remus, Romulus, and the founding of Rome, provides a foundation of origin for the people. The exile allows the people to (re)claim the land. Together the exodus and the exile create, present, and sustain identity.

Lemche develops a stimulating and plausible theory that deserves attention from biblical scholarship. His inability to disengage from debilitating polemics and his tendency to see today's historiography as bi-polar hinder the consideration of his ideas. Ironically, his effort to find central themes in his book evokes images of some previous and quite "traditional" scholarship, particularly as found in biblical theology. He replaces Old Testament "theology" with Old Testament "ideology." And, where von Rad would have named the theology "YHWH's salvation history," Lemche names the ideology "the elites' creation of ethnic identity."

Lemche has much to offer the scholarly discussion. He raises pertinent and often helpful questions about the socio-historical context of biblical material. He calls scholars to recognize and name their tasks and methodology as historians. He recognizes operating and underlying assumptions within biblical scholarship. He tries to understand how and why biblical scholarship has tended to use the biblical material as a primary source for history and he encourages writers of history to be deliberate in designation and use of source material. He takes issue with an assumption of ancient Israel as unilaterally unique.[37] He challenges his readers to evaluate whether and how it is possible to see historical Israel "as it was."

Ethnicity in Palestine," in *Western Scholarship and the History of Palestine* (ed. Michael Prior; London: Melisende, 1998), 23–39, and "Defining History and Ethnicity in the South Levant," in *Can a "History of Israel" Be Written?* (ed. Lester Grabbe; JSOTSup 245; Sheffield: Sheffield Academic Press, 1997), 166–78.

36. Lemche, *The Israelites in Tradition and History*, 130.

37. But, in his own way, Lemche too implies a unilateral Israel when he suggests a singular, unilateral ideology for that biblical material, an ideology that both

For this study of the Zadokites in history, Lemche's approach encourages certain questions. So, biblical references to the Zadokites, few as they are, reflect the socio-political milieu of the time in which the references were written. As fully discussed in Chapter 4, the priestly lists in Ezra–Nehemiah and Chronicles, as well as the sparse mentions of Zadok, reflect the periods in which they were written. The evidence of the presence and role of the Zadokites depends heavily upon the dating of the pericopes. Because of the paucity of references and the current historiographic difficulties in dating the biblical material, it is necessary to employ other historiographic means to create a portrait of the Zadokites. Lemche correctly challenges the use of the biblical material directly as history and necessarily as a primary source, which, for a study of the Zadokites, has the potential to reconfigure any portrait of the ancient priesthood. Lemche also raises a serious challenge to the early and often still dominant view that the biblical material provides contemporaneous history as a starting point for historians. If another starting point is chosen, our understanding of the Zadokites will be altered. Finally, his insights into the importance of land and the creation of identity provide a critical lens with which to view ancient Israel in the Persian period, providing at least one context for a portrait of the Zadokites. While Lemche's work seemingly deconstructs many historical portraits of ancient Israel, particularly those using the biblical material in a linear fashion to generate a historical chronology, it also opens the way for scholars to employ additional historiographic methodologies, such as social-scientific analysis, to create a fuller historical portrait of the Zadokites.

Thomas L. Thompson

If Lemche is polemical, Thomas L. Thompson is logomachic. He readily names the operating assumptions of traditional scholarship; he is less eager to clarify his own, although he should be applauded for providing, in the Preface of *The Mythic Past: Biblical Archaeology and the Myth of Israel*, a description of his own socio-historical context.[38] For Thompson, the purpose of writing history is "to explain evidence of the past that has survived"—"to give clarity and coherence to what we know about the

advocates and creates a national and ethnic identity. Lemche's response to this comment would probably be that he agrees that the biblical material presents an ideology, but that this ideology does not represent the whole of ancient Israel. And most would likely disagree with Lemche about a biblical theology representing the whole of ancient Israel.

38. Thomas L. Thompson, *The Mythic Past: Biblical Archaeology and the Myth of Israel* (London: Basic Books, 1999).

past."[39] The historian's starting point is critical for Thompson. He insists that historians should begin with an insular history of ancient Israel generated independent of textual data. Only then can scholars scrutinize textual evidence for its possible contributions to a written history of any period. Textual evidence must be designated as primary or secondary source material. Primary source material, contemporaneous with the events described, is rarely available and can be used, albeit carefully, to shape a historical portrait of a period. Secondary source material is principally helpful for understanding the historical context of the writers as opposed to providing useful information about the referent period. While secondary sources may contain information collected from historical events, historians today have little means of separating fact from fiction. Textual evidence is best evaluated, then, by literary analysis. His eristic style continues to fan the flames of the so-called minimalist/maximalist debate, although he does not use those labels in this book.[40] Often condescending, he faults traditional scholarship—sometimes biblical scholars, sometimes biblical archaeologists, sometimes historians, and sometimes historical scholarship—for raiding the Bible "for whatever they found illustrative or useful for their own historical interests"; for "historicizing" the origin stories; for its "indolent habit of offering paraphrases of ancient historians and correcting them only when evidence proves them wrong"; for using a "feckless excuse: Everyone has been doing it"; for pointing "to the transcendent theological value of these unexamined traditions to justify the lack of academic integrity in research"; for being solipsistic in their work; for being an "embarrassment" by "posing as an historical and critical scholarly discipline"; for "resisting change vigorously"; for using the Bible as an "illustration for their archaeological research"; for functioning in a "more apologetic and theological than critical and historical mode"; for accepting plausibility instead of evidence"; for inflicting nineteenth-century European need for unique

39. Ibid., 7.

40. Current debates about histories of biblical periods often are reduced to the labeling of participant scholars as "minimalist" or "maximalist." Both appellations serve derisive purposes and hearken back to the earlier controversy between Alt/Noth and Albright. "Minimalist" has been used to label Davies, Thompson, and Lemche as nihilists or dilettantes who show disrespect for *the* tradition and write only to serve their own agendas, disregarding anything and everything that cannot be substantiated by coeval evidence. The label "maximalist" has been used less frequently, but when used has generally been applied to Dever to suggest that he uses the Hebrew Bible to build a real-time, historically accurate, chronological framework for his subsequent history of biblical periods. Few scholars would label themselves either "maximalist" or "minimalist"; few push their work to either extreme.

self-identification upon ancient Israel; and for confusing stories with historical evidence—just to mention a few.[41]

Historicity,[42] for Thompson, is an irrelevant question that cannot, in any event, be answered. He resolves his dissonance between history and historicity by specifying that "our question involves more complicated issues of literary historicality and reference, of metaphor and literary postures, evocation and conviction."[43] For Thompson, questions about the Bible and history are not really about history but about how the text functions. He delights in investigating the structure, themes, plot-lines, repetitive patterns, genres, settings, motifs, chain-narratives, scenes, roles, polarities, tropes, metaphors, characters, typologies, traditions, and morals of biblical narratives. For Thompson, historians, biblical scholars, and biblical archaeologists can do no better than to shatter the false dichotomy between faith and science, between theology and history. We

41. Thompson, *The Mythic Past*, 4, 5, 10, 31–32, 35, 36, 288, 229.

42. Regarding archaeology specifically, Thompson applauds the rise in importance of archaeology as a distinct discipline as well as the abundance of data now available to scholars through the efforts of archaeology. He contends that most primary evidence in fact comes from archaeology and that this evidence should be used as the basis for the independent historical framework. Yet, in his complaints against biblical archaeology, Thompson emphasizes that "Archaeology has need for a sound historical perspective of ancient Palestine as a background and canvas on which to work." Perhaps Thompson thinks archaeology can do both—provide the data for an initial historical framework and, at the same time, stand in need of a historical canvas on which to work—but the coexistence of these notions presents a quandary for Thompson's work. Thompson both compliments biblical archaeology for demanding external evidence in the historical proof of any matter and decries it for its dysfunctional relationship with biblical studies. He challenges biblical archaeology to "give up its historicized Bible as the intellectual centre of its historiography."

It is in regard to historiography, history, and historicity that Thompson most clearly finds his antinomies. He writes about writing history of ancient Israel but does not really think a history is possible. Thompson's discontinuity surfaces in his understanding of ancient history. Sometimes he says that the biblical writers never intended to write history—that the biblical stories often regarded as historical were written and transmitted for reasons other than history. He continues, the "Bible's language is not an historical language." On the other hand, he often refers to the Bible or parts of the Bible as ancient historiography. Reading Thompson as a whole, one must assume that he finds history a modern concept. His idealized, objectified, often naïve view of a pure history can never be attained. Although he sometimes refers to the ancient writers as ancient historians, he most often sees them as creators of identity, origins, and continuity.

43. Thompson, *The Mythic Past*, 34. This is Thompson's segue to his passion—literary analysis of the Bible.

can do no better than to understand the Hebrew Bible as a theology borne out of critical self-reflection, to recognize ourselves—biblical scholars, historians, archaeologists—as theologians.[44]

Thompson's often acrimonious work assists the general discussion on historiography and the Zadokites in one particular way. Thompson invokes questions about why there are so few mentions of the Zadokites in the biblical material. Like Lemche, Thompson reminds historians that we cannot develop a picture of a Zadokite priesthood based on any assumption that the biblical literature presents a historical portrait of the period to which it refers.[45] Thompson, along with Lemche, assist the further development of historiographic method by provoking historical self-reflection. The critical mass of evidence regarding the Zadokites, or actually the lack thereof, demands a historical re-examination of the Zadokites.

William G. Dever

William Dever's work is no less filled with contradictions and polemics than that of Thompson, and still offers insights into how we might successfully approach a history of the Zadokites. Lashing out at the so-called minimalists with name-calling of his own, Dever casts labels such as "disaffected anti-establishment figure," "revisionist," "small but vocal minority," "the new nihilists," "outsider," presenters of history that is "full of errors, misrepresentations and unbalanced judgments," "outrageous," and without "even a superficial acquaintance with socio-anthropology or archaeology."[46] He can neither abide nor enter into a scholarly discussion with these so-called minimalists. Dever, sometimes labeled as a maximalist, has at times served as a minimalist in his own right.

In 1985, writing about "Syro-Palestinian and Biblical Archaeology" for *The Hebrew Bible and Its Modern Interpreters*, Dever called for an understanding of biblical archaeology as its own unique chapter of American biblical studies.[47] He rightly recognized archaeology related to ancient Israel as an autonomous discipline developing from the decreasing influence of colonialism, the increasing commonalities in archaeological field methods, the necessity of cooperative efforts in the areas of

44. The "minimalist" Thompson becomes the "maximalist."

45. In this, Thompson, like Dever, agrees with Wellhausen.

46. William G. Dever, *What Did the Biblical Writers Know, and When Did They Know It? What Archaeology Can Tell Us About the Reality of Ancient Israel* (Grand Rapids: Eerdmans, 2001), passim.

47. William G. Dever, "Syro-Palestinian and Biblical Archaeology," in Knight and Tucker, eds., *The Hebrew Bible and Its Modern Interpreters*, 31–74.

fundraising and recruitment of workers, and the juxtaposition of expense and intellectual sophistication for the field of study. He chastises biblical scholarship for engaging in a debate that was clearly *passé*. In the methodology and theory of this work, Dever presents as a "minimalist."

Over a decade later, in 1997, Dever[48] historiographically analyzes the limitations of philological and theological approaches and acknowledges the values inherent in new histories of ancient Israel as found in the works of Soggin, Lemche, Miller and Hayes, and Garbini.[49] Israelite historiography, he says, is in crisis. Instead of focusing on facts, historians must ask meaningful questions of data; these questions should include: What is history? What are the goals of history? How do we distinguish between primary and secondary sources? What are the criteria for verifying facts? What is the appropriate balance between objectivity and relativity? What kind of history do we want? He rightly asserts that biblical texts can and do provide a history of ideas. He calls on an interdisciplinary archeology to write a techno-environmental and socio-economic history of ancient Israel.

In his most recent work, *What Did the Biblical Writers Know and When Did They Know It? What Archaeology Can Tell Us about the Reality of Ancient Israel*, Dever makes what appears to be a radical change of direction from his previous methodological and theoretical approach as they relate to historiography. In this largely defensive work, Dever should be commended as he carefully begins by offering a description of his own background. Unfortunately, the description is quite brief. He acknowledges having "immersed myself in 'revisionist' and 'postmodern' literature" based on intuition that led him to write the book, he states his purpose as being "not only to counter the 'revisionists' abuse of archaeology, but to show how modern archaeology brilliantly illuminates a real 'Israel' in the Iron Age, and also to help foster the dialogue between archaeology and biblical studies."[50] Writing an apology for some of his previously published points of view, Dever presents an outcry against what he regards as personal attacks against his work. His stated thesis—"While the Hebrew Bible in its present, heavily edited form cannot be taken at face value as history in the modern sense, it nevertheless contains much history" that is obscured "to all but the most critical and

48. William G. Dever, "Philology, Theology, and Archaeology: What Kind of History Do We Want, and What Is Possible," in *The Archaeology of Israel: Constructing the Past, Interpreting the Present* (ed. Neil Asher Silberman and David Small; JSOTSup 237; Sheffield: Sheffield Academic Press, 1997), 290–310.

49. Dever, "Syro-Palestinian and Biblical Archaeology."

50. Dever, *What Did the Biblical Writers Know?*, x.

discerning eye"[51]—is his fundamental response to the "crisis" in biblical and historical studies, especially to those he considers postmodern revisionists.[52] "If all this makes me a positivist," says Dever, "so be it... At least I have not unwittingly put myself out of business as a historian by denying the existence of my fundamental data, which I think the revisionists have done."[53] Dever conflates his response to his "minimalistic," "nihilistic" opponents with a caricature of postmodernism and its promulgation of deconstruction. He suggests a possible conspiracy theory: "And in my judgment the revisionists are carrying out a classic, deliberate, single-minded deconstructionist agenda."[54]

Dever agrees with his opponents that the biblical material is largely propaganda before proceeding to accuse them of jumping "from the conclusion that because the Hebrew Bible's 'Israel' is really couched in idealistic terms, there is no *real* 'Israel' of the biblical period, that is... the Iron Age of ancient Palestine."[55] In fact, Dever differs little from his apparent opponents.[56] And it is in these commonalities that those seeking to write histories of ancient Israel may find possibilities for making productive progress. Dever acknowledges and stresses the difference between "fact" and "data."[57] He defends the importance of context.[58] For

51. Ibid., 97. There might be some disagreement about how to discern appropriately "the most critical and discerning eye."

52. Ibid., 97. There might be some disagreement about how to discern appropriately "the most critical and discerning eye." Chief among Dever's revisionists are Lemche, Thompson, Davies, Whitelam, and Finkelstein (whom Dever calls an inherent iconoclast).

53. Ibid., 17. Goals and objectives become critical here.

54. Ibid., 27.

55. Ibid., 46. In fact, Dever's revisionists do not say there is no *real* Israel—only that we cannot know much of the Israel of the biblical period. Philip R. Davies, *In Search of "Ancient Israel"* (JSOTSup 148; Sheffield: Sheffield Academic Press, 1993), does not claim that there was no ancient Israel, only that historians must separate the idea of a real, historical Israel from the biblical literature which must be appreciated as an ideological construct. Davies challenges not the concept of a history of ancient Israel but the historians who solipcistically create history from a chronological interpretation of the Hebrew Bible and then use the same history to generate a socio-historical context for interpreting the Bible. Davies, like Wellhausen, suggests that the biblical literature reflects the socio-political context of the time in which it was constructed.

56. Ironically, in much the same fashion that Alt/Noth differed little from their rhetorical/polemical opponent, Albright—despite their disagreements, they all used biblical narrative to form the bases of their histories.

57. Dever, *What Did the Biblical Writers Know?*, 72.

58. Ibid., 74.

Dever, and his "opponents," "All historians deal with possibilities, at best with probabilities, never with certainties. The degree of subjectivity can and should be reduced, but can never be eliminated."[59]

Dever furthermore shares assumptions with his opponents: "That the Hebrew Bible is in that sense 'propaganda' is not in dispute among responsible scholars."[60] He then qualifies this notion:

> There is merit in recognizing that the ideal *theological* "Israel" of the Hebrew Bible, as well as that of many Jewish and Christian commentators and believers, is not to be automatically equated with the *real* Israel of the Iron Age of ancient Palestine... Furthermore, the revisionists are right in asserting that our relatively recent rediscovery of data on the latter Israel has resulted in a theoretical historical "reconstruction," rather than an absolutely certain and fully accurate portrait. No responsible historian or archaeologist would claim otherwise. In that sense, all "histories of ancient Israel" are indeed "social constructs." But it is obvious that so is all our knowledge of the human past, the external world, or any other purported "reality." Religion is a "social construct"; is it thereby irrelevant? The question is not whether claims to knowledge are "social constructs"—intellectual formulations within a social context that gives them particularity, relevance, and meaning—but a question of whether the constructions are based on facts or merely on fancies. In short, the fundamental historiographical and epistemological presuppositions of the revisionists with regard to writing a history of Israel are either naïve, or even when unobjectionable, banal. There is nothing sophisticated or new here.[61]

Methodologically, Dever, once again in agreement with his opponents, presents concise and potentially productive considerations: the opportunity for "the advance of real and lasting knowledge comes not so much from chance discovery (as the popular misunderstanding assumes) but rather from the systematic investigation of specific questions."[62] "Responsible, serious" historians of ancient Israel should build upon "pertinent observations on the limitations of the biblical texts as sources for history-writing."[63] Dever recommends that these "responsible, serious" historians should turn "to the now primary source for new data, archaeology, in order to write *truly* revisionist histories of ancient Israel."[64] For Dever, all

59. Ibid., 78.
60. Ibid., 47.
61. Ibid., 45.
62. Ibid., 78.
63. Ibid., 46.
64. Ibid., 46. Once again, Dever is caught in the trap of his own brilliance and insight, just as he was with "Death of a Discipline," *BAR* 21 (1995): 50–55, 70. He names what must and should be done but he himself has not done it.

evidence falls under the rubric of artifact—all evidence is therefore "encoded messages." There are few (if any) "facts" in archaeology.[65]

Finally, Dever basically, if not fundamentally, agrees with his "opponents" in his conclusions about what remains when the dust of the current polemical controversy settles. We have, at the most, historical kernels available from pre-monarchical periods. We know little of a united monarchy, except that Dever says the biblical texts have a "ring of truth."[66] Dever agrees with many others that demographic changes occurred in the central highlands during Iron I. Dever, along with many others, takes an anthropological view of Saul and David as "chiefs" and posits a state of some sort for Solomon. As for the divided monarchy, Dever and his opponents find little about which to disagree. Clearly, Dever's greatest point of disagreement with some scholars, his opponents, lies not in substance but in rhetoric and polemics. By and large, Dever and his opponents agree on commendable practices and assumptions (and many conclusions).[67]

65. Dever, *What Did the Biblical Writers Know?*, 70–72.

66. Ibid., 268. "In short, there is nothing inherently improbable in the main outline of the biblical story as it now stands" (ibid.). In other words, Dever demands acknowledgement that the narrative presents a plausible portrait—a conclusion that almost no scholar would deny. In fact, the suggestion of one of Dever's archaeological colleagues becomes increasingly important; in his "The Archaeology of the United Monarchy: An Alternative View," *Levant* 28 (1996): 181–91, Israel Finkelstein presents his development of the so-called low chronology for monarchic Israel. He argues "The Low Chronology that I proposed for the Philistine pottery carries far-reaching implications for the archaeology of the tenth–ninth centuries BCE. To start with the conclusion, it would be fair to say that the identification of the archaeology of the United Monarchy is far from being a decided matter. Actually, it is a classic case of circular reasoning and dead reckoning. In what follows, I wish to discuss the search for the archaeology of the United Monarchy free of any conventional wisdom, text bias, or irrelevant sentimentality. I will try to demonstrate that there is an alternative hypothesis to the prevailing theory, though I will not be able to prove it (nor would any scholar be able to prove the prevailing view); the alternative approach is no less appealing and historically sound than the generally accepted one" (p. 178). Finkelstein presents a credibly plausible portrait.

67. In the end, Dever's primary methodological suggestion is perhaps the weakest portion of his book—that a dialogue between artifacts and text "holds the best hope yet for writing an adequate history of ancient Israel" (*What Did the Biblical Writers Know?*, 81). His fallacy is that both the text and the artifact require reading and interpretation and, for Dever, his hermeneutic is *the* only acceptable hermeneutic. Dever's other fault is in continuing to defend his early conclusions—ethnicity, Iron I gates issues—in spite of his agreement with evidence that does not support these earlier conclusions.

How then does Dever assist with a study of the Zadokites? His earlier works call for clear, concise, and deliberate historiography.[68] He demands that historiography be driven by specific questions. Even in this work, despite his defensive rhetoric, the ideals raised by Dever set an appropriate interrogative framework for any historiographic study of the Zadokites. What are the goals of writing a history of the Zadokites? How do historians distinguish between primary and secondary sources as they relate to the Zadokites? And how should these sources be used? What criteria should be used to verify facts about the Zadokites? What kind of history of the Zadokites can and/or should historians write? What can contexts tell us about the Zadokites? What can we infer about the Zadokites from the encoded messages of our written sources and their contexts? What role should archaeology play in writing a history of the Zadokites? How can an interdisciplinary approach assist in developing a fuller portrait of the Zadokites? Dever is right about something else. Historiography of ancient Israel is in crisis.

Post-Dever–Lemche–Thompson

Post the Dever–Lemche–Thompson appellative period, new histories address similar issues. Iain Provan, often stridently polemical, joins with V. Phillips Long and Tremper Longman III, in *A Biblical History of Israel* (2003), to provide readers with first a commentary on historiography and then a retelling of biblical history.[69] Their analysis of historiography yields an often cogent description of the path and pitfalls of historiographic development—concluding that the positivistic, objective oriented historiography of the nineteenth and twentieth centuries and the relativism of postmodern historiography collapse in failure under their inherent inadequacies.[70] In almost tongue-in-cheek fashion, they suggest three options for today's historians. The first option is the ostrich approach, putting one's head in the sand in a denial of reality—what they term the "modernist" approach.[71] Option two they label the give-up approach. Historians simply throw their hands in the air, concluding that

68. Especially see Dever, "Syro-Palestinian and Biblical Archaeology," and "Philology, Theology, and Archaeology."

69. Provan, Long, and Longman, *A Biblical History of Israel.*

70. Their analysis often generalizes toward some type of empirical positivism predominating modern historiography. Although the influence of positivism continues in historiography, its function was (and is) nuanced. For further discussion, see Lester L. Grabbe's review of the book for the *Review of Biblical Literature* (August 2004), n.p. Online: http://bookreviews.org/pdf/3961_3828.pdf.

71. Provan, Long, and Longman, *A Biblical History of Israel*, 43.

the writing of a history of ancient Israel just cannot be done, evidencing the type of historiography produced by postmodern approaches.[72] For the third option, they agree with postmodernism in criticizing modernism for self-delusional grandeur but deny its so-called subjectivism. The correct approach is to give a "proper place to philosophy and tradition."[73] This is indeed the appropriate question—and in this they have tried to move the discussion to a new and helpful point. Their answer, however, is not as helpful as their question. Their answer is to say that there are many histories—and that they want to present a biblical history; in this, they seek to use the Hebrew Bible to build a real-time, historically accurate, chronological framework for their history of biblical periods. To do this, they make a case for depending on "testimony." Their premise here cannot be sustained. They argue the wrongness of "marginalizing the biblical text." While they call hesitating to use the biblical text as a basic starting point "marginalization," I call it a methodological choice fully present in the art of history writing.

Mario Liverani attempts to write a new kind of history with his 2003 *Israel's History and the History of Israel*, prompted by the progress (and lack of progress) in historiography of ancient Israel.[74] For Liverani, "The history of ancient Israel has always been presented as a sort of paraphrase of the Biblical text," so that biblical studies has expended most of its effort over the last century toward deconstruction. Liverani thinks it is time for a change: "If the critical *de*construction of the Biblical text is accepted, why not also attempt a *re*construction, referring literary texts to the time in which they were written and not to the period they speak about?"[75] He seeks to write a history in two parts; the first, a "'normal' (i.e. not unique) and quite insignificant history of two kingdoms in Palestine," a best history created from all available data, and the second, an "invented" history, an analysis of the ideology undergirding the biblical material as it seeks to persuade and to create identity.[76]

Lester L. Grabbe, prolific analyst of the Second Temple period, deals directly with the question: "To what extent can we use the biblical text as a historical source?"[77] He suggests a "multiple-source approach": one

72. Ibid., 44. Their characterization of postmodern approaches is simplistic and somewhat dismissive while their analyses of the presuppositions of both the ostrich and the give-up approaches are solipsistic.

73. Ibid., 44.

74. Liverani, *Israel's History and the History of Israel*.

75. Ibid., xv–xvi.

76. Ibid., xvi.

77. Lester L. Grabbe, "The Kingdom of Judah," in *Good Kings and Bad Kings* (ed. Lester L. Grabbe; LHBOTS 393; ESHM 5; New York: T. & T. Clark, 2005),

that uses "archaeological, inscriptional, contemporary textual, biblical" data, each analyzed independently prior to being synthesized in a history. The biblical text, one source, should be analyzed critically with regard to genre and should be "controlled by external data."[78] Distinctions should be made with regard to primary and secondary sources.[79]

Historiography and Ancient Israel

Often polarities are named where they do not exist; they are false dichotomies. Dever, Lemche, and Thompson, are correct: the history of ancient Israel faces a critical and defining period. Evidence the significant corpus of scholarly exchange and engagement on the topic over the last decade or so.[80] Rendtorff's 1992 seminal essay, "The Paradigm is

79–122 (114). For Liverani (*Israel's History and the History of Israel*, xv), "The history of ancient Israel has always been presented as a sort of paraphrase of the Biblical text," so that biblical studies has expended most of its effort over the last century toward deconstruction. Liverani thinks it is time for a change: "If the critical *de*construction of the Biblical text is accepted, why not also attempt a *re*construction, referring literary texts to the time in which they were written and not to the period they speak about?" (p. xv). He seeks to write a history in two parts; the first, a "'normal' (i.e. not unique) and quite insignificant history of two kingdoms in Palestine" (p. xvi), a best history created from all available data and the second an "invented" history, an analysis of the ideology undergirding the biblical material as it seeks to persuade and to create identity.

78. Grabbe, "The Kingdom of Judah," 114–15.

79. Lester L. Grabbe, "Reflections on the Discussion," in Grabbe, ed., *Good Kings and Bad Kings*, 339–50 (345). Grabbe states, "Primary sources are those demonstrably written at or near the time of the events they describe, whereas secondary sources are those further removed from the events. Not all members of the discussion were impressed by this distinction, since no rule of methodology is absolute: primary sources may contain false or distorted data and secondary sources may have been copied accurately from reliable sources. A primary source may also deliberately distort the truth. Nevertheless, historical reconstruction has to take into account he laws of probability: primary sources are more often and more likely to have usable historical data than secondary sources. This is why a number argue that primary sources should be given priority in historical reconstruction, where available" (ibid.).

80. Marc Zvi Brettler, *The Creation of History in Ancient Israel* (London: Routledge, 1995); Van Seters, *In Search of History*; Rendtorff, "The Paradigm Is Changing," 34–55; Davies, *In Search of "Ancient Israel"*; Finkelstein, "The Archaeology of the United Monarchy"; Israel Finkelstein and Neil Asher Silberman, *The Bible Unearthed: Archaeology's New Vision of Ancient Israel and the Origin of Its Sacred Texts* (New York: Free Press, 2001); Diana V. Edelman, ed., *The Fabric of History: Text, Artifact and Israel's Past* (JSOTSup 127; Sheffield: JSOT Press, 1991);

Changing: Hopes—And Fears," named a phenomenon that has not yet come to fruition. Though several years have passed, a new paradigm has yet to form.[81] Perhaps Dever is right once again when he reminds us of Thomas S. Kuhn's work on paradigms: "But as Thomas S. Kuhn has stated in *The Structure of Scientific Revolutions*, theory often follows rather than precedes the practical 'shift in paradigm' that he regards as constituting a revolution in most research disciplines."[82] Perhaps the practice of a new paradigm is coming into place with the theory to follow. Perhaps we as historians of ancient Israel should acknowledge an axiom of philosopher of history, Michael Stanford:

> It is therefore not a weakness of history that it generates unending debates… Therefore history is to be seen not as a set of cast-iron facts, but rather as an ongoing conversation with one's fellows about affairs of importance or interest—past, present or future. The discussion can at times become debate, or fierce argument… History is not a concept but an activity—an activity of a unique kind… History is…best understood as an endless debate, constituting an important part of the continuing conversation of mankind [*sic*].[83]

Contemporary historians continue to press forward by contemplating increasingly complex questions. Perhaps it is in conversation with the broader discipline of history and philosophy of history that historians of

Grabbe, *Judaism from Cyrus to Hadrian*; idem, "Reconstructing History from the Book of Ezra," in *Second Temple Studies*. Vol. 1, *Persian Period* (ed. Philip R. Davies; Sheffield: JSOT Press, 1991), 98–107; Halpern, *The First Historians*; Long, "The Future of Israel's Past"; Thompson, *Early History of the Israelite People*; Lemche, *The Israelites in History and Tradition*; idem, "On the Problems of Reconstructing Pre-Hellenistic Israelite (Palestinian) History," *Journal of Hebrew Scriptures* 3 (2000), n.p. Online: http://www.arts.ualberta.ca/JHS/Articles/article_13.htm; Paula McNutt, *Reconstructing of Society of Ancient Israel* (Library of Ancient Israel; London: SPCK; Louisville, Ky.: Westminster John Knox, 1999); J. Maxwell Miller, "Reading the Bible Historically: The Historian's Approach," in *To Each Its Own Meaning: An Introduction to Biblical Criticisms and Their Applications* (ed. Stephen R. Haynes and Steven L. McKenzie; Louisville, Ky.: Westminster John Knox, 1993), 11–28; John Hayes, "The History of the Study of Israelite and Judaean History," in Hayes and Miller, eds., *Israelite and Judaean History*, 1–69.

81. Rendtorff, "The Paradigm Is Changing," 34–55. Brettler, *The Creation of History*, 6, reiterates, "The old consensus is gone, and there is no indication that a new one is developing to replace it."

82. Dever, *What Did the Biblical Writers Know?*, 69, discussing Thomas S. Kuhn, *The Structure of Scientific Revolutions* (3d ed.; Chicago: University of Chicago Press, 1996).

83. Stanford, *An Introduction to the Philosophy of History*, viii.

ancient Israel will find acceptable foundations for a new paradigm.[84] Historiography in general, and historiography of ancient Israel specifically, finds itself at an extended crossroad, in need of an agreed-upon historiographic framework. In establishing this framework, the discipline must acknowledge the tradition upon which it stands; it must acknowledge the corrective challenges that have and continue to modify that tradition; it must push that tradition to ask itself challenging questions; it must reformulate itself to meet its current circumstances (data, interpretation, and questions). This necessary framework requires territorial and methodological boundaries that, at the very least, recognize the role of the historian; that allow for heterogeneity, an inclusiveness that recognizes the contributions of histories from many perspectives; that accepts both the existence of a past reality "as it really was" and the impossibility of ever seeing that reality; that recognizes that many histories can be written about the same topic and that these histories may even contradict each other and still both contribute to a fuller portrait of the topic.

The need for a historical framework grounded in the broader discipline of history has not gone entirely unnoticed by biblical scholars.[85] Throughout his academic career, but especially in his 1988 work, *The First Historians: The Hebrew Bible and History*, Baruch Halpern grapples with historiographic issues within the broader framework of the field of history. Frustrated with conventional approaches that often hamstring critical historical analysis, Halpern calls on historians to determine what the ancient writers meant to say. To do this, historians must appropriate three stages of work: they must identify acceptable evidence, interpret this evidence, and present a reconstruction based on the evidence. No single historian can or should present a complete history; each history has its own subject and makes its own contribution to the many portraits of periods and events. Halpern correctly seeks to steer historians away from historicity issues: "History is susceptible to evidence but not to proof."[86] He agrees wholeheartedly with literary critics that the line of distinction "falls not between history and fiction—all history is fictional, imaginative, as the literary critics say. The distinction is between history and romance, or fable; it is a distinction in authorial intention."[87] History attempts to "get at" the past. For Halpern, "appropriate" history writing

84. As already suggested by Long, "The Future of Israel's Past," passim, and Halpern, *The First Historians*, passim. See also Diana V. Edelman's essay, "Doing History in Biblical Studies," in idem, ed., *The Fabric of History*, 13–25.

85. As noted above.

86. Halpern, *The First Historians*, 3.

87. Ibid., 8.

"demands author-centered interpretation."[88] Focus on ancillary criteria—events, states, particular people—only, and eventually, allows historians to "get at" the author's intention. Halpern recognizes the tensions inherent in contemporary historiography of ancient Israel. The von Ranke ideal of reclaiming a universal history is not possible. The history of ancient Israel cannot be romanticized as Wellhausenian studies have led it to be. Nor can it be positivistic as philology demands. Halpern calls on historians to re-engage substantive issues such as "how the historians came to believe what they wrote, what they thought writing history demanded."[89]

Important strides are being made in the creation of a vital historical framework. V. Phillips Long edited a 1999 collection of works contending with just such issues. In *Israel's Past in Present Research: Essays on Ancient Israelite Historiography*,[90] Long brings together scholars from a broad spectrum within biblical scholarship, each speaking to the crisis facing historiography of ancient Israel. Long's concluding essay appropriately summarizes the situation. Historians no longer should, or can, create a "grand synthesis" but should instead "seek to reconstruct the past not in its entirety but as it pertains to specific questions they are asking. This means that written histories are partial and perspectival."[91]

88. Ibid., 11.
89. Ibid., 26.
90. Long, ed., *Israel's Past in Present Research.*
91. Long, "The Future of Israel's Past," 583. At the end of his article he makes three methodological suggestions. First, he wants scholars to re(de)fine the canons of the historical-critical method. He calls on W. J. Abraham, *Divine Revelation and the Limits of Historical Criticism* (Oxford: Oxford University Press, 1982), who conjoins belief and scholarship so that a believer may be a scholar if this believer correctly defines and utilizes criticism, analogy, and correlation. Criticism, then, is "thoughtful appraisal of the evidence in keeping with its source" (p. 589). This seems to me to produce only insipid history. Analogy allows the historian to stretch any narrow understanding of plausibility. Correlation allows for divine agency as opposed to natural cause or human agency. To me, this first point seems like semantic gymnastics aimed at co-opting conservative scholars to continue in scholarship. Secondly, Long seeks to ensconce social-scientific study into a secondary role in regards to history-writing. He wants to do this to prevent contemporary issues from seeping into our writing of histories about ancient periods. In other words, he here, as well as with his first point, contradicts his entire article. Finally, he calls on historians of ancient Israel to seek once again the worth of literary studies. In his opinion, the value of literary studies has increasingly diminished with increasing criticisms of Wellhausen's literary criticism. I would contend that Long is incorrect here. Historical studies of ancient Israel continue to rely heavily on Wellhausenian models. To be sure, challenges have been mounted against much of the content of

The questions asked produce the histories written. Long calls scholars to consider and specify the models on which their work is based, their philosophy of history, their initial questions, their criteria for acceptable evidence, their own perspectives inherently operational in the writing of history, and their own contribution to the larger picture of history in ancient Israel.

Fundamentally at stake is the existence and perpetuation of a scholarly consensus concerning the history of ancient Israel.[92] William Dever's defensive posture in his latest book stems from his desire to defend his idea of the prevailing, traditional consensus. This consensus faces increasingly insurmountable challenges. Albert Baumgarten summarizes the situation succinctly:

> When a consensus is reigning, its adherents advance knowledge by working on questions requiring clarification within the context it provides. The consensus itself is rarely challenged: ...challenges, if any, are either resisted or overlooked. In some senses, the consensus matters more than any mere facts for these facts only have meaning within a consensus. A dying consensus, however, attracts challengers like flies. As the realization spreads that the old intellectual thought patterns are no longer adequate to the job, many scholars try their hands as suggesting replacement systems.[93]

Historical studies as a discipline continually repeats this pattern, continually renews itself in response to new data, new approaches, or new ideas

Wellhausen's work, but his framework permeates almost every facet of history writing, even today. Even more so, the solipsistic relationship between history and this kind of literary study seduces scholars into an avoidance of substantive issues. The created history produces a certain understanding of the literature, particularly as it relates to the historical context of the literature. The historical context of the literature, then, establishes the historical framework. The solipsism is a fundamental vulnerability in Wellhausen's work as well as in contemporary literary criticism today. Furthermore, by focusing on Wellhausenian literary studies, we fail to see the subtle but pervasive consequences of "old" history on contemporary literary studies. So, although I heartily agree with and appreciate Long's attention to historiography in the bulk of his essay, I disagree with his three methodological suggestions and hope that he reconsiders them in light of his other work.

92. Too late for engagement in this study, but crucial to the discussion, is John J. Collins' book *The Bible after Babel: Historical Criticism in a Postmodern Age* (Grand Rapids: Eerdmans, 2005). In particular, see his chapter on "The Crisis in Historiography."

93. A. I. Baumgarten, "Crisis in the Scrollery: A Dying Consensus," *Judaism* 44 (1995): 399–416 (405). Baumgarten wrote about the prevailing consensus regarding interpretation of the Dead Sea Scrolls. His concept is applicable to consensus in biblical history and history of ancient Israel.

on how to organize data or approaches. Historical studies as a discipline has always been about change, about improving upon previous understanding, about further developing and enhancing our knowledge of the past. As stated by William Stubbs, Regius Professor of Modern History at Oxford, 1866–84, "History knows that it can wait for more evidence and review its older verdicts; it offers an endless series of courts of appeal, and is ever ready to re-open closed cases."[94] Stubbs offers a helpful metaphor, a court of law, and in so doing, provides a suggestion for how the discipline of historical studies might proceed.[95] The discipline does not require that historians agree about everything. In fact, the discipline demands opposing agendas, points of view, and proffering of evidence. What the discipline most readily supplies is an appropriate framework for the hearing and substantiation of claims.

Historiography—A Suggestion for Creating Vital Histories

That historiography of ancient Israel is and has been in crisis is not in question. That new questions, evidence, and approaches are available is not in question. What remains is for historians to acknowledge the complexity of writing history and concurrently to recognize the futility of simple explanations. As such, an actual reality of the past exists but is unattainable to us. The historian's task is seeking to give a best presentation of an approximation of that reality. By acknowledging the current state of historiography, not only within biblical studies but as a broader discipline, historians will recognize that actual historical consensus is no longer possible, and will seek consensus in method and basic framework. Historians will include self-reflection as fundamental to any historical work and will therefore specify philosophy of history, goals, originating questions, underlying presuppositions, starting points, sources and criteria for judging them, issues of concern, and privileged notions. Historians will be consciously interdisciplinary, seeking to include environmental, ethnographic, archaeological, social-scientific, literary, rhetorical, anthropological, ideological, cultural, psychoanalytic, deconstruction, feminist, womanist, liberationist, and critical theory concerns. Historians will consciously avoid polemics and seek to engage fellow scholars and previous scholarship on common grounds. Historians must acknowledge that histories do not achieve an end and will be modified in response to new data, new approaches, or some combination of the two. Respective histories

94. Quoted in John R. Hale's introduction to *The Evolution of British Historiography: From Bacon to Namier* (ed. John R. Hale; New York: World Publishing, 1964), 58.

95. Also see Long, "The Future of Israel's Past," passim.

may stand in juxtaposition or even opposition to histories of fellow scholars, but nevertheless contribute to the ever-growing and ever-complex picture of ancient Israel.

Metaphors and Maps

A metaphor of maps may aid in understanding historical application of data and perspectives. A map is "a form of symbolization with a special utility for encoding and transmitting human knowledge of the environment...a graphic symbolization of one's milieu."[96] Michael Polanyi suggests that all theory "is a kind of map extended over space and time."[97] Although the origins of cartography are unknown, the earliest specimens of maps date, appropriately, to Babylonia in the third millennium B.C.E. Maps provide charts of known information which are used by inhabitants who are already familiar with details as well as by newcomers who want to understand a broad overview of the area. Maps are fashioned as a means to visualize the object, the territory. They do not construct the territory itself so that description does not necessarily match reality. Sources used in the construction of maps are partially determinative of the product. The orientation of maps is critical. Starting point, final objective, setting for use, vantage point, and methodology play crucial roles in both the reading and interpretation of maps. Two different maps can cover the same territory and offer similar or dissimilar renderings. Different types of maps can offer compatible or even non-compatible conceptualizations of the same territory. No map can show everything. No matter what type of map is developed, the cartographer must first select applicable and appropriate source material. Features on a particular map are selected to fit particular purposes. Series of maps can show evolutionary dynamics. Some maps locate only visible features while others depict invisible aspects. Abstract features, such as boundaries or lines of latitude and longitude, may or may not appear. Some types of maps are more costly to produce. Some maps are distorted, permitting the map-reader to see only a portion of the desired territory. Maps have their own particular jargon which enables communication. Map scales are, at best, relative absolutes.

Obviously this description could continue to pursue numerous avenues, but the objective here is to advance the map metaphor as another way to conceptualize historiography in relation to ancient Israel. Why not view

96. Mary C. Boys, *Educating in Faith: Maps and Visions* (Kansas City: Sheed & Ward, 1989), viii.

97. Michael Polyani, *Personal Knowledge: Towards Post-Critical Philosophy* (Torchbooks; New York: Harper & Row, 1964), 4.

our various histories as coeval cohabitants operating in symbiosis? After all, as James Barr says at the beginning of his seminal work, *The Semantics of Biblical Language*, "It is the main concern of both scholarship and theology that the Bible should be soundly and adequately interpreted!"[98] Without exception, scholars would consent to this goal, yet they apparently continue to vie for position as the reigning historical paradigm. Why not have several history maps standing by still other, also useful maps? In fact, having adequate history demands the existence of numerous such maps.[99] Perhaps instead of vying for supremacy, historians of ancient Israel should philosophically examine the task at hand. As seen in the discussion above, most contemporary practitioners of a discipline related to ancient Israel (biblical scholars, archaeologists, historians) do not overtly claim absolute dominance for their own theory. Faced with the challenge of moving beyond a confirmation and (re)description of what has already been seen, there may be a way to overcome current contentious rhetoric by recognizing new possibilities for historiography of ancient Israel, new possibilities that value available data and incorporate new data.[100] Critical to this approach is a recognition that a history is never completely abstract and that data is never completely absolute.[101]

98. James Barr, *The Semantics of Biblical Language* (London: Oxford University Press, 1961), 1.

99. Important to any discussion of maps is postmodern analyses of spatiality. James Flanagan, "Ancient Perceptions of Space / Perceptions of Ancient Space." *Semeia* 87 (1999): 15–43, summarizes current engagement as related to biblical studies. Pertinent to this study is Flanagan's observation that notions about maps tend toward exclusivity in dependence on positivism. For Flanagan, "Contrary to the belief that maps are neutral, mimetic representations of real physical and social worlds...[they] disguise social contexts and impose their own hegemonies of power and privilege. The hegemonic strategies are first the 'rule of ethnocentricity,' the tendency for societies to put themselves at the center of maps, and second the 'rule of social order,' the tendency of cartographers to use verbal text on maps as commentary in order to convey information and impressions about classifications and measurements of social and political factors beyond the physical or human landscape" (p. 21). Flanagan's admonishments are well taken and not altogether dissonant with my suggestion that an appropriate historical portrait can only come with a combination of many histories.

100. These ideas formed during the reading of Craig Calhoun, "Social Theory and the Public Sphere," in *The Blackwell Companion to Social Theory* (ed. Bryan S. Turner; Cambridge: Blackwell, 1996), 429–70.

101. Clearly some maps are more useful than others. Some might even be mutually exclusive with others. Inappropriate maps are maps that exclude all other maps. Maps developed out of response to a critical mass of evidence last longer and draw consensus.

Social-Scientific Approach—A Fruitful Map

One particularly fruitful set of maps follows the pattern of social-scientific studies. History uninterested in social context is boring, uninformative, and basically useless.[102] Virtually all practitioners of biblical studies scholarship employ a social-scientific approach, either overtly or covertly. I suggest that we become deliberate and conscientious about this employment. Traditional historiography relies on social-scientific approaches in its generation of a context. Even literary biblical studies use social-scientific approaches to provide their social contexts. As Philip R. Davies points out in an unpublished article, "Taking Up Social Scientific Investigations of the Second Temple Period,"[103] meaningful explanations can only be provided in terms of social systems which in turn must be understood through social-scientific approaches. Facts have little signification without their accompanying social context that answers the questions how and why. For social-scientific approaches two elements, then, are necessary—empirical data and theory—each standing in a complex and self-conscious relationship to the other.[104]

Social science is a "description of the familiar world with slightly differing contexts and particulars."[105] Practitioners of this approach accumulate facts [data], test the facts [data] for validity, and then rely on narrative to sort the facts [data] into patterns based on perspective, language, and culture. The social-scientific approach, then, is both empirical and theoretical, providing a systematic framework for knowledge. The social-scientific approach demands empirical depth while recognizing its implicit dependence on the inductive development of ideas. Descriptions resulting from such social-scientific approaches offer broad explanations, syntheses of data, and ways to think about the world of ancient Israel.

102. Here I am disclosing my own presupposition. I should further disclose my own presuppositions. I presume traditional history to be narrow in that it seems to have focused primarily on the elite of society, providing a limited portrait of ancient life. As a white, affluent, educated female, I assume that I likely give some priority to the elite in society even as I recognize the errors of doing so. I assume the positive value of progress over time, influencing my historiographical methodology and content.

103. Philip R. Davies, "Taking Up Social Scientific Investigations of the Second Temple Period" (unpublished essay, Sheffield University, 1992). Davies suggests the following: "1. Social-scientific investigation is not a method but an approach which deploys many methods; 2. It is the only proper approach to be adopted in the case of ancient history; and 3. Members of the Sociology of the Monarchy Seminar ought, in my opinion, go out into all the SBL and even the real world too, and preach the gospel, whether in the Seminar on Second Temple or any other form."

104. We might use other terms but the connotations remain clear.

105. Calhoun, "Social Theory and the Public Sphere," 431.

Social-scientific approaches rightly yield a multiplicity of such descriptions "not because we are confused or have not yet reached correct scientific understanding of the problems before us, but because all problems—like all people—can be seen in different ways."[106] No single theory or description can serve as the only, uniquely comprehensive theory. No history can serve as such and provide an adequate historical picture. Instead, histories serve as points of dialogue standing in present and reflexive tension with the past and the future.

Social-scientific approaches to histories of ancient Israel cross traditional disciplinary boundaries to provide broad theoretical modes for description. While social-scientific approaches often fall into one or the other distinctive categories of either a functionalist approach or a conflict-oriented approach, I suggest that any social-scientific approach to a history of ancient Israel should combine the strengths of both approaches.

Functionalist practitioners theoretically approach their questions in view of society as a natural whole in which described components necessarily comprise the entirety and fulfill the needs of the complex social system. Social stratification is a given. Common interests of society members are assumed. Supply-and-demand remains operative. Observable consequences between components and the overall system generate change. Often criticized for their positivistic tendencies, their presumptive favor for the elite in society, their frequent inability to account for change over time and space, their predilection toward maintaining *status quo*, and especially their penchant for ignoring tensions and divisions within social systems, functionalist approaches nevertheless have significant contributions to make toward social-scientific approaches to ancient Israel. In particular, functionalism provides system frameworks and, more importantly, a common descriptive language.

Conflict theories begin with an assumption of inequality within a social system. Instead of identifying how societal components serve the system, these approaches focus on tensions and conflict within society, examining exploitation and the ideological roles of power and privilege while raising questions about silences within the dominant system. Often labeled "Marxist" and summarily dismissed, the concerns of conflict-oriented approaches nonetheless continue to appear and share common interests with the likes of Claude Lévi-Strauss, Michel Foucault, Hans-Georg Gadamer, Jürgen Habermas, Thomas Kuhn, and Jacques Derrida. Criticized for dismissing scientific objectivity, conflict approaches respond by calling on all approaches to articulate their underlying assumptions. While occasionally bent toward overgeneralization, conflict approaches

106. Ibid., 435.

provide profitable points of departure for social-scientific approaches to ancient Israel. Conflict theories challenge the structure and maintenance of social systems, noting the fragmentary and incomplete nature of both systems and languages.

Macrosociological approaches might be seen as coins with two sides —functionalist and conflict—and having generally been able to utilize these positive features while minimizing the difficulties with each approach. Macrosociological approaches seek to examine broad social structures, using the functionalist assumption that society interacts with its components to produce reality in conjunction with the truculent questions raised by conflict approaches. N. Elias, in his *History of Manners*, provides an example of this type of application in that his work is interdisciplinary, presents a broad picture of society, and demonstrates a concern for theory.[107] Immanuel Wallerstein provides another example with his world-systems theory.[108] These and other macrosociological studies provide broad impetus for further dialogue, place significant emphasis on research, and seek to synthesize the best of functional and conflict theories.

Gerhard Lenski makes a case for the viability of macrosociological theory in his 1988 article, "Rethinking Macrosociological Theory."[109] For Lenski, critical to such approaches is an underlying assumption of the falsifiability of all theories. Macrosociological theory must clearly articulate concepts [variables] and their interrelationships; must incorporate constants, data, and theoretical concepts from a variety and broad spectrum of disciplines; must be presentable "diagrammatically"; must be multivalent so that the basic theory encompasses key concepts and spawns derivative theories; must explicitly state assumptions; and must be constructed with intense rigor.[110]

Lenski, in his seminal 1966 work, *Power and Privilege: A Theory of Social Stratification*, meets these criteria by reformulating issues and concepts through "transforming categorical concepts into variable concepts" and "breaking down compound concepts into their constituent elements."[111] He provides an examination of the nature of phenomena

107. N. Elias, *The Civilizing Process*. Vol. 1, *The History of Manners* (Oxford: Blackwell, 1978).

108. Immanuel Wallerstein, *The Modern World-System*, Vol. 1 (New York: Academic Press, 1974).

109. Gerhard Lenski, "Rethinking Macrosociological Theory," *American Sociological Review* 53 (1988): 163–71.

110. Ibid., 163, as this forces certain and sophisticated conceptual development.

111. Gerhard E. Lenski, *Power and Privilege: A Theory of Social Stratification* (paperback ed.; Chapel Hill: University of North Carolina Press, 1984 [1966]), 20–23.

causality and consequences as he builds a theoretical model that is both deductive and inductive. Particular signification for Lenski lies in the processes of change resulting from new factors within a society.

As would be expected, Lenski is criticized for the typical problems in both functionalist and conflict approaches as well as for operating from caricatures of functionalist and conflict theories in a manner that is "both plausible and oddly artificial," and for claiming uniqueness in his offering of a synthesis when many sociologists produce meta-theories.[112] Lenski is nonetheless applauded for raising pertinent questions and for applying the questions to a long view of history.[113] Lenski maximizes social-scientific possibilities as he gathers data, sorts and then proceeds to analyze the collection.

The final portion of this study will follow this social-scientific analytical path in an attempt to provide a necessarily new starting point for understanding the Zadokites and their place in the history of ancient Israel. The chapters on biblical evidence collect data and perform some analysis. The chapter on extrabiblical evidence does the same. The chapter on the social context of the Zadokites collects historical data and provides a social-scientific model for analyzing them.

112. Ralf Dahrendorf, "Review Symposium: Gerhard E. Lenski, *Power and Privilege: A Theory of Social Stratification*," *American Sociological Review* 31 (1966): 714–18. Note that Lenski calls the functionalist approaches "conservative" approaches and the conflict approaches "radical" approaches.

113. Lloyd A. Fallers, "Review Symposium: Gerhard E. Lenski, *Power and Privilege: A Theory of Social Stratification*," *American Sociological Review* 31 (1966): 718–19; Stephan Thernstrom, "Review Symposium: Gerhard E. Lenski, *Power and Privilege: A Theory of Social Stratification*," *American Sociological Review* 31 (1966): 719–20.

Chapter 4

BIBLICAL EVIDENCE OF THE ZADOKITES: SAMUEL–KINGS–EZRA–NEHEMIAH–CHRONICLES

Introduction

The Hebrew Bible contains few references to the Zadokites. In fact, all four references to the בני צדוק, "sons of Zadok," occur in one small section of the book of Ezekiel (Ezek 40:45–46; 43:18–19; 44:6–16; 48:9–11). Second Chronicles 31:10 makes reference to בית צדוק, "house of Zadok." צדוק is mentioned fifty-three times. At least twenty-two of the twenty-six occurrences in Samuel–Kings refer to a priest named Zadok. The other four refer to Ahimaaz, son of Zadok (three times) or Jerusha, daughter of Zadok. Chronicles has seventeen references to someone named "Zadok" (of these, eight seem to refer to a priest). Ezra–Nehemiah contains six references to persons named "Zadok."

These represent the entirety of references to Zadok or the Zadokites in the Hebrew Bible. In examination of these references we will find no evidence for a Zadokite priestly dynasty during either the united or the divided monarchy. We will find a hint of interest in Zadokites in two places, Chronicles and Ezek 40–48, but neither of these texts can be appropriately placed in historical context.

Samuel–Kings

Introduction

Historians' reliance on Samuel–Kings as a history of its referent period has informed and continues to inform our understanding about ancient Israelite priesthoods. Yet Samuel–Kings yields very little information about priesthoods or the Zadokites. Samuel–Kings clearly does not mention בני צדוק. Samuel–Kings does, by referring to Zadok, provide a foundation for a potential Zadokite priesthood. Second Samuel 8:17; 15:24–37 (with seven mentions of צדוק); 17:15; 18:19–27 (with three mentions of צדוק); 19:12 (ET 11); 20:25; 1 Kgs 1:8, 26–45 (with seven mentions of צדוק); 2:35; 4:2–4 (with two mentions of צדוק); and 2 Kgs 15:33 provide the 26 references in Samuel–Kings to צדוק. Second Samuel 8:17; 15:24–36; 17:15; 19:12; and 20:25 refer to Zadok as a priest and in his role *vis-à-vis* David.

2 Samuel 8:17

Naming Zadok son of Ahitub and Ahimelech son of Abiathar as priests, 2 Sam 8:17 is set in the context of a summary of David's reign that begins in 8:15:

> And David reigned over all Israel and David was an observer of justice and righteousness for all his people. Joab, son of Zeruiah, was over the army. Jehoshaphat, son of Ahilud, was recorder. *Zadok*, son of Ahitub, and Ahimelech, son of Abiathar, were priests. Seraiah was secretary. Benaiah, son of Jehoiada, [was over] the Cherethites, and the Pelethites. David's sons were priests. (2 Sam 8:15–18)[1]

Providing the first mention in Zadok in Samuel–Kings, this text names Zadok and Abiathar as David's priests. Aside from Theophile J. Meek, who notes that these early Samuel–Kings references to Zadok "give him no lineage at all," most discussions center around text-critical issues and how the text does or does not situate Zadok in priestly circles.[2] Kyle P. McCarter's work on Second Samuel yields:

> Zadok shared the high priesthood with Abiathar until David's death, when his colleague and rival was banished (I Kings 2:26) and he took full title to the office (cf. I Kings 2:35). Deuteronomistic tradition saw in this the fulfillment of a divine decree of priesthood analogous to the divine decree

1. Translations are mine unless otherwise noted.

2. Meek, "Aaronites and Zadokites," 159. The Syriac and Ethiopic texts have Abiathar and Ahimelech in reverse order. P. Kyle McCarter attributes these witnesses to a secondary correction; see his *II Samuel: A New Translation with Introduction, Notes and Commentary* (AB; Garden City, N.Y.: Doubleday, 1984), 253. The MT version of 1 Chr 18:16 repeats the representation of Ahimelech as son of Abiathar. For McCarter, this is an obvious error since 2 Sam 20:25 names Abiathar and Zadok as David's priests. Various scholars have offered explanations. McCarter notes that Wellhausen, followed by many others, amended the text to read "Abiathar son of Ahimelek son of Ahitub and Zadok." Cross (*Canaanite Myth and Hebrew Epic*, 213), attributing the error to a haplography, amends the text to "Zadok son of Ahitub and Abiathar son of Abimelech." Many (e.g., Cody, *A History of the Old Testament Priesthood*, 89–93, 100, 107) see the text, following Wellhausen, as a late modification by a Zadokite partisan in an effort to boost the status of Zadok and hence the Zadokites. Peter R. Ackroyd, *The Second Book of Samuel* (The Cambridge Bible on the New English Bible; Cambridge: Cambridge University Press, 1977), 89, calls the text "muddled." Rowley, "Zadok and Nehushtan," 114, says it is "manifestly out of order."

> of kingship found in chap. 7 (see the oracle in I Sam 2:27–36 and the notice of its fulfillment in I Kings 2:27). It offered a justification for the exclusion of non-Jerusalemite priests from temple service that the cultic centralization of the Deuteronomic reform produced. Eventually only those priests who traced their descent to Zadok were regarded as eligible for temple duties (Ezek 40:46; etc.).[3]

Notice McCarter's acceptance and imposition of a chronologically linear view of priesthood in ancient Israel which promulgates the assumption that Zadokites assumed and maintained the institution of the high-priesthood. In particular, this interpretation relies heavily on a particular interpretation of Ezek 40–48 (which will be discussed below.)

2 Samuel 15

> And all the country wept aloud as all the people passed by; and the king crossed Wadi Kidron, and all the people passed on toward the wilderness. [Abiathar came up] And behold, *Zadok* also, and all the Levites with him, were carrying the ark of the covenant of God. They set down the ark of God. And Abiathar came up until all the people had passed out of the city. Then the king said to *Zadok*, "Carry the ark of God back into the city. If I find favor in the eyes of the Lord, he will bring me back and let me see it as well as the place where it dwells. But if he says this, 'I take no pleasure in you,' then behold, here I am, let him do to me what seems good in his eyes." The king also said to *Zadok*, the priest, "Are you a seer? Go back to the city in peace, you and Ahimaaz your son and Jonathan the son of Abiathar, your two sons, with you. See, I will wait at the fords of the wilderness until word comes from you to inform me." So *Zadok* and Abiathar carried the ark of God to Jerusalem, and they remained there. But David went up the ascent of the Mount of Olives, weeping as he went. His head was covered and he went (with) barefoot. And all the people who were with him had covered their heads and they went up, weeping as they went. And David told it like this, that Ahithophel was among the conspirators with Absalom. And David said, "Turn, I pray, O Lord, into foolishness, the counsel of Ahithophel." When David came to the summit where God was worshiped, behold, Hashai the Archite came to meet him with his coat torn and earth upon his head. David said to him, "If you go on with me, you will be a burden to me. But if you return to the city and say to Absalom, 'I will be your servant, O king; as I have been your father's servant in time past, so now I will be your servant,' then you will defeat for me the counsel of Ahithophel. Will not the priests *Zadok* and Abiathar be there with you? So it will be that whatever you hear from the king's house, tell it to *Zadok* and Abiathar, the priests. Behold, with them there are their two sons, Ahimaaz, son of *Zadok*, and Jonathan, son of Abiathar. You will send to me by their hands everything that you hear." So Hushai, David's friend, came into the city, just as Absalom was entering Jerusalem. (2 Sam 15:23–37)

3. McCarter, *II Samuel*, 255–56.

Second Samuel 15:23–37 comes on the heels of the story of Absalom's usurpation of the throne and David's subsequent flight. Zadok is mentioned seven times in the account of David commanding the ark to be returned to Jerusalem. Zadok and Abiathar are here presented as acting in accord. The text also recounts David's assignment of Ahimaaz, son of Zadok, and Jonathan, son of Abiathar, as messengers between David's refuge and the events within the city.

2 Samuel 17; 18; 19

Second Samuel 17:15 mentions Zadok and Abiathar as the priests in communication with David's friend, Hushai the Archite. In 2 Sam 19:12, David sends a message to the priests Zadok and Abiathar. Second Samuel 18:19–27 recounts David's grief over the death of Absalom and refers several times to Ahimaaz, son of Zadok, as a messenger who is pronounced a "good man" by the king.

2 Samuel 20

Second Samuel 20:23–26 provides another list of David's officials, naming Zadok, Abiathar, and Ira as David's priests:

> Joab was over all the army of Israel. Benaiah, son of Jehoiada, was over the Cherethites and the Pelethites and Adoram was over the corveé. Jehoshaphat, son of Ahilud, was the recorder and Sheva was the scribe. *Zadok* and Abiathar were the priests. And also Ira, the Jairite was a priest of David. (2 Sam 20:23–26)[4]

This list differs from the 2 Sam 8 list on several counts. In 2 Sam 8, lineage is provided for Joab, and perhaps for Zadok and Abiathar. Joab is over the army in both lists. Jehoshaphat is the recorder in both lists. Someone whose name begins with a ש is a scribe in both lists. Benaiah is somehow related to the Cherethites and the Pelethites in both lists. There is no Adoram or mention of corveé in the 2 Sam 8 list. While David's sons are mentioned as priests in the 2 Sam 8 list, Ira is not mentioned. The reverse is the case for the 2 Sam 20 list.

1 Kings

First Kings 1:8, 26–45; 2:35; and 4:2–4 refer to Zadok as priest in his role *vis-à-vis* Solomon. First Kings 1:8 mentions "the priest Zadok" in the context of the struggle for the succession to David's throne when

4. There are numerous text-critical issues with this text. The *BHS*'s critical apparatus refers to the list in 2 Sam 8 for v. 23. The text in this list, however, is more complete for v. 23b, including the ל (when listing Benaiah and the Cherethites and the Pelethites.)

Zadok and the prophet Nathan did not take the side of Adonijah. First Kings 1:26–45, still part of the succession struggle, portrays the priest Zadok and the prophet Nathan coming before the old king David to receive his order to anoint Solomon as king over Israel. In v. 39, Zadok anoints Solomon. First Kings 2 recounts the end of the succession struggle. Benaiah, son of Johaiada, receives orders from King Solomon to kill Joab, who chose to support Adonijah.[5] Solomon then places Benaiah in Joab's place over the army and sets Zadok as priest in place of Abiathar. The pronouncement that Zadok was put in Abiathar's place when Second Samuel consistently presents Zadok and Abiathar as "co"-priests is somewhat puzzling.

First Kings 4:1–6 presents a list of Solomon's officials.

> And so Solomon was king over all Israel. These were his chief officials. Azariah, son of *Zadok*, was the priest, Elihoreph and Ahijah, sons of Shisha, were scribes, Jehoshaphat, son of Ahilud, was recorder. Benaiah, son of Jehoiada, was over the army. *Zadok* and Abiathar were priests. Azariah, son of Nathan, was over the deputies and Zabud, son of Nathan, was priest and the king's friend. Ahishar was over the palace and Adoniram, son of Abda, was over the corveé. (1 Kgs 4:1–6)

צדוק is mentioned twice. In v. 2, somewhat surprisingly given the Samuel texts, Azariah, son of Zadok, is priest. (The Samuel texts mention only Ahimaaz as "son of Zadok."[6]) Also surprisingly, given the previous 1 Kings texts regarding the roles of Zadok and Abiathar in the succession conflict as well as the just mentioned Azariah son of Zadok as priest, v. 4 names Zadok and Abiathar as priests. Finally, and curiously, this text lists Zabud, son of Nathan, as priest and a friend of the king. Clearly textual issues abound in understanding this text.[7]

Finally, 2 Kgs 15:33, in a portion of the kings lists of Samuel–Kings, mentions the mother of King Jotham, Jerusha, daughter of צדוק. This צדוק is considered to have no connection to the priest צדוק.[8]

5. 1 Kgs 1 presents Abiathar and Joab as siding with Adonijah throughout the succession issue.

6. 2 Sam 15:27, 36; 17:17, 20; and 18:19, 22, 23, 27, 28, 29. Other mentions of Ahimaaz include 1 Kgs 4:15 where Ahimaaz is one of Solomon's officials over Israel. Also, 1 Sam 14:50 indicates that Saul's wife, Ahinoam, is the daughter of Ahimaaz.

7. Some interpret the אליחרף after Azariah as אלי חרף, translated as "over the year," so that the text would read "Azariah, son of Zadok, was the priest over the year"; see James A. Montgomery, *The Books of Kings* (ICC; Edinburgh: T. & T. Clark, 1951), 113–16.

8. For more information, see Mordechai Cogan and Hayim Tadmor, *II Kings: A New Translation with Introduction and Commentary* (AB 11; New York: Doubleday,

Summary of Samuel–Kings References

These 26 references provide our only Samuel–Kings evidence regarding Zadok. A Zadokite dynasty having its beginnings in the reigns of David and Solomon and continuing until the Maccabean revolt would require that its members be descendants of David's Zadok and these descendants would have served as priests. Of the 26 Samuel–Kings references to צדוק, 2 Sam 8:17; 15:24–36; 18:19–27; and 1 Kgs 4:2–4 give some lineage information that may assist in the consideration of בני צדוק. Second Samuel 8:17 lists Zadok as the son of Ahitub.[9] Second Samuel 15:27 and 15:36 list Ahimaaz as Zadok's son. Second Samuel 18:19 and 18:27 likewise note that Ahimaaz was Zadok's son. First Kings 4:2 lists Azariah as the son of Zadok.[10] Was Ahimaaz Zadok's son? Was he a priest? Was Azariah Zadok's son? Was he a priest? Furthermore, if there was a Zadokite dynasty, where does it go from this point? An already murky portrait of Zadokite priestly succession immediately becomes murkier. So, as far as Samuel–Kings is concerned, the succession of

1988), 182; J. J. Stamm, "Hebräische Frauennamen," in *Hebräische Wortforschung. Festschrift zum 80. Geburstag von Walter Baumgartner* (ed. Benedikt Hartmann et al.; VTSup 16; Leiden: Brill, 1967), 301–39; and Linda S. Schearing, "Jerusha," *ABD* 3:768. Also see 2 Chr 27:1.

9. Cross, *Canaanite Myth and Hebrew Epic*, 196, 212–13. In his article "Priestly Houses of Early Israel," Cross unequivocally names this genealogical information as "corrupt" for he sees Ahitub as the grandfather of Abiathar of the house of Eli from Shiloh. He does not believe that Zadok is "an Elid" and therefore this must be a corruption of the text. He cites 2 Sam 2:30–36 as evidence that Zadok stood in opposition to the house of Eli. Hans Wilhelm Hertzberg, *I & II Samuel* (OTL; Philadelphia: Westminster, 1964), 293–94, notes the new figure, Zadok, stands alongside Abiathar, who is from the Aaronic priesthood of Shiloh. Hertzberg attributes the confusion regarding Zadok's lineage to this text, which names Ahitub as Zadok's father. Hertzberg accepts 1 Sam 1:3 in naming Ahitub as the grandson of Eli and 1 Sam 22:9 in naming Ahitub as the father of Ahimelech, implying that he is thus the grandfather of Abiathar. He suggests that some later tradition wanted to incorporate Zadok into the Aaronite line. But, as discussed throughout this study, the Aaronite line apparently only came into prominence during the postexilic period.

10. Still in this same list, v. 5 names an Azariah as the son of Nathan. Also important in analyzing these lists, numerous scholars note the textual difficulties with these lists and question their value for historical reconstruction. See, e.g., John Raymond Bartlett, "Zadok and His Successors at Jerusalem," *JTS* 19 (1968): 1–18 (11); Tryggve N. D. Mettinger, *Solomonic State Officials: A Study of the Civil Government Officials of the Israelite Monarchy* (ConBOT 5; Lund: Gleerup, 1971), 9. Mettinger notes the "considerable problems of textual and literary criticism connected with this list." Also see Donald B. Redford, *Egypt, Canaan, and Israel in Ancient Times* (Princeton: Princeton University Press, 1992), 329.

Zadokite priests ends with Zadok's son, Ahimaaz—a short dynasty indeed. Even if we accept the text as providing historical records of priestly succession, only our assumptions can carry us further.

Excursus: The Issue of Zadok's Successors

The issue of Zadok's successors was dealt with in detail by John Bartlett in 1968. The purpose of his article is the same as the originating idea of this study. He begins his article with "It has often been assumed that the office of leading priest in the Jerusalem temple from the time of David onwards was held only by direct descendants of Zadok, and that the succession was handed on from father to son" and he then proceeds to examine these assumptions.[11] He first analyzes the issue of hereditary priestly succession. Bartlett compares the lists from (in the following sequence) 1 Chr 6:1–15; 6:50–53; Ezra 7:1–5; Neh 11:10–11; 1 Chr 9:10–11; 1 Esd 8:1–2; and 2 Esd 1:1–3. He argues that Zadokites never gained exclusive control over the priesthood and sees the Zadokites as more important during the exilic and postexilic periods. He designates "house of Zadok" as a misleading and artificial phrase, suggesting Zadokite descent was arbitrary.[12] Bartlett finds little available evidence for assuming that the priesthood was provided by hereditary succession noting that "Apart from Zadok and his son Azariah…no priest is clearly said to have his son as his successor." He contrasts this lack of hereditary evidence with the later concern in Chronicles for lineage: "We may put this point another way by saying that if the leading priest's descent from Zadok was important at Jerusalem before the exile, the Deuteronomistic historian does not make an explicit point of it as the Chronicler does."[13] Bartlett concludes that "it is far from clear that Zadok's sons or son followed him in his priestly position."[14] All this Bartlett regards as "negative" evidence; for "positive" evidence, he reminds us that "Zadok's was not the only priesthood in Jerusalem under David and Solomon" and that "the Jerusalem priesthood in David's time was not entirely in the hands of Zadok and his family."[15] He further concludes that pre-exilic priests were neither "chief cultic officers of the nation" nor necessarily appointed by patrilineal succession.[16] Bartlett's main

11. Bartlett, "Zadok and His Successors at Jerusalem," 1. He footnotes here Bright, *A History of Israel*, 421, and de Vaux, *Ancient Israel*, 75ff., 394.

12. For Bartlett, all of the genealogical lists are "artificial" ("Zadok and His Successors at Jerusalem," 1). He thinks Zadok had two sons, Ahimaaz and Azariah. Based on his reconstruction of 1 Kgs 4.2, which uses the LXX, he posits Azariah as the priest who took over after Zadok (pp. 6–8).

13. Ibid., 8.

14. Ibid., 9.

15. Ibid., 10. Consideration of semantics is important here; even the choice of saying *the* priesthood influences the way we regard priesthoods during the history of ancient Israel.

16. Ibid., 15. "In view of all this, we have some reason for believing that the leading priests in Jerusalem between Zadok and the exile were not yet primarily the chief cultic officers of the nation, taking their office from their lineage, but were

argument regarding our lack of information and evidence about a Zadokite priesthood has gone basically unchallenged and, unfortunately, unused by biblical scholars and historians of ancient Israel.

Frank Moore Cross, considered an influential authority on priesthoods in ancient Israel, does not mention Bartlett's work in either *Canaanite Myth and Hebrew Epic* or *From Epic to Canon*.[17] Neither does Benjamin E. Scolnic in *Chronology and Pappynomy*.[18] Julia O'Brien, author of *Priest and Levite in Malachi*, acknowledges Bartlett's contention and, probably because it is immaterial for her study, proceeds with the view of "most other scholars."[19]

Deborah Rooke, in her published dissertation, *Zadok's Heirs: The Role and Development of the High Priesthood in Ancient Israel*, likewise acknowledges Bartlett's point of view but dismisses his arguments with the following footnote:

> Despite Bartlett's argument in "Zadok and his Successors," 6–11, that there is little evidence for an hereditary line of actual Zadokites as chief priests before the Exile, the fact that subsequent priests took on the mantle of Zadok would make it legitimate to call them "sons of Zadok" regardless of their biological descent. As discussed in Ch. 2 above on the Deuteronomistic History, there certainly was a priestly group associated

rather men chosen and appointed by the king for their outstanding ability to take office as 'the chief priest,' and as one of the 'rulers of the house of God,' with administrative oversight of the temple. Doubtless they were chosen from the priestly families, but we have seen that even in Zadok's time Zadok's was not the only priestly family, and we have seen little evidence that Zadok's family controlled the Jerusalem priesthood in later reigns" (ibid.). W. Boyd Barrick, "Genealogical Notes on the 'House of David' and the 'House of Zadok,'" *JSOT* 96 (2001): 29–58 (44 n. 58), says, "For discussion of the lists see J.R. Bartlett, 'Zadok and his Successors at Jerusalem', *JTS* NS 19 (1968): 3–9, and especially R.W. Klein, 'The High Priestly Genealogies: A New Reconstruction' (unpublished paper delivered at the 1999 annual meeting of the Society of Biblical Literature [Boston, 23 November 1999], kindly shared with me by the author); cf. also, for example, H. J. Katzenstein, 'Some Remarks on the Lists of the Chief Priests of the Temple of Solomon', *JBL* 81 (1961), pp. 377–84; M.D. Rehm, 'Levites and Priests', in *ABD* IV, pp. 297–310 (307); J. Blenkinsopp, 'The Judaean Priesthood during the Neo- Babylonian and Achaemenid Periods: A Hypothetical Reconstruction', *CBQ* 60 (1998), pp. 39–41." Barrick names but does not engage with these studies. He claims the priesthood is hereditary while acknowledging "the evidence for this is slim," footnoting Bartlett and Blenkinsopp before claiming somewhat surprisingly, "I see no *a priori* reason why the tradition of hereditary high-priestly succession from Zadok should be more difficult to accept than the tradition of royal succession from David" (p. 48 n. 70).

17. Cross, *Canaanite Myth and Hebrew Epic*.

18. Benjamin E. Scolnic, *Chronology and Papponymy: A List of the Judean High Priests of the Persian Period* (The Hebrew Scriptures and Their World; Atlanta: Scholars Press, 1999).

19. Julia O'Brien, *Priest and Levite in Malachi* (SBLDS 121; Atlanta: Scholars Press, 1990), 9.

> with Zadok which was based at the Jerusalem Temple, and this would have led quite naturally to their association with the chief (and later high) priesthood since it too was associated with the Temple.[20]

Rooke fails to note the dearth of evidence regarding a Zadokite priesthood. She also fails to acknowledge the late nature of any priests that "took on the mantle of Zadok"[21] as can only be seen in biblical material in Ezek 40–48, if indeed this mantle assumption ever took place. In discussing the Deuteronomistic History and the "antecedents" of the high priesthood in the pre-exilic period, Rooke notes that the Priestly material presents Aaron as the eponymous head in the ideology of priesthood.[22] She connects this priesthood to Phinehas and by implication to Zadokites "who are thought later to have monopolized the Jerusalem priesthood in general and the high priesthood in particular." She cites Num 25:10–13 and 1 Chr 5:29–41 (ET 6:3–15) in support of this argument. In another footnote, she acknowledges that there is

> no specific mention in Numbers 25 of the high priesthood of Zadok (who of course does not appear until the time of the monarchy), it seems reasonable to interpret this "covenant of a perpetual priesthood" as referring to the high priesthood, since all sons of Aaron were priests anyway in P's scheme, and so making a specific covenant of priesthood with one of those sons would be meaningless unless it signified something different from what was promised to all the others. Making Phinehas the ancestor of the high-priestly line is in effect the same as making him the ancestor of the Zadokites, since, as already noted, the Zadokites later monopolized the high priesthood, and indeed in 1 Chronicles 5:34 (ET 6:8) Zadok himself is included in the line of high priests who are the descendants of Phinehas.[23]

She attempts to make a case for a Zadokite priesthood in the Deuteronomistic History by extrapolating from the Priestly material. Returning to the Phinehas story, she writes, "The oracle of judgment in 1 Sam 2:27–36, prophesying the downfall of the Elide house and its replacement by what can only be a Zadokites line of priests...provides divine legitimation of the Zadokites' rise to prominence."[24] There is no reference to Zadok or Zadokites in this text and the connection between Zadokites and the faithful priest with a sure house can only be achieved by Rooke on the basis of numerous unexamined presuppositions regarding the biblical texts, the history of ancient Israel, and the history of priesthoods in ancient Israel. Rooke cannot and does not leave her initial assumption about Zadok and hence the Zadokites: "Whatever Zadok's origins, though, he became a key figure in the genealogical

20. Deborah W. Rooke, *Zadok's Heirs: The Role and Development of the High Priesthood in Ancient Israel* (Oxford Theological Monographs; Oxford: Oxford University Press, 2000), 16.
21. Ibid., 116.
22. Ibid., 43–79.
23. Ibid., 52 n. 18.
24. Ibid., 57.

contest whereby Jerusalemite priests claimed precedence from the time of the late monarchy onwards."[25]

In fact, very little at all is found in Samuel–Kings regarding priesthood. Of the 117 references to "priest," the vast majority are references to an individual priest in some narrative account. An exception to this is found in 1 Sam 2 which presents the story of the dishonor of the sons of Eli the priest. YHWH declares (speaking to Eli):

> And this is the sign for you: your two sons, Hophni and Phinehas, both of them will die on a single day. And I, for myself, will raise up a dynastic priest, one who will do what is in my heart and in my mind. I will build for him an established house and he will go in and out before my anointed forever. (1 Sam 2:34–35)

I conclude, with Bartlett, that we cannot find evidence in Samuel–Kings for a Zadokite priestly dynasty.[26] Neither can we find evidence in Samuel–Kings for a dominant Zadokite priesthood from the time of David. What can we say? According to the writers and redactors of Samuel–Kings, there was a priest named Zadok who served King David.[27]

Ezra–Nehemiah

Introduction

In terms of questions asked of history, the past twenty-five years show notable shifts regarding the study of Ezra–Nehemiah.[28] While some topics

25. Ibid., 69. Her chapter on the Deuteronomistic History does not in fact spend much time on Deuteronomistic History but concentrates on Priestly material and the work of the Chronicler.

26. In fact, we cannot substantiate a genealogical succession of any priestly family with the Samuel–Kings material. As early as 1877, Samuel Curtiss (*The Levitical Priests*, 79) says of Samuel–Kings, "we approach a period in the history of Israel which is said by the modern theorists to yield no trace of an Aaronitic priesthood, and which, if it reveals a priesthood at all, only presents the Levitical."

27. This study concludes with Scolnic and Blenkinsopp (*Sage, Priest, Prophet*) that the notion of succession does not become prominent until well into the Persian Period. So here we must ask: Was there a Zadokite dynasty? When did dynastic successions in priesthood become prominent and what is the impact of these dates on study of these texts and priesthood?

28. From the early twentieth-century until about 1976 or so, studies are characterized by Albright's assumptions. For example, see William Foxwell Albright, "The Date and Personality of the Chronicler," *JBL* 40 (1921): 104–24. Pre-1900 they were more like today, see Scolnic, *Chronology and Pappyonmy*, 6–7. He cites William Hendrik Kosters, *Die Wiederherstellung Israels in der persischen Periode* (Heidelberg: J. Hornung, 1895), who denied that there was any return connected with Zerubbabel and historically disregarded over half of the book of Ezra, suggesting that they were nothing more than propaganda for the priesthood. C. C. Torrey, in *The Composition and Historical Value of Ezra–Nehemiah* (BZAW 2; Giessen:

remain constant, the nature of the questions has changed. In 1965, Jacob Myers puzzled over the authorship, date, and order of Ezra–Nehemiah as they fit into the larger work of the Chronicler.[29] In a seminal volume of its day, Hayes and Miller's *Israelite and Judaean History*, Geo Widengren identified primary issues concerning the development of a clear historical picture of the Persian period: chronological order of Ezra–Nehemiah; administrative relationship of Judah and Samaria; the Samaritan schism and the construction of the Samaritan temple; and the identity of Ezra's law book.[30]

In the last decade, the issues have been defined more broadly.[31] The relationship of Ezra–Nehemiah to the Chronicler is fairly well settled by the work of Sara Japhet, who shows rather conclusively that they are separate works.[32] The outstanding issues remaining include: the identity

J Ricker, 1896), builds on Koster's conclusions. Scolnic (*Chronology and Papponymy*, 7) writes that "Albright claims that while Torrey's textual work was brilliant beyond anything in Biblical scholarship, scholarship disregarded it because it involved accepting Koster's views and rejecting the Ezra memoirs as a total fabrication of the Chronicler. It is to Albright's credit that just as he looks at the neglected traditional order of Ezra and Nehemiah, he is also willing to appreciate what is valuable in Torrey's radical work." Even historical studies regarding the priesthood of ancient Israel show the same pattern as discussed above.

29. Jacob M. Myers, *Ezra–Nehemiah* (AB 14; New York: Doubleday, 1965).

30. Widengren, "The Persian Period," 503–9.

31. In his extensive history, Pierre Briant, *Historie de l'empire perse: De Cyrus à Alexandre* (Paris: Fayard, 1996), is reluctant to engage these issues. He says, "Grâce aux livres bibliques (Ezra et Néhémie), on peut également mener une analyse de la situation intérieure de Juda—à cette reserve près que bien des difficulté exégètiques paraissent encore aujourd'hui insurmontables" (p. 569), and further, "mon incompetence en la matière m'interdit d'y prendre part…je ne ferai part que d'une impression: à suivre la literature récente, le non-spécialiste a du mal à se situer dans les debates et les polémiques, don't les fondements scientifiques lui échappentde plus en plus au fur et à mesure qu'il multiplie les lectures; on a l'impression qu'a l'heure acutelle, aucune tradition ne jouit du statut de 'fait historique': bref, les dates adoptées dans le texte le sont par pureconvention: ma seule justification, c'est que je suis en bonne compagnie; mais je ne le serais pas moins dans l'hypothèse inverse!" (p. 1002).

32. Sara Japhet, "Composition and Chronology in the Book of Ezra–Nehemiah," in *Second Temple Studies*. Vol. 2, *Temple and Community in the Persian Period* (ed. Tamara C. Eskenazi and Kent H. Richards; JSOTSup 175; Sheffield: JSOT Press, 1994), 189–216; idem, *I & II Chronicles: A Commentary* (OTL; Louisville, Ky.: Westminster John Knox, 1993); and idem, "The Relationship between Chronicles and Ezra–Nehemiah," in *Congress Volume: Leuven, 1989* (VTSup 43; Leiden: Brill, 1991), 209–313. Joseph Blenkinsopp (*Ezra–Nehemiah* [OTL; London: SCM Press, 1989]), disagrees based on his discernment of similar themes and ideology, suggesting an editorial *inclusio* (Knoppers, *1 Chronicles 1–9*, 95, calls it a doublet) in Ezra

and role of the "people of the land";[33] the historicity, context, content, and role of the Torah book of Ezra;[34] the mission and historicity of Ezra and Nehemiah;[35] the authorship of the so-called Ezra Memoirs;[36] the socio-historical context of the authors;[37] the socio-political status of Yehud;[38] leadership in Judah during the Persian period;[39] religion and sectarianism in Yehud;[40] the role of Samaria;[41] the purpose/ideology of

1:1–3a and 2 Chr 36:22–23 as well as a reinterpretation of "linguistic and stylistic features" (pp. 48–49). I suggest separate initial authorship joined by a minimalistic final editor. As a historian, Lester Grabbe (*Ezra–Nehemiah* [Old Testament Readings; New York: Routledge, 1998], 11), states, "Ezra 1:1–3a is the same as 2 Chron. 36:22–23. This has the clear aim of making Ezra a continuation of Chronicles." Questions surrounding multiple redactions and a final integrative editor remain. For a full discussion, see Knoppers, *1 Chronicles 1–9*, 72–127.

33. Tamara C. Eskenazi, "Book of Ezra," in *Eerdmans Dictionary of the Bible* (ed. David Noel Freedman and Allen C. Myers; Grand Rapids: Eerdmans, 2000), 449–51.

34. Berquist, *Judaism in Persia's Shadow*, 110; Eskenazi, "Book of Ezra"; Japhet, "Composition and Chronology in the Book of Ezra–Nehemiah"; Blenkinsopp, *Ezra–Nehemiah*, 152–57; Juha Pakkala, *Ezra the Scribe: The Development of Ezra 7:10 and Nehemiah 8* (BZAW 347; Berlin: de Gruyter, 2004).

35. Robert P. Carroll, "What Do We Know About the Temple? The Temple in the Prophets," in Eskenazi and Richards, eds., *Second Temple Studies*, 2:34–51; Eskenazi, "Book of Ezra"; Lester L. Grabbe, "What Was Ezra's Mission?," in Eskenazi and Richards, eds., *Second Temple Studies*, 2:286–99; idem, *Judaism from Cyrus to Hadrian*, 1:88–92; idem, "Reconstructing History from the Book of Ezra," in Davies, ed., *Second Temple Studies*, 1:98–107; Japhet, "Composition and Chronology in the Book of Ezra–Nehemiah"; McNutt, *Reconstructing of Society of Ancient Israel*, 183; Etienne Nodet, *A Search for the Origins of Judaism: From Joshua to the Mishnah* (trans. Ed Crowley; JSOTSup 248; Sheffield: Sheffield Academic Press, 1997), 189 and passim; Rooke, *Zadok's Heirs*, 153; Paolo Sacchi, *The History of the Second Temple Period* (JSOTSup 285; Sheffield: Sheffield Academic Press, 2000), 132.

36. Eskenazi, "Book of Ezra." Addressing the question of whether there is an Ezra Memoir, see Pakkala, *Ezra the Scribe*, passim; Grabbe, *Ezra–Nehemiah*, 133, 152–54; Blenkinsopp, *Ezra–Nehemiah*, 135.

37. Berquist, *Judaism in Persia's Shadow*, 27; Blenkinsopp, *Ezra–Nehemiah*, 60–69.

38. Grabbe, *Judaism from Cyrus to Hadrian*, 1:73, 79–83, 93–4, 99–100; Nodet, *A Search for the Origins of Judaism*, 378.

39. Grabbe, *Judaism from Cyrus to Hadrian*, 1:75–79, 88–92; Nodet, *A Search for the Origins of Judaism*, 29–37; Grabbe, *Ezra–Nehemiah*, passim.

40. Grabbe, *Judaism from Cyrus to Hadrian*, 1:100–10; Nodet, *A Search for the Origins of Judaism*, 389.

41. Grabbe, *Judaism from Cyrus to Hadrian*, 1:83–88; Nodet, *A Search for the Origins of Judaism*, 35–37.

Ezra–Nehemiah;[42] plausible sources for the period;[43] the place and role of prophecy;[44] focus on ethnicity issues;[45] the role of Ezra–Nehemiah in literature and authority of ancient periods;[46] the role of genealogies;[47] and others including the role of archaeology, questions about decrees, sabbath, and the reconstruction of the temple.

In general, historical studies of Ezra–Nehemiah have both expanded in scope and have become increasingly interdisciplinary in approach.[48] This can be attributed in part to a shift from using the Bible as a starting point to using a wider range of questions which tend to focus on how history relates to the biblical accounts or, more specifically, how the biblical accounts about the Persian period fit into the history of Persian period Yehud.[49] Contemporary studies attempt to broaden the view of the period and, in so doing, have recognized the critical nature of the period to biblical studies, the paucity of source material, the necessity for comparative studies, the difficulties with arguing from silence, the need to test accurately historical hypotheses, the need to be deliberate about history as well as to specify underlying assumptions and methodological approaches, and the need for a variety of input in order to present a full portrait of the period.[50]

42. McNutt, *Reconstructing of Society of Ancient Israel*, 183; Nodet, *A Search for the Origins of Judaism*, 29; Sacchi, *The History of the Second Temple Period*, 131; Grabbe, *Ezra–Nehemiah*, 11–68, 183–97; Blenkinsopp, *Ezra–Nehemiah*, 41–59, passim.

43. Grabbe, "Reconstructing History from the Book of Ezra," 98–106; *Ezra–Nehemiah*, passim; Nodet, *A Search for the Origins of Judaism*; Sacchi, *The History of the Second Temple Period*, 133.

44. Carroll, "What Do We Know About the Temple?"; Nodet, *A Search for the Origins of Judaism*, 389; David L. Petersen, "The Temple in Persian Period Prophetic Texts," in Davies, ed., *Second Temple Studies*, 1:125–45; Blenkinsopp, *Ezra–Nehemiah*.

45. Davies, ed., *Second Temple Studies*, Vol. 1; Eskenazi and Richards, eds., *Second Temple Studies*. Vol. 2; Grabbe, *Ezra–Nehemiah*, 177–82 and passim; Blenkinsopp, *Ezra–Nehemiah*, 173–201.

46. Nodet, *A Search for the Origins of Judaism*, 25–33, 337–74; Sacchi, *The History of the Second Temple Period*, 131.

47. Japhet, "Composition and Chronology in the Book of Ezra–Nehemiah," 207; Nodet, *A Search for the Origins of Judaism*, 27; Sacchi, *The History of the Second Temple Period*, 131.

48. While study of a single issue often leads to a particular conclusion, a collection of such conclusions often creates a null set, making synthesis difficult if not impossible.

49. This stands in contrast to previous efforts to reconcile inconsistencies within the biblical material.

50. Grabbe, *Judaism from Cyrus to Hadrian*, 1:111.

This section re-examines ideas of the Zadokite priesthood as they relate to Ezra–Nehemiah in light of these contemporary historical issues. As the בני צדוק are not mentioned specifically in Ezra–Nehemiah, how do the references to Zadok inform our understanding of Zadokites? If we cannot retain the assumption that Zadokites priests were necessarily among those members of society taken into exile, how must we reformulate the questions we ask about the reconstruction period? What does it mean for our understanding of the Persian and Hellenistic periods that "sons of Zadok" are not mentioned in Ezra–Nehemiah?

Numerous scholars assume that Zadokite priests were taken into exile with the fall of Jerusalem. In his discussion of the priests and Levites in the period of Ezra and Nehemiah, Roland de Vaux clearly assumes a Zadokite lineage for the priests that went into exile as well as those that returned: "Though the biblical texts give no precise information about the origin of the four priestly families which returned, all four of them very probably claimed Sadoqite ancestry… Besides, it was principally the Sadoqite priests who had been deported."[51] Coote and Ord find "the Zadokites of the late Davidic monarchy" as severely diminished, killed or deported by the Babylonians; these same Zadokites "again came into their own" in the Persian period, returning more powerful than before.[52]

The first and most logical explanation for this assumption is that if Zadokites were the dominant priesthood throughout the united and divided monarchy, they must have been the priests taken into exile as mentioned in various biblical texts related to the exile. Second Kings 25:18–21 (cf. Jer 52:24–27) provides a brief list of priests at the time of the exile:

> The captain of the guard took Seraiah, the chief priest, and Zephaniah, the second priest, and three keepers of the threshold. From the city he took the officer who had been commander of the soldiers, five men who were on the king's council who had been found in the city, the secretary of the commander of the forces who had served the people of the land, and sixty men from among the people of the land who had been found in the city. Nebuzaradan, the captain of the guard, took them and brought them to the king of Babylon at Riblah. The king of Babylon put them to death at Riblah in the land of Hamath. Judah was taken out of its land into exile. (2 Kgs 25:18–21)

But note here that Seraiah, Zephaniah, and the three guardians of the threshold were killed by the king of Babylon at Riblah. We have no

51. De Vaux, *Ancient Israel*, 388.

52. Robert B. Coote and David Robert Ord, *In the Beginning: Creation and the Priestly History* (Minneapolis: Fortress, 1991), 34–35.

textual evidence that priests were taken into exile. We certainly have no names of priests taken into exile. We have no primary evidence associating even these two priests, Seraiah and Zaphaniah, with Zadokites (or any particular priestly family for that matter).[53] If we cannot retain the initial presupposition that Zadokite priests were exiled, and if we cannot even know which priests went into exile, we must certainly examine more closely the notion that many if not most of the priests returning from exile were Zadokites.

Ezra 2:1–2

Ezra 2:1–2 gives an introduction to the list of returnees:

> These were the sons of the province who came up from the captivity of the exile, those who Nebuchadnezzar, king of Babylon, carried to exile in Babylonia. They returned to Jerusalem and Judah, each to their own city. Those who came with Zerubbabel were Jeshua, Nehemiah, Seraiah, Reelaiah, Mordecai, Bilshan, Mispar, Bigvai, Rehum, Baanah. The number of the men of the people of Israel… (Ezra 2:1–2 [= Neh 7:7–8])

This Jeshua, considered to be the same person as Joshua and frequently designated as high priest during the restoration period, is generally understood to be a critical figure in the period.[54] Jeshua/Joshua is found elsewhere in biblical material as the head of one of the Aaronite ancestral houses of priests (1 Chr 24:11); one of six people from the time of Hezekiah who was assisting Kore, the keeper of the east gate, in the distribution of goods to the people (2 Chr 31:15); a priest, the son of Jehozadak, who, along with his brothers, and Zerubbabel, built the altar of the God of Israel, made a beginning, supervised those working on the

53. Even if we can demonstrate that there were priests in exile (which there surely must have been), and while it is beyond the scope of this study to examine the activities of any priests in exile, conclusions of this study must surely be brought to bear on studies of life in exile. Notions that might be affected include restoration plans and the writing and compilation of biblical texts.

54. In his reconstructed list of high priests, Frank Moore Cross argues for a date of ca. 570 for the birth of Jeshua; see "A Reconstruction of the Judean Restoration." But see James C. VanderKam, *Second Temple Studies*, "Jewish High Priests of the Persian Period: Is the List Complete?," in *Priesthood and Cult in Ancient Israel* (ed. G. Anderson and S. Olyan; JSOTSup 125; Sheffield: Sheffield Academic Press, 1991), 67–91. Also see Widengren, "The Persian Period"; Lester L. Grabbe, "Josephus and the Reconstruction of the Judean Restoration," *JBL* 106 (1987): 231–46, and idem, *Judaism from Cyrus to Hadrian*, Vol. 1, for a discussion of the difficulties with Cross' reconstruction. Also see Scolnic, *Chronology and Pappynomy*, 213–21; VanderKam, *From Joshua to Caiaphas*, 18–42 (with mentions of Zadokites, 18 n. 56, 19, 37, 40).

house of God, decided with Zerubbabel who would work on the house of God (Ezra 3:2, 8, 9; 4:3; 5:2); high priest (Hag 1:1, 12; 2:2, 4; Zech 3:1, 8; 6:11); a high priest in the process of cleansing and ordination (Zech 6:10–15); an ancestor of some people living in the land (Ezra 2:6); an ancestor of Levites living in the land (Ezra 2:40; Neh 7:43; 12:8, 24); father of Jozabad who was with the priest Meremoth in the house of God (Ezra 8:33); father of Ezer who repaired part of the wall (Neh 3:19); father of Joiakim, ancestor of Jaddua (Neh 12:10); one of eight who stood on the stairs of the Levites and cried out to the Lord their God (Neh 9:4–5); a Levite who signed a sealed document with Nehemiah (Neh 10:9); and one of thirteen Levites who helped the people understand the law (Neh 8:7). Tamara Eskenazi notes that, given the attention to Jeshua/Joshua's role in Haggai, Zechariah, and Ezra–Nehemiah, his absence from the priestly genealogies in Chronicles raises questions.[55] His father, Jehozadak, does appear in the genealogical list in 1 Chr 5, which names Jehozadak as the priest sent into exile by Nebuchadnezzar.[56] Other than Jeshua/Joshua, Seraiah and Baanah may have some connection to priesthood according to biblical material.[57]

Ezra 2:36–70

Ezra 2:36–70 (= Neh 7:39–73) provides a list of the family names of returning priests included in the group of the sons of the province that came up from exilic captivity from Babylon (Ezra 2:1):[58]

> The priests, the sons of Jedaiah of the house of Jeshua, nine hundred seventy-three, the sons of Immer, one thousand fifty-two, the sons of Pashhur, one thousand two hundred forty-seven, the sons of Harim, one thousand and seventeen. (Ezra 2:36–39)

55. Tamara C. Eskenazi, "Jeshua," *ABD* 3:769–71. For Blenkinsopp (*Ezra–Nehemiah*, 84–85), "Zech. 3:1–10 suggests that he was given the high priesthood after the return even though he or his 'house' had been involved in apostasy or suspect religious practice."

56. Jeshua/Joshua's father in Hag 1:1, 12, 14; 2:2, 4; Zech 6:11 but interestingly not in Ezra–Nehemiah (although Jozadak does appear in Ezra–Nehemiah: Ezra 3:2, 8; 5:2; 10:18).

57. Neh 12:1–3, 12; 1 Chr 24:8; 2 Kgs 25:18–21 (Jer 52:24–27); Ezra 7:1; Neh 11:11.

58. Conclusions about the nature of these lists remain unanswered. See Blenkinsopp, *Ezra–Nehemiah*, 83; D. J. A. Clines, *Ezra, Nehemiah, Esther* (NCB; Grand Rapids: Eerdmans, 1984), 44–45; Antonius H. J. Gunneweg, *Esra* (KAT 19; Gütersloh: Gütersloher Verlagshaus Mohn, 1985); W. Rudolph, *Ezra und Nehemia* (HAT; Tübingen: J. C. B. Mohr, 1949), 13; H. G. M. Williamson, *Ezra and Nehemiah* (OTG 13; Sheffield: JSOT Press, 1987), 30–31.

With no specific names of priests, Ezra 2 delineates the returning priests as coming from the sons of Jedaiah,[59] the sons of Immer,[60] the sons of Pashhur,[61] and the sons of Harim.[62]

In speaking of these priestly families, Blenkinsopp correctly notes, "Significantly, they are not called 'sons of Aaron.'"[63] I would add: Neither

59. Jedaiah is seen elsewhere in biblical material as the son of Shimri, a clan leader of the tribe of Simeon (1 Chr 4:37); an ancestor of a priestly house, a descendant of the house of Aaron (1 Chr 9:10; 24:7); a son of Harumaph who helped to restore the walls (Neh 3:10); a priest who lived within the newly constructed walls of Jerusalem (Neh 11:10); a priest who came up with Zerubbabel and served as priest in the days of Jeshua (Neh 12:7); the ancestral house for Uzzi, a priest during the days of Joiakim (Neh 12:19); the ancestral house for Nethanel, a priest during the days of Joiakim (Neh 12:21); one of three exiles who arrived from Babylon carrying silver and gold (Zech 6:10, he is not specified as a priest here); one of four who were to care for the crown of the high priest Joshua (Zech 6:14); ancestor of some returning from exile (1 Esd 5:24).

60. Immer is seen elsewhere in biblical material as an ancestor of a priestly house, a descendant of the house of Aaron (1 Chr 24:14); father of the priest Pashhur who was the chief officer in the house of the Lord (Jer 20:1); ancestor of Maasai who returned as priest from exile (1 Chr 9:12); ancestor of Amashsai who lived within the newly constructed walls of Jerusalem (Neh 11:13); ancestor of Hanani and Zebadiah who married foreign women (Ezra 10:20; 1 Esd 9:21); father of Zadok who made repairs on the wall (Neh 3:29); ancestor of some returning from exile (1 Esd 5:24).

61. Pashhur is seen elsewhere in biblical material as ancestor in the line of Immer of Adaiah, a priest who returned from exile (1 Chr 9:12); ancestor in the line of Malchijah of Adaiah who lived in the newly constructed walls of Jerusalem (Neh 11:12); ancestor of the priests Elioenai, Maaseiah, Ishmael, Nethanel, Jozabad, and Elasah who married foreign women (Ezra 10:22; 1 Esd 9:22); priest, son of Immer, chief officer in the house of the Lord, who struck the prophet Jeremiah and put him in stocks before releasing him the next morning; named by Jeremiah "Terror-all-around" and condemned by Jeremiah to captivity in Babylon (Jer 20:1–6); son of Malchiah, sent by King Zedekiah along with Zephaniah to Jeremiah to inquire about impending attack by Nebuchadrezzar (Jer 21:1); father of Gedaliah who heard the words of Jeremiah (Jer 38:1); son of Malchiah, who heard the words of Jeremiah (Jer 38:1); priest whose name was among many on the sealed document during Nehemiah's time (Neh 10:3); ancestor of those returning from exile (1 Esd 5:25).

62. Harim is mentioned elsewhere in biblical material as a descendant of the house of Aaron who becomes a head of ancestral houses of priests (1 Chr 24:8); ancestor of Maaseiah, Elijah, Shemaiah, Jehiel, and Uzziah, priests who were found to have married foreign women (Ezra 10:21); ancestral head of the house whose descendant, Adna, served as priest in the days of Joiakim (Neh 12:15); priest whose name was among many on the sealed document during Nehemiah's time (Neh 10:5; also see Neh 10:27); father of Malchijah who worked with Hasshub toward restoring the wall (Neh 3:11).

63. Blenkinsopp, *Ezra–Nehemiah*, 88.

are they called Zadokites, which is somewhat odd if the Zadokites were the dominant priestly family making up the priests who were taken into exile.

Ezra 7:1–5

Ezra is often assumed to be a priest who returned from exile.[64] Frequently in this regard, Ezra 7:1–5 forms the basis for the traditional notion that Ezra was a priest, not only a priest but a high priest, not only a high priest but a Zadokite high priest.[65] Ezra is often referred to as a priest (Ezra 7:11, 12, 21; 10:10, 16; Neh 8:2, 9; 12:1, 13, 26). A thoroughgoing discussion of Ezra as a priest is better left for another project and is only connected to this study when Ezra is considered a Zadokite priest. The notion that Ezra was a priest is connected to the assumption that he was a Zadokite in that, if he was a priest and returned to Yehud from exile, he must have been a Zadokite because, so the assumption goes, the Zadokites were the ones who went into exile and therefore were the ones who returned from exile. Sufficient questions have been raised regarding Ezra as a Zadokite high priest to require significant examination before a presumptive use of that association. Grabbe and Scolnic both recall the work of K. Koch in concluding that the idea of Ezra as a high priest is based on Ezra 7:1–6.[66] The Ezra text reads as follows:

64. Ezra is mentioned in the biblical material in Ezra 7:1, 6, 10, 11, 12, 21, 25; 10:1, 2, 5, 6, 10, 16; Neh 8:1, 2, 4, 5, 6, 9, 13; 9:6; 12:1, 13, 26, 33, 36. In *Antiquities* (11.121, 123, 127), Josephus describes Ezra as the leading priest who reads the laws in Babylonia. 1 Esd 9:39–40 sets him as the chief priest. *Cant. Rab.* 5:5 makes Ezra a contemporary of Zerubbabel and Jeshua. *b. Meg.* 15a and Targum on Mal 1:1 associate him with Malachi. *B. Meg.* 16b says he was a disciple of Baruch. For *b. Sukk.* 20a, Ezra's primary function was the restoration of the Torah.

65. De Vaux, *Ancient Israel*, 397. De Vaux even uses Ezra 7:1–5 as part of his proof that the Zadokites were the dominant priesthood from the time of David until the collapse of the Temple (pp. 360–61).

66. Grabbe, "What Was Ezra's Mission?," 292. Although Grabbe (*Ezra–Nehemiah*, 26–27), raises questions, he notes about Ezra, "He is identified by means of his genealogy which goes back ot Aaron the high priest. Ezra is a priest; furthermore, he is of the line of the pre-exilic high priests. This is significant because he nowhere claims the office of high priest, but the text seems to be implying that he deserves this office even if he does not have it formally. His immediate predecessor was Sariah (7:1), the last of the pre-exilic high priests, who was executed when Nebuchadnezzar took Jerusalem (2 Kings 25:21). It cannot be literally true that Ezra was son of Sariah, for he would have been at least 120 years old. Yet it seems that this is what the text wants us to believe. It is not uncommon for a more distant ancestor to be used as a patronymic, and there is nothing linguistic to make us think Sariah is anything but Ezra's father. It is only when we calculate the chronology

> Now after these matters, in the reign of Artaxerxes, king of Persia, Ezra, son of Seraiah, son of Azariah, son of Hilkiah, son of Shallum, son of *Zadok*, son of Ahitub, son of Amariah, son of Azariah, son of Meraioth, son of Zerhiah, son of Uzzi, son of Bukki, son of Abishua, son of Phinehas, son of Eleazar, son of Aaron, the chief priest, this Ezra went up from Babylonia and he was a skilled scribe in the torah of Moses which YHWH, God of Israel, had given. The king gave to him all that he asked because the hand of YHWH, his God, was on him.

Although the text never states that Ezra was a high priest, some read it as so by implication since, using sixteen generations, Ezra is presented in the lineage of Aaron. As noted by Grabbe and Scolnic, the narrative shows Ezra performing tasks frequently associated with those of high priesthood, thus contributing to the idea that Ezra was a high priest.[67] Various scholars regard the purpose of this genealogical list in Ezra 7:1–5 as something other than a historical accounting for the priesthood.[68] As Blenkinsopp so effectively states, "...the list must be either defective or selective, most probably both."[69] The historicity of the list must certainly be questioned since Ezra cannot be the son of the pre-exilic priest Seraiah who was executed by the king of Babylon according to 2 Kgs 25:18–21.[70] Some see this list as a "secondary insertion in its context" making the determination of its purpose and context all the more difficult.[71]

from data outside Ezra that the absurdity of the situation becomes clear." Also see Blenkinsopp, *Ezra–Nehemiah*, 136. Scolnic, *Chronology and Papponymy*, 149–204. Klaus Koch, "Ezra and the Origins of Judaism," *JSS* 19 (1974): 173–97.

67. Grabbe, "What Was Ezra's Mission?," 292; Scolnic, *Chronology and Papponymy*, 195.

68. For example, see Robert H. Pfeiffer, "Books of Ezra and Nehemiah," *IDB* 215–19 (218). Also see Klaus Koch, "Ezra and Meremoth: Remarks on the History of the High Priesthood," in *"Sha'arei Talmon": Studies in the Bible, Qumran, and the Ancient Near East Presented to Shemaryahu Talmon* (ed. Michael Fishbane and Emanuel Tov with the assistance of Weston W. Fields; Winona Lake, Ind.: Eisenbrauns, 1992), 173–97 (190–93).

69. Blenkinsopp (*Ezra–Nehemiah*, 136) notes that "Ezra was not, of course, high priest. He appears in none of the lists (Neh. 12:10–11, 22) and is nowhere described as such (see also on Ezra 8:33). If the genealogy is to be considered at all historical, he must have stood in the collateral line of descent. But it is much more likely that the genealogy is a fiction designed to convey the message that Ezra's function with respect to the law and the cult continued that of the preexilic priesthood."

70. Of course it is possible that Ezra's father was named Seraiah.

71. Loring Woart Batten, *A Critical and Exegetical Commentary on the Books of Ezra and Nehemiah* (ICC 15; Edinburgh: T. & T. Clark, 1972), 303; de Vaux, *Ancient Israel*, 365; Arvid S. Kapelrud, *The Question of Authorship in the Ezra–Narrative: A Lexical Investigation* (Oslo: Universitetsforlaget, 1944), 19–20; Scolnic, *Chronology and Papponymy*, 187. Also see Pakkala, *Ezra the Scribe*, 22–32.

Clearly Ezra is missing from any other biblical lists of priests or high priests.[72]

Let us review current scholarly ideas concerning the purpose of Ezra 7:1–5, a text which: demonstrates a concern for "purity of blood line";[73] is a "bulky lacuna"[74]; provides a genealogy for Ezra;[75] seeks to legitimize the priestly role of Ezra.[76]

While most scholars would agree with Robert Wilson that genealogical lists, both in the Bible and more generally from the ancient Near East, primarily served social and political purposes and only secondarily and infrequently served as historical records, discussion continues on the historical specifics related to the lists in Ezra–Nehemiah.[77] Contrary to Blenkinsopp, who thinks the writer of the list used, as a source, the already incomplete 1 Chr 6 (ET 5) list, Sara Japhet finds the Ezra list as the older and more original of the two.[78] At the time of its writing, Ezra 7:1–5 fills a "need to establish an unequivocally legitimate ancestry for the priests…"[79] Japhet and Scolnic both see it as an "attempt to provide an Aaronide lineage for the last High Priests of the First Temple period."[80] In her analysis, Japhet suggests that the list intentionally

72. Blenkinsopp, *Ezra–Nehemiah*, 136. It could very well be, as suggested by Scolnic, that the notion of high priesthood was not operative at that time. Scolnic (*Chronology and Papponymy*, 195–99) even goes so far as to "wonder if the model of the Papacy does not subconsciously affect modern scholars as they discuss the 'High Priesthood' of Israel." Of course, if this notion is unavailable to the reconstruction of history for the restoration period, we must (re)ponder ideas of hereditary lineages. He also suggests that the "later High Priesthood" may be serving as a model (pp. 203–4).

73. Scolnic, *Chronology and Papponymy*, 200.

74. Japhet, *I & II Chronicles*, 151.

75. Rooke, *Zadok's Heirs*, 162; Japhet, *I & II Chronicles*, 151. Japhet sees the text as "ostensibly the genealogical tree of Ezra."

76. Scolnic, *Chronology and Papponymy*, 199.

77. Robert R. Wilson, "The Old Testament Genealogies in Recent Research," *JBL* 94 (1975): 169–89. For a detailed discussion of priestly genealogies, see Gary N. Knoppers, "The Relationship of the Priestly Genealogies to the History of the High Priesthood in Jerusalem," in *Judea and the Judeans in the Neo-Babylonian Period* (ed. Oded Lipschitz and Joseph Blenkinsopp; Winona Lake, Ind.: Eisenbrauns, 2003), 109–34.

78. Blenkinsopp, *Ezra–Nehemiah*, 136. For Blenkinsopp, Azariah, Amariah, Ahitub, and Zadok are omitted by haplography.

79. Japhet, *I & II Chronicles*, 151.

80. Scolnic, *Chronology and Papponymy*, 200. Also see Japhet, *I & II Chronicles*, 151–2. If this is so, what are the implications for our understanding of pre-exilic priesthood? If the pre-exilic priests were "Zadokites," would not that have been known?

ignores "altogether priests known from the historical records."[81] The missing persons/priests are: Amariah, Ahitub, Zadok, Ahimaaz, Azariah as they appear in the 1 Chr 5 list.[82] Frank Moore Cross attributes these absences to redaction and textual corruptions, but, as Japhet notes, "the nature of the missing names makes these solutions doubtful."[83] The missing names are all associated in some way with the צדוק of Samuel–Kings. Apparently the list in Ezra 7:1–5 serves as a connection with late pre-exilic figures. As previously discussed, the Aaronite line appeared only in the postexilic period. The Ezra 7 list serves to connect both Ezra and the late pre-exilic priests with Aaron and seems intentionally to avoid, or at least to be unconcerned with, priests known from the deuteronomistic historian's accounts. An appropriate study at this point would be an attempt to understand when, how, and why the Aaronite name

81. Japhet, *I & II Chronicles*, 152.

82. Amariah (only mentioned in Chronicles, Zephaniah, Ezra, and Nehemiah); Ahitub (1 Sam 14:3 as one of the two sons of Phinehas and the father of Ahijah; 1 Sam 22:9 as the father of Ahimelech; 2 Sam 8:17 as the son of Amariah and the father of Zadok; 1 Chr 6:7–8 as the son of Amariah and the father of Zadok; 1 Chr 9:11 and Neh 11:11 as the grandfather of Zadok; 1 Chr 6:11–12 as a son of Amariah and grandfather of Zadok; Judg 8:1 as an ancestor of Judith, son of Elijah, and father of Raphain); Zadok (cited passim); Ahimaaz (1 Sam 14:50 as the father of Saul's wife Ahinoam; 2 Sam 15:27, 36: 17:20 as the son of Zadok; 2 Sam 18:19–30 as a messenger for the king; 1 Kgs 4:15 as one of Solomon's officers); Azariah (1 Kgs 4:2 as priest under Solomon and son of Zadok; 1 Kgs 4:5 as son of Nathan who was in charge of officials; 2 Kgs 15:13; 2 Chr 26:1–23 as the name of King Uzziah, son of Amaziah and Jecoliah; 1 Chr 2:8 as the great-grandson of Judah; 1 Chr 2:38–39 as a descendant of Judah; 1 Chr 6:9 as a descendant of Aaron and grandson of Zadok; 1 Chr 6:10 as a priest in Solomon's temple; 1 Chr 6:13 as a priest, father of Hilkiah and son of Seraiah; 1 Chr 6:36 as a Levite of the Kohathite family; 1 Chr 9:11 as a priest in the early restoration period; 2 Chr 15:1–7 as a prophet, the son of Oded; 2 Chr 21:2 as a son of Jehoshaphat (two "Azariahs" are mentioned in the list of 2 Chr 21:2); 2 Chr 23:1 as a military officer, son of Jeroham; 2 Chr 23:1 as a military officer, son of Oded; 2 Chr 26:17–20 as a priest during the time of Uzziah; 2 Chr 28:12 as Ephramite chief; 2 Chr 29:12 as the father of Joel; 2 Chr 29:12 as the father of Jehallelel; 2 Chr 31:10 as a priest for Hezekiah; Ezra 7:1 as the grandfather of Ezra; Ezra 7:3 as the father of Amariah; Neh 3:23–24 as a person who repaired the wall; Neh 7:7 as a leader who returned with Zerubbabel; Neh 10:2 as one signing a document with Nehemiah; Neh 8:7 as one who interpreted the law for the people; Jer 43:2 as one who led people to Egypt; Dan 1:6–7 as the other name of Abednego). As is discussed in the section on Chronicles, it is only at a later period that there is an interest in incorporating a "house of Zadok" into the Aaronite line.

83. Cross, *Canaanite Myth and Hebrew Epic*, 208–15. See also Japhet, *I & II Chronicles*, 151–52. As will be discussed in the section on Chronicles, Japhet suggests that the Zadokite strand was added at a later time.

arose and served as an eponym for these priests.[84] But what does that tell us about Zadokites? How does that associate Ezra with Zadok as so often seen in traditional histories of ancient Israel?

Certainly one could argue that there is a צדוק in this Ezra 7 list. The question is: What does it tell us? Does this Zadok refer to David's Zadok? Does the Zadok and its placement in this list constitute a reference to Zadokites? Japhet correctly notes that the position of Zadok, son of Ahitub, in the Ezra 7 list "makes it very unlikely that the priest of David's time is meant."[85]

What, then, can we make of the צדוק in Ezra 7:1–5? Were the names in this list chosen specifically for this list? Were "priestly" names floating around and written down to fill a specific number of places? Nowhere in Ezra–Nehemiah is the בני צדוק mentioned. Nowhere in Ezra–Nehemiah are Zadokites exalted. If any priestly group is exalted, it is the "house of Aaron." Thus, there is only potential to assume that Ezra is Zadokite if the Zadokites indeed went into and returned from exile. At this point we have no evidence that Ezra was a Zadokite.

Consider for a moment that even if Ezra–Nehemiah gives a fairly time-proximate description of late restoration events and if the books of Haggai and Zechariah[86] are speaking to events of the restoration period, then, from the point of view of a search for a Zadokite priesthood, we must ask why Zadokites are not mentioned in any of this period's material. Why do we not hear of בני צדוק or בת צדוק? As there are no references to בני צדוק or בת צדוק in Ezra–Nehemiah, this section will examine the remainder of references to צדוק: Neh 3:4, 29; 10:22 (ET 21); 11:11, and 13:13.

Nehemiah 3:4, 29; 10:22; 13:13

Nehemiah 3:4, 29; 10:22; and 13:13 clearly do not refer to the pre-exilic, historical Zadok. Nehemiah 3 presents a list of builders working on the wall. The secondary nature of this list becomes apparent in a literary analysis. The list interrupts an on-going narrative with a change of person and subject matter.[87] Nehemiah 10 lists those members of the community who signed a document with Nehemiah; צדוק is listed among the

84. If this does give an indication of the rising notion that all priests should be Aaronite—this could come as part and parcel of the creation of the Exodus to the twelve tribe system as a foundation myth per Lemche, *Israelites in Tradition and History*, 96–132, esp. 101–2.

85. Japhet, *I & II Chronicles*, 151.

86. Along with, possibly, Isa 56–66.

87. Blenkinsopp, *Ezra–Nehemiah*, 231.

leaders of the people. Nehemiah 13:4–14 seems to provide some sort of epilogue, discussing administrative details. Nehemiah appoints officers over the treasury, including Zadok as a scribe.[88]

Nehemiah 11:10–14

It has already been noted that in the entirety of Ezra–Nehemiah there are only two possible references to Zadok, the priest of David/Solomon: Ezra 7:1–5, as discussed above, and Neh 11:10–14, which reads:[89]

> From (among) the priests: Jedaiah, the son of Joiarib, son[90] of Seraiah,[91] son of Hilkiah, son of Meshullam, son of *Zadok*, son of Meraioth, son of Ahitub, ruler of the house of God (אלהים) and their brothers, the ones doing the work of the house, eight hundred and twenty-two, and Adaiah, son of Jeroham, son of Pelaliah, son of Amzi, son of Zechariah, son of Pashur, son of Malchijah and his brothers, heads of ancestral homes, two hundred forty-two, and Amashsai, son of Azarel, son of Ahzai, son of Meshillemoth, son of Immer, and their brothers, mighty men of strength, one hundred and twenty-eight, and their overseer, Zabdiel, son of Haggedolim.

As Blenkinsopp notes, this text presents six priestly houses, including three of the four seen in Ezra 2.[92] More parallels are apparent with the 1 Chr 9 list which supplies a shorter version of this list. Whether Nehemiah served as a source for the Chronicles list or the writer(s) used related source material, the lists apparently served different purposes. Where this Nehemiah list records the "chiefs of the province," the Chronicles list details "those who lived in Jerusalem." The Nehemiah list gives

88. Note 13:10: "I discovered also that the portions of the Levites were not given to them so that every one of them, as well as the singers responsible for the work, had gone to their farms. Then I brought a case against the leaders." Could this be a possible referent for Ezek 44?

89. De Vaux, *Ancient Israel*, 388, uses this text as a 'prooftext' that Jedaiah is a Zadokite.

90. The Hebrew here reads מן־הכהנים ידעיה בן־יויריב יכין with the ending emended in the critical apparatus to יויקים בן־ based on Neh 12:10; 1 Chr 9:10/11. See the following footnote about Rudolph's reconstruction.

91. Following the reconstruction of W. Rudolph, *Chronikbücher* (HAT; Tübingen: Mohr, 1955), 84, which takes יכין to be a corruption of בן. This reconstruction is accepted by and discussed in Japhet, *I & II Chronicles*, 211. Also see W. F. Albright, "Notes on Early Hebrew and Aramaic Epigraphy," *JPOS* 6 (1926): 75–102 (96–97); Raymond A. Bowman, "The Book of Nehemiah," *IB* 549-69, 662-819 (774); Myers, *Ezra–Nehemiah*, 184–85. Rudolph further adds "son of Azariah" between "son of Seraiah" and "son of Hilkiah."

92. Blenkinsopp, *Ezra–Nehemiah*, 325–26.

a total of approximately 1200 priests where the Chronicles total reaches 1760. Japhet finds the section on the priests to be the most similar between the two lists.[93]

Other than a comparison of its "partner" list in 1 Chr 9, this text is notable for its differences from the Ezra 7 pericope.[94] Here Zadok is the son of Meraioth[95] who in turn is the son of Ahitub whereas the Zadok of Ezra 7:1–5 is listed as the son of Ahitub.[96] As with the Zadok of Ezra 7:1–5, the position of צדוק in this list makes it unlikely that this refers to the *pre-exilic* Zadok of Samuel–Kings, Davidic fame.[97]

Summary of Ezra–Nehemiah References

There is some discussion about whether the lists in Ezra 7:1–5 and Neh 11:10–14 provide lists of high priests (הכהן הגדול) and how these lists relate to other lists of priests.[98] Given the total number of lists of priests, the absence of references to בני צדוק is somewhat surprising. We certainly do not see any leaning toward an elevation of a family of Zadokites at this point. Whenever Ezra–Nehemiah was written and produced, "Zadokites" were not on the tip of the writer's pen.

Chronicles

Introduction

Interpretation of references in the work of the Chronicler to צדוק relies heavily on what is understood regarding the date, provenance, authorship, and ideology of the material. Of these, date, provenance, and authorship seem to elude consensus.[99] Language and rhetoric are frequently used as

93. Japhet, *I & II Chronicles*, 210.
94. Which is discussed in the section on Chronicles.
95. As is also found in 1 Chr 9:11.
96. As is also found in 2 Sam 8:17; 1 Chr 6:8, 12; 8:16.
97. Rooke, *Zadok's Heirs*, 144. Rooke claims that the Ahitub in this list is "the preexilic Ahitub" but she does not address the complications of his position in the list.
98. Batten, *A Critical and Exegetical Commentary on the Books of Ezra and Nehemiah*, 269; Blenkinsopp, *Ezra–Nehemiah*, 325, 353–54; Bowman, "The Book of Nehemiah," 775, 805; L. H. Brockington, *Ezra, Nehemiah, and Esther* (Century Bible New Series; London: Nelson, 1969); Clines, *Ezra, Nehemiah, Esther*, 215, 239; Myers, *Ezra–Nehemiah*, 214; Rooke, *Zadok's Heirs*, 76, 168–69; Williamson, *Ezra–Nehemiah*, 351, 386.
99. Japhet (*I & II Chronicles*, 25) attributes this difficulty to the lack of availability of "precise historical events." Actually, the presence of historical events in narrative material can sometimes obscure an appropriate understanding of date and

one means to determine the date, if not the provenance of material. While a wide consensus exists regarding the late biblical Hebrew language of Chronicles, giving the text a dating window from the mid-Persian period to the end of the Hasmonean period, no such consensus is available regarding the date as discerned from the book's rhetoric.[100] Japhet finds no material that suggests a relationship to the Persian empire, but the implications of this finding are uncertain.[101]

Dating Chronicles presents a challenge to scholars. Although difficult to date with precision, the date of Chronicles is often placed toward the end of the Persian period.[102] Dating analyses are typically based on presuppositions about sources, style, language and the use of Persian words, the position of Chronicles in relationship to other extant texts and indications of institutionalized "cultic practice."[103] Some scholars, including Welch, situate Chronicles in the sixth century B.C.E.[104] Scholars dating Chronicles to an earlier date around 400 B.C.E. include Rudolph, Elmslie, and Myers.[105] Williamson, Coggins, and Ackroyd place Chronicles in the mid-fourth century B.C.E.[106] Still other scholars, including Japhet and Michaeli, choose to date Chronicles to the end of the Persian period.[107]

provenance. In this way, study of Chronicles is "ahead of the game" in comparison to much of the biblical material. Also see Gary N. Knoppers, *I Chronicles 1–9: A New Translation with Introduction and Commentary* (AB 12; New York: Doubleday, 2003), 101–37.

100. Thus setting the parameters of the text between mid-Persian period and the end of the Hasmonean period. Japhet (*I & II Chronicles*, 23–28) notes that the text shows no Greco-Hellenistic influence, further narrowing the parameter/window.

101. Ibid., 25.

102. Dating ranges from the end of the sixth century B.C.E. through the second century B.C.E. The 1987 study of Mark Throntveit (*When Kings Speak: Royal Speech and Royal Prayer in Chronicles* [SBLDS 93; Atlanta: Scholars Press, 1987], 97) characterizes the state of the question in the late 1980s.

103. Japhet, *I & II Chronicles*, 5, 23–28; Rooke, *Zadok's Heirs*, 185.

104. Welch, *The Work of the Chronicler*, 155. Knoppers, *1 Chronicles 1–9*, 101–17, effectively dispenses with a date as early as late sixth century B.C.E. for the book.

105. W. A. L. Elmslie, "The First and Second Books of Chronicles," *IB* 340–548; Jacob M. Myers, *I Chronicles: Introduction, Translation, and Notes* (AB 12; New York: Doubleday, 1965), lxxxvii–lxxxix; Rudolph, *Chronikbücher*, x.

106. Peter R. Ackroyd, *I & II Chronicles, Ezra, Nehemiah* (TBC; London: SCM Press, 1973); R. J. Coggins, *The First and Second Books of the Chronicles* (CBC; Cambridge: Cambridge University Press, 1976); H. G. M. Williamson, *1 and 2 Chronicles* (NCB; Grand Rapids: Eerdmans, 1982).

107. Japhet, *I & II Chronicles*, 5, 27. Also see Frank Michaeli, *Les Livres des Chroniques, d'Esdras et de Néhémie* (CAT 16; Neuchâtel: Delachaux & Niestlé, 1967), 25.

Knoppers sets a point at mid-third century B.C.E. as *terminus ante quem*.[108] Spinoza is among scholars who date Chronicles to the Maccabean period.[109] Within the dating discussion, the lists are the most difficult to date. Williamson begins his commentary on Chronicles with a section on the genealogies and opens with the following comment: "Few biblical passages are more daunting to the modern reader than the opening chapters of 1 Chronicles."[110] In fact, even if consensus could be reached about the date and provenance of the majority of the book, scholars often regard the genealogical lists as secondary.[111]

Bartlett contends that the construction of these, and other, genealogical lists are devised to serve specific purposes.[112] They are deliberately artificial and demonstrate that intent in the number of names included, in the chosen order of the names, and in the inclusion and exclusion of certain names.[113] Williamson comments on the sophisticated structure of lists such as the one found in 1 Chr 5.[114] On the other hand, numerous scholars note the extended redaction history of these lists.[115] Certainly scholars would agree that the final form of many of these lists reflects an intentionally imposed structure and that counting generations within the lists does not provide helpful historical information.[116] Likewise,

108. Knoppers, *1 Chronicles 1–9*, 111. He sets the earliest possible date at late fifth century B.C.E.

109. Benedict de Spinoza, *A Theologico-Political Treatise and a Political Treatise* (trans. R. H. M. Elwes; New York: Dover, 1951), 146.

110. Williamson, *1 and 2 Chronicles*, 2. Also see Knoppers, *1 Chronicles 1–9*, 245–65, for a full discussion of genealogies.

111. Martin Noth, *The Chronicler's History* (JSOTSup 50; Sheffield: JSOT Press, 1987), 29–35; Welch, *The Work of the Chronicler*, passim. Japhet, *I & II Chronicles*, 26. Many other scholars regard other parts of the book as secondary; for example, Rudolph, *Chronikbücher*, 153–55; Thomas Willi, "Late Persian Judaism and Its Conception of an Integral Israel According to Chronicles," in Eskenazi and Richards, eds., *Second Temple Studies*, 2:194–204; Williamson, *1 and 2 Chronicles*, passim; Japhet, *I & II Chronicles*, 27. For a summary of the discussions concerning Chronicles' redaction history, see Gary N. Knoppers, "Hierodules, Priests, or Janitors? The Levites in Chronicles and the History of the Israelite Priesthood," *JBL* 118 (1999): 49–72 (51–55).

112. Bartlett, "Zadok and His Successors at Jerusalem."

113. Ackroyd, *I & II Chronicles, Ezra, Nehemiah*, 38; Bartlett, "Zadok and His Successors at Jerusalem," 1–3, although those intentions are often obscure to modern-day exegetes. Also see Williamson, *1 and 2 Chronicles*, 70.

114. Williamson, *1 and 2 Chronicles*, 68–69.

115. Japhet, *I & II Chronicles*, 146; Noth, *The Chronicler's History*, 39–40; Rudolph, *Chronikbücher*, 51–64; Williamson, *1 and 2 Chronicles*, 68.

116. Japhet, *I & II Chronicles*, 26–27, 147.

most scholars agree that these lists are meant to serve as tools of legitimation.[117] R. North states emphatically, "The Chronicler…does not think he is fooling anybody. He is inculcating a principle of legitimacy."[118] Sara Japhet says it well, "However, the genealogical picture which eventually crystallized must be regarded as a reflection, not of biological processes, but of social ones."[119] The lists could be an effort to legitimize past events, to secure a place for those who intend to serve in the future, to present an idealized plan for the future, or some combination of the above. Knoppers posits the genealogies as a means to "convey pedigree, hierarchy, and status," a way by which "recent immigrants…are given the patina of a native pedigree."[120] He further concludes:

> Each ancient writer was attempting to create an intelligible network of lineages that would fit his own conceptions and reconcile, if not select from, available traditions. Genealogists employed a variety of literary conventions to structure their works. If political or social conditions changed, the genealogy created by one writer in one geopolitical or social conditions changed, the genealogy created by one writer in one geopolitical setting might be adjusted by a later writer working in another setting. Or, alternatively, a new genealogy could be fashioned to comport with current social and religious realities.[121]

Rooke rightly identifies the purpose of these lists in Chronicles as serving to legitimize the priestly institution as opposed to any particular

117. They further agree that the lists are not meant to present "real" history. An exception to this understanding can be found in the work of F. M. Cross. In his chapter on the "Priestly Houses of Early Israel," in *Canaanite Myth and Hebrew Epic*, 196 n. 6, Cross claims textual corruptions to explain the historical deficits of the lists, particularly that of 1 Chr 5:30–41. On the other hand, and in the same chapter (pp. 207, 212), he recognizes the paucity of historical value in these genealogical lists. He further acknowledges that many of the genealogical lists are secondary while concurrently using these lists historically, seemingly as a matter of convenience.

118. Ackroyd, *I & II Chronicles, Ezra, Nehemiah*, 38; Robert North, "Theology of the Chronicler," *JBL* 82 (1963): 369–81 (371); Rooke, *Zadok's Heirs*, 198.

119. Japhet, *I & II Chronicles*, 427.

120. Knoppers, *1 Chronicles 1–9*, 250, 252.

121. Knoppers, *1 Chronicles 1–9*, 259. He continues, "The lines of descent provide vital information to the readers or hearers about the identity of the persons introduced. If so, this would parallel the purpose that may be ascribed to the genealogies in 1 Chr 1–9. These lines of descent introduce readers to the Israelites—their identity, their land, and their internal kinship relationships." Also see Scolnic, *Chronology and Papponymy*, 2, 45–48. So also Michaeli, *Les livres des Chroniques*, 73–74, and Rooke, *Zadok's Heirs*, 199.

priest.[122] If we accept the reasoning of those scholars who have completed detailed studies of this material, we find ourselves with even less historical material about Zadokites than we might have previously thought possible.

References to Zadok

Chronicles contains 17 references to צדוק: 1 Chr 5:34 (ET 6:8) (two references); 5:38 (ET 6:12) (two references); 6:38 (ET 6:53); 9:11; 12:29 (ET 12:28); 15:11; 16:39; 18:16; 24:3, 6, 31; 27:17; 29:22; 2 Chr 27:1; 31:10. Of these, 1 Chr 5:34–38 (ET 6:8–12); 6:38 (ET 6:53); 9:11; 18:16; and 27:17 include צדוק in some sort of genealogical listing and will be discussed below. Second Chronicles 31:10, which refers to a בית צדוק, will also be discussed below.

1 Chronicles 12; 15; 16; 29; 2 Chronicles 27

Of the non-genealogical references to צדוק, 1 Chr 12:29 (ET 12:28) is part of a description of the troops who came to David at Hebron. Zadok is a young warrior who brought twenty-two commanders from his family. Although Christian Hauer argues an implication for "priestly status" here, the connection is more circumstantial and interpretation-bound than apparent from the text as it stands.[123] First Chronicles 15:11 relates an account of David summoning his priests Zadok and Abiathar. The inclusion of the phrase "the priests Zadok and Abiathar" is often considered a late addition, primarily because of the Chronicler's supposed interest in the Levites and apparent lack of attention to the lineage of Abiathar.[124] First Chronicles 16:39 tells of David leaving his priest Zadok before the tabernacle of YHWH at the high place at Gibeon.[125] This pericope is often

122. Rooke, *Zadok's Heirs*, 199–204. Although she also allows the genealogies occasionally to serve the purpose of legitimizing individual priests, like Zadok or Hilkiah, she notes a lack of clarity regarding roles and status in priesthood of the pre-exilic period and suggests that these postexilic genealogies seek to provide continuity as opposed to any particular historical information.

123. Hauer, "Who Was Zadok?," 91. But see Cody, *A History of the Old Testament Priesthood*, 92–93.

124. See Rudolph, *Chronikbücher*, 115; Welch, *The Work of the Chronicler*, 65–66; Williamson, *1 and 2 Chronicles*, 123. Japhet disagrees (*I & II Chronicles*, 294). Japhet sees the pericope as an explanation for David's delegation of authority (p. 299), as does Knoppers, *1 Chronicles 1–9*, 604–33.

125. See Japhet, *I & II Chronicles*, 320–23; Williamson, *1 and 2 Chronicles*, 130–32. For Japhet, it presupposes a ministry for Zadok at Gibeon prior to his tenure in Jerusalem and thus presents both a lineage for Zadok and a continuity for cultic ministry from the time of Moses until the united monarchy. For Williamson, the

seen as critical in the discussion of Zadok's lineage and fundamental for completing the historic portrayal of cultic establishment in Jerusalem. First Chronicles 29:22 recounts David's second anointing and maybe that of Zadok as David's priest.[126] Second Chronicles 27:1 mentions the marriage of Jerusha, daughter of Zadok.[127]

The references to צדוק in genealogical lists are found in 1 Chr 5:27–41 (ET 6:1–15); 6:38 (ET 6:53); 12:29 (ET 12:28); 18:16; 24:3–7, 31; 27:17; and 2 Chr 31:10.[128]

1 Chronicles 5

The list found 1 Chr 5:27–41 presents itself as 26 generations descending from Levi through Kohath, Amram, Aaron, and Eleazar:[129]

> The sons of Levi: Gershon, Kohath, and Merari. The sons of Kohath: Amram, Itzhar, and Hebron and Uzziel. The sons of Amram: Aaron and Moses and Miriam. The sons of Aaron: Nadab and Abihu, Eleazar and Ithaamar. Eleazar was the father of Phinehas, Phinehas was the father of Abishua, Abishua was the father of Bukki, Bukki was the father of Uzzi, Uzzi was the father of Zerahiah, Zerahiah was the father of Meraioth, Meraioth was the father of Amariah, Amariah was the father of Ahitub, Ahitub was the father of *Zadok*, *Zadok* was the father of Ahimaaz, Ahimaaz was the father of Azariah, Azariah was the father of Johanan, and Johanan was the father of Azariah (it was he who served as priest in the house that Solomon built in Jerusalem). Azariah was the father of Amariah, Amariah was the father of Ahitub, Ahitub was the father of *Zadok*, *Zadok*

Chronicler's purpose and historical assumptions remain an open issue. For Knoppers (*1 Chronicles 10–29*), it demonstrates that David has the "opportunity to reorganize Israel's national cultus" (p. 651) and allows David to "honor" both Gibeon and Jerusalem (p. 652).

126. Some read this, the apparent anointing of a priest (which is shared in biblical material only with the anointing of Aaron and his sons in the wilderness by Moses—Exod 40:15 and Lev 8), as bestowing a particularly unique status upon Zadok; see Japhet, *I & II Chronicles*, 512. But this reading relies heavily on presuppositions. Alternatively, Ackroyd (*I & II Chronicles, Ezra, Nehemiah*, 95) suggests that it was customary for postexilic priests to be anointed. Williamson (*1 and 2 Chronicles*, 187), suggests that the reference does not fit the context and may be a corruption.

127. Also see 2 Kgs 15:33.

128. See the discussion of genealogical lists on pp. 100–102, above.

129. Ackroyd (*I & II Chronicles, Ezra, Nehemiah*, 38) posits a possibly intentionally "balanced structure" of this list with twelve names "to the time of Solomon" and twelve names "to the fall of Jerusalem." His "balanced structure" depends heavily on Cross' reconstruction which, while helpful, has been questioned on several fronts.

> was the father of Shallum, Shallum was the father of Hilkiah, Hilkiah was the father of Azariah, Azariah was the father of Seraiah, Seraiah was the father of Jehozadak; and Jehozadak went into exile when the Lord sent Judah and Jerusalem into exile by the hand of Nebuchadnezzar.[130]

Set in the genealogical prologue of the book, the Chronicler clearly emphasizes the prominence of the sons of Levi.[131] Japhet sees the list as a "purported representation" of the entire high priesthood from Aaron via Eleazar to the destruction of the First Temple.[132] Williamson suggests Phinehas as the Chronicler's chief target, seeing the entire intent of the Chronicler come to fruition in the listing of the genealogy and role of the "high priest."[133] Knoppers, on the other hand, sees Zadok (the first one) as the emphasis.[134] Clearly the text represents continuity for the postexilic community with its pre-exilic heritage. A focus on the high priesthood, however, remains implicit at best. Listed first in the overall list among the sons of Levi, these sons of Aaron attain an apparent prominence. Still, connection to a high priesthood comes tangentially. Biblical texts naming Jeshua/Joshua as high priest[135] and son of Jehozadok[136] create the link.

The purpose of this list bears similarities with that of the Ezra 7 list:

1 Chronicles 5	*Ezra 7*[137]
Kohath	
Amram	
Aaron	
Eleazar	Eleazar

130. Knoppers (*1 Chronicles 1–9*, 400–401) emends the text so that Ahitub was the father of Zadok, Zadok the father of Ahimaaz, Ahimaaz the father of Azariah. And it was Azariah then who officiated at the temple and was the father of Johanan.

131. Along with Judah and Benjamin; cf. Ackroyd, *I & II Chronicles, Ezra, Nehemiah*, 38; Williamson, *Ezra–Nehemiah*, 70–76.

132. Japhet, *I & II Chronicles*, 150–56.

133. Williamson, *1 and 2 Chronicles*, 68–75. Also see Ackroyd, *I & II Chronicles, Ezra, Nehemiah*, 38.

134. Knoppers (*1 Chronicles 1–9*, 258) states, "There are twenty-five descendants from Qohath to Jehozadaq. If Qohath is the first pertinent scion of Levbi and Jehozadaq the last, the midpoint is Zadoq." For a different view on prominence in genealogical lists in general, see Jack M. Sasson, "A Genealogical 'Convention' in Biblical Chronography?," *ZAW* 90 (1978): 171–85.

135. Hag 1:1, 12; 2:2, 4; Zech 3:1, 8; 6:11. Interestingly, Ezra–Nehemiah does not refer to Jeshua/Joshua as high priest (using "high priest" only in reference to Eliashib in Neh 3:1, 20; 13:28), although Ezra 7:5 designates Aaron as chief priest.

136. Hag 1:1, 12, 14; 2:2, 4: Zech 6:11; Jeshua is son of Jozadak in Ezra 3:2, 8; 5:2, 10:18; Neh 12:26.

137. In reverse order.

Phinehas	Phinehas
Abishua	Abishua
Bukki	Bukki
Uzzi	Uzzi
Zerahiah	Zerahiah
Meraioth	Meraioth
Amariah	
Ahitub	
Zadok	
Ahimaaz	
Azariah	
Johanan	
Azariah	Azariah
Amariah	Amariah
Ahitub	Ahitub
Zadok	*Zadok*
Shallum	Shallum
Hilkiah	Hilkiah
Azariah	Azariah
Seraiah	Seraiah
Jehozadak	Ezra

The lists duplicate each other with two exceptions. The Ezra list ends with Ezra, while the Chronicler's list ends with Jehozadak. Also, there is a "gap" in the Ezra 7 list where the Chronicler's list contains the names: Amariah, Ahitub, Zadok, Ahimaaz, Azariah, and Johanan. Ackroyd regards this "supplement" in Chronicles as fulfilling the Chronicler's need to produce "a much fuller treatment of a family…whose concern with the temple and its institutions is so great."[138] Cross explains this difference as either textual corruption or redaction. Regarding this text, as well as that found in 1 Chr 6:35–38; 9:10–13 and Neh 11:10–14,

> The problems of these genealogies are manifold and need not be examined here. We note however, that the sequence Meraioth, Amariah, Ahitub, Zadok is followed later by the sequence Amariah, Ahitub, Zadok in 1 Chron. 5:27–51, producing a haplography (Amariah to Amariah II) in Ezra 7:1–5. That the lists are highly confused with doublets and omissions is evident in the omission of known preexilic high priests, and in the secondary intrusion of Meraioth in the document underlying 1 Chron. 9:11 = Neh. 11:11.[139]

138. Ackroyd, *I & II Chronicles, Ezra, Nehemiah*, 38. He does not discuss the ideological/theological intent behind this supplement.

139. Cross, *Canaanite Myth and Hebrew Epic*, 196 n. 6.

Cross' conclusions have been seriously challenged.[140] Japhet correctly notes the critical "nature of the missing names"; Amariah, Ahitub, Zadok, Ahimaaz, and Azariah are all priests familiar to us from Samuel–Kings. "Can a coincidental textual corruption be responsible for the omission from the genealogy of all the names connected explicitly with Zadok?"[141] Japhet suggests an earlier date for the Ezra list coinciding with a community need to establish a connection with their heritage during a time when concern for purity of blood line functioned as a source of legitimation. The priests that received legitimation during this time were those who verified their Aaronite lineage. Wilson demonstrates the political and ideological nature of genealogical lists.[142] With this in place, the purpose for the additions in the Chronicler's list may become clearer; where the writer of Ezra–Nehemiah sought to legitimate an Aaronite priesthood, the Chronicler sought to integrate the Zadokites, or at least those associated with Zadok.

1 Chronicles 6

Zadok appears again in 1 Chr 6:34–41 (ET 6:49–56) in an apparent supplement to the 5:30–41 (ET 6:4–14) list of priests from the Aaronite–Kohathite branch of Levites:

> Aaron and his sons made offerings upon the altar of burnt offering and upon the altar of incense for all the work of the most holy place, and to propitiate for Israel, according to all that Moses the servant of God had commanded. These are the sons of Aaron: Eleazar his son, Phinehas his son, Abishua his son, Bukki his son, Uzzi his son, Zerahiah his son, Meraioth his son, Amariah his son, Ahitub his son, *Zadok* his son, Ahimaaz his son. These are their dwelling places according to their settlements in their borders. To the sons of Aaron of the families of Kohathites, because to them was the lot, to them they gave Hebron in the land of Judah and its surrounding pasture lands but the fields of the city and its villages they gave to Caleb the son of Jephunneh. (1 Chr 5:34–41 [ET 5:49–56])

Most scholars see this list as secondary. Even Williamson, who argues for unity of composition for the genealogical listings, agrees with the

140. Grabbe, *Judaism from Cyrus to Hadrian*, 1:112–14; Japhet, *I & II Chronicles*, 151–52; Widengren, "The Persian Period," 506–9. Criticism of Cross' ingenious reconstruction coalesces around his assumption of a functioning pappynomy, his assumption of twenty-five-year generations, and his reliance on Josephus for accurate historical information. Furthermore, even if his emendations based on possible haplographies can be accepted, other assumptions cannot be explained.

141. Japhet, *I & II Chronicles*, 151–52.

142. Wilson, "The Old Testament Genealogies in Recent Research."

secondary nature of this list.[143] For Japhet, this list introduces subsequent information about priestly cities.[144] Knoppers suggests this repetition allows for a linking of priests and singers through a common lineage.[145] Ackroyd, however, suggests that this apparent supplement is designed to accentuate the distinction between the Levites and the Aaronites from whom special duties are required.[146] For Ackroyd, the Chronicler's "incorporation of Zadok into the family of Aaron is to be regarded as a pious fiction, designed to stress the legitimacy of the Jerusalem priesthood over against all others."[147] Ackroyd presumes an on-going prominence of the Zadokites. If, as concluded above, the Chronicler is initiating the legitimation of the Zadokite name, this list assumes a different tone; the list is merely a copy of that found in the 1 Chr 5:30–41 establishing this particular line of Aaronites as the legitimate functionaries in the temple.[148]

1 Chronicles 9

Zadok appears again at the conclusion of the genealogical listings that open the book of Chronicles. Chapter 9 begins, "So all Israel was enrolled by genealogies. These are written in the Book of the Kings of Israel." This list that includes Zadok begins with v. 10:

> Of the priests: Jedaiah, and Jehoiarib and Jachin and Azariah, son of Hilkiah, son of Meshullam, son of *Zadok*, son of Meraioth, son of Ahitub, the chief officer of the house of God; and Adaiah the son of Jeroham, son of Pashhur, son of Malchijah, and Maasai the son of Adiel, son of Jahzerah, son of Meshullam, son of Meshillemith, son of Immer; besides their kinsmen, heads of their father's houses, one thousand seven hundred and sixty, very able men for the work of the service of the house of God. (1 Chr 9:10–13)[149]

143. K. Möhlenbrink, "Die levitischen überlieferungen des alten testaments" *ZAW* 52 (1934): 205; Williamson, *1 and 2 Chronicles*, 68–69. Contra T. Willi, *Die Chronik als Auslegung: Untersuchungen zur literarischen Gestaltung der historischen Überlieferung Israels* (Göttingen: Vandenhoeck & Ruprecht, 1972), 214, who claims priority for this shorter list based on *lectio brevior*.

144. Japhet, *I & II Chronicles*, 152, 159.

145. Knoppers, *1 Chronicles 1–9*, 428.

146. Ackroyd, *I & II Chronicles, Ezra, Nehemiah*, 39.

147. Ibid., 39–40.

148. Of course, we must ask why the writer chose to stop with Ahimaaz.

149. Textual issues abound within this list. The parallel list in Neh 11 designates Jedaiah the sons of Joiarib (Jehoiarib). On the other hand, Jedaiah and Jehoiarib both receive lots as heads of priestly houses in 1 Chr 24 and Neh 12:6, 19. Following Rudolph's text-critical work, I have reconstructed the text from "Jedaiah

Ackroyd advocates a comparison of this list to other priestly lists, determining that "The opening list of the leading house of *Zadok* is at some points confused."[150] Certainly the list is "confused" but perhaps we are not able to assume the list's focus on a "leading house of *Zadok*." Zadok here is the son of Meraioth and the grandson of Ahitub; in the 1 Chr 5:30–41 list, Zadok is the son of Ahitub, who is the grandson of Meraioth. Without any prior assumption of a house of Zadok, this list offers no particular prominence for Zadokites. At best, Zadok is a priest in the line of Immer, also seen in the division of the priestly courses in 1 Chr 24 and as the ancestor of a priestly house in the Ezra 2 listing of those who lived in the province after returning from captivity.[151]

1 Chronicles 12

Zadok's next appearance in Chronicles is found in 1 Chr 12:29 (ET 12:28) in the broader context of a listing of those who came to David prior to his ascension to the monarchy (1 Chr 12:24–41):

> These are the numbers of the chiefs of the armed troops, who came to David in Hebron, to turn the kingdom of Saul over to him, according to

and Jehoiarib and Jachin and Azariah son of Hilkiah…" This contra Myers, *Ezra–Nehemiah*, 187, and Williamson, *1 and 2 Chronicles*. See F. Charles Fensham, *The Books of Ezra and Nehemiah* (Grand Rapids: Eerdmans, 1982), 242–54, for a discussion of all the textual difficulties of the text. Also see Japhet's discussion of Jehoiarib, *I & II Chronicles*, 429–30. For Japhet (pp. 202–12), Neh 11:3–19 serves as the Chronicler's source based on content as well as duplicated textual issues, although when discussing vv. 7–9, she suggests that the Chronicler used a different *Vorlage* from that used by the author of Neh 11. As in the Nehemiah text, she follows Rudolph (*Chronikbücher*, 84) in reconstructing the text, regarding יכין to be a corruption of בן. She sees the Nehemiah list as "a fuller and more authentic version of the document, while Chronicles is actually an abridgment." Japhet suggests that the portions of the list dealing with priests and Levites (vv. 9, 10–14, 15–18) are most likely to be representative of the original source material. As further evidence that the Nehemiah list served as a source for this list, Japhet notes that the last verse of the Chronicles list in fact is a combination of key phrases from three of the Nehemiah verses—"and their brethren who did the work of the house, 822" (11:12a); "and his brethren, heads of fathers' houses, 242" (11:13a); "and their brethren, heads of their fathers' houses, 128" (11:14a)—which are condensed into 1 Chr 9:13: "and their brethren, heads of their fathers' houses, 1,760, mighty men of valour, for the work of the service of the house of God." Thus she sees the differences between the two lists as either textual corruptions or intentional changes; it is these intentional changes which may reflect the agenda of the writer(s).

150. Ackroyd, *I & II Chronicles, Ezra, Nehemiah*, 45.

151. Also mentioned as ancestor of Pashhur in Jer 20:1, Ezra 10:20; Neh 3:29; 7:40 (= Ezra 2:37); 11:13.

> the word of YHWH. The men of Judah bearing shield and spear were six thousand eight hundred armed troops. Of the Simeonites, mighty men of valour, for war, seven thousand one hundred. Of the Levites, four thousand six hundred. The prince Jehoiada, of the house of Aaron, and with him three thousand seven hundred. *Zadok*, a young man mighty in valor, and twenty-two commanders from his own father's house. (1 Chr 12:24–29 [ET 12:23–28])

As with the other lists of the Chronicler, this list shows "little regard for chronology" or historical accuracy, focusing instead on presenting the commitment of all tribes of Israel to the impending kingship of David.[152] The last two verses, about the Levites, are often considered secondary additions placed by an advocate of the priesthood.[153] Some see this as the division of the Levites between sons of Aaron and members of the ancestral house of Zadok reflecting some time well into the postexilic period.[154] If, however, this is the case, these verses reflect a view of contemporary priesthood quite different from other Chronicler lists that include Zadok in the Aaronite line. The selection of Jehoiada and Zadok are likewise interesting, as are their respective descriptions: Jehoiada is a prince and Zadok, a young man mighty in valor.

1 Chronicles 18

First Chronicles 18:14–17 brings another list and another reference to Zadok:

> So David reigned over all Israel. He administered justice and equity to all his people. And Joab, son of Zeruiah, was over the army, and Jehoshaphat, son of Ahilud, was recorder. *Zadok*, son of Ahitub, and Ahimelech, son of Abiathar, were priests, and Shavsha was secretary. Benaiah, son of Jehoida, was over the Cherethites and the Pelethites, and David's sons were the chief officials in the service of the king. (1 Chr 18:14–17)

Similar to the text in 2 Sam 8, the pericope summarizes David's reign and presents a list of his officials:

152. Japhet, *I & II Chronicles*, 258, passim; J. G. McConville, *I & II Chronicles* (The Daily Study Bible; Philadelphia: Westminster, 1984), 32.

153. For example, Rudolph, *Chronikbücher*, 190–11, Williamson, *1 and 2 Chronicles*, 111. Contra Japhet, *I & II Chronicles*, 232–33, 255. Furthermore, Hauer ("Who Was Zadok?," 89–94) argues for the authenticity of the numerical facts in v. 29 due to the small number as compared to the other numbers in the list. But this small number of twenty-two only reflects the number of commanders, not total troops.

154. Japhet, *I & II Chronicles*, 258–59.

1 Chronicles 18		*2 Samuel 8*
Joab son of Zeruiah	over the army	Joab son of Zeruiah
Jehoshaphat son of Ahilud	recorder	Jehoshaphat son of Ahilud
Zadok son of Ahitub Abimelech son of Abiathar	priests	Zadok son of Ahitub Ahimelech son of Abiathar
Shavsha	secretary	Seraiah
Benaiah son of Jehoiada	over the Cherethites and the Pelethites	Benaiah son of Jehoiada
David's sons priests		David's sons chief officials in service of the king

Clearly, either the respective writers used the same source material or one used the other as its source. Differences between the two lists provide points of departure for discussion. In the Chronicles list, Abimelech, son of Abiathar, serves as priest whereas in Samuel, Zadok serves with Ahimelech; a simple scribal error can explain this difference. In other Samuel–Kings texts, however, Zadok serves alone or alongside Abiathar. To further add to the confusion, for both this text and a variety of references to Zadok in Samuel–Kings, 1 Sam 22:20 presents Abiathar as the son of Ahimelech who is the son of Ahitub. Driver suggests that the original reading was "Abiathar the son of Ahimelech the son of Ahitub and Zadok," but that would clumsily alter the tight literary composition of the text and, if that were the case, an outstanding issue would remain regarding the many other times Zadok is presented as the son of Ahitub.[155]

155. Samuel S. Driver, *An Introduction to the Literature of the Old Testament* (New York: Meridian, 1957), 283. See Knoppers, *1 Chronicles 10–29*, 705, for further discussion. Cross (*Canaanite Myth and Hebrew Epic*, 196), clearly thinks that Ahitub, as grandfather of Abiathar, had no connection to Zadok. He attributes that conclusion to Wellhausen, *Prolegomena*, as opposed to the Chronicler. It is true enough that Wellhausen (*Prolegomena*, 126) does not see Zadok as Aaronite—that Zadok "does not figure as an intermediate link in the line of Aaron, but as the beginner of an entirely new genealogy." And, even though Cross identifies issues with Wellhausen's presupposition about Zadok, he cannot apply that same method to his own. It is not the purpose of this study to discuss the finer merits of Cross'

Japhet suggests that one possible emendation would be to reverse the order of Ahimelech and Abiathar, so that the text would read "Zadok son of Ahitub and Abiathar son of Ahimelech."[156]

1 Chronicles 24

First Chronicles 24:1–6 presents yet another accounting of the sons of Aaron:

> The divisions of the sons of Aaron were these. The sons of Aaron: Nadab and Abihu, Eleazar and Ithamar. But Nadab and Abihu died before their father. They had no children so Eleazar and Ithamar became the priests. So David, and *Zadok* of the sons of Eleazar, and Abiathar of the sons of Ithamar, organized them according to the appointed duties in their service. Since more chief men were found among the sons of Eleazar than among the sons of Ithamar, they organized them under sixteen heads of fathers' houses of the sons of Eleazar, and eight of the sons of Ithamar. They organized them by lot, all alike, for there were officers of the sanctuary and officers of God among both the sons of Eleazar and the sons of Ithamar. And the scribe Shemaiah the son of Nethanel, a Levite, recorded them in the presence of the king and the princes, and *Zadok* the priest, and Ahimelech the son of Abiathar, and the heads of the fathers' houses of the priests and of the Levites; one father's house being chosen for Eleazar and one chosen for Ithamar.[157]

attribution of lineage to Zadok. It would however be appropriate to re-examine those conclusions in light of this study regarding historical assumptions about Zadok and Zadokites.

156. Japhet, *I & II Chronicles*, 350–52. Also interesting in this pericope, where the 2 Samuel text lists David's sons as priests, this pericope lists David's sons as chief officials. Some, including Cody, *A History of the Old Testament Priesthood*, 103, attribute this to the Chronicler's careful attention to the details of the priesthood and its distinction from monarchic functions, but that does not fit with the Chronicler's presentation elsewhere of the priestly duties of David and Solomon (e.g. 1 Chr 14:27; 16:2–3, 43; 21:26).

157. Interestingly, VanderKam, *From Joshua to Caiaphas*, 270 n. 90, notes concerning this list, "The priestly line to which the Hasmoneans belonged is traced to Joiarib in 1 Macc 2:1, and Joiarib is the first of the twenty-four priestly groups in 1 Chr 24:7–19. The groups in 1 Chronicles 24 are divided into two, with sixteen from the line of Eleazar and eight from Ithamar (v. 5); Zadok is listed as being from Eleazar (v. 3). The chapter offers no further evidence for which of the twenty-four belonged to which line, but it is likely (two chances out of three) that Joiarib and hence the Hasmoneans were Zadokites. Also, the appeal to the zeal of Phinehas in 1 Macc 2:26, 54 could point in the same direction, as Phinehas was Eleazar's son. For these arguments, see Rooke, *Zadok's Heirs*, 281–82. The possibility, even the likelihood, that the Hasmoneans were Zadokite should be emphasized in opposition to the frequently repeated idea that they were non-Zadokites (see, for example,

Here again we see a different division of the priestly houses. Zadok is of the lineage of Eleazar and Ahimelech is of the lineage of Ithamaar. Aside from Ahimelech the priest of Saul in 1 Samuel (21:1, 2, 8; 22:9, 11, 14, 16, 20; 23:6; 26:6 [perhaps]), Ahimelech is the son of Ahitub in 1 Sam 22:9, 11, and 20. Ahimelech is the father of Abiathar in 1 Sam 22:20; 23:6; 30:7; 2 Sam 8:17; 1 Chr 18:16, and here in v. 6. First Chronicles 24:6 names Ahimelech as the son of Abiathar. Other than this list, Ahimelech's connection with Ithamaar comes circuitously at best and is based largely on assumptions of when particular literature was written. Second Esdras 1:1–3 traces Ezra's lineage through Phinehas, son of Eli back to Eleazar son of Aaron; Ahitub is mentioned as the father of Zadok and the son of Ahijah (Ahitub's other son besides Ahimelech) in that list. Josephus (*Ant.* 5.11.5) makes the association between Eli and Ithamaar.

Reliance on the Chronicler for reconstructing a pre-exilic priesthood places scholarship in the difficult position of selectively, occasionally, and inappropriately choosing to pluck historical data from lists that serve deliberate purposes while frequently rejecting data if it does not suit the current historical theory. We can recognize at least a partial intention of the writer; this list gives Zadok Aaronite lineage through Eleazar. Clearly the list does not intend to provide a full genealogical list for the priesthood; instead, with Japhet, Liver, and Williamson, I see this text as an organizational chart of the priesthood, a portrait of priesthood at a given time.[158] Once again, and consistent with the Chronicler's work, the official priesthood traces its origins to Aaron. David's Zadok is merely part of that organizational plan, here alongside Ahimelech. Genealogy, while clearly important in this pericope, does not receive the same emphasis as in the other lists referring to "Zadok."[159] Here instead we see

Smith, 'A Study of the Zadokite High Priesthood,' 107–8). They were perhaps not Oniads, but they may indeed have been Zadokites."

158. Japhet, *I & II Chronicles*, 423–29; Knoppers, *1 Chronicles 10–29*, 826–42; Jacob Liver, *Chapters in the History of Priests and Levites: Studies in the Lists of Chronicles and Ezra and Nehemiah, Publications of the Perry Foundation for Biblical Research in the Hebrew University of Jerusalem* (Jerusalem: Magnes Press, 1968), 33; Williamson, *1 and 2 Chronicles*, 162. Paul Winter, "Twenty-Six Priestly Courses," *VT* 6 (1956): 215–17, emphatically dates this pericope to the Hasmonean period; Williamson convincingly argues for the secondary nature of this list, in "The Origins of the Twenty-Four Priestly Courses," in *Studies in the Historical Books of the Old Testament* (ed. J. A. Emerton; VTSup 30; Leiden: Brill, 1979), 251–69.

159. Williamson sees this entire section as a secondary addition to the original genealogical list. Note that this is apparently the first association of Ahimelech with Ithamaar.

a focus on institutional organization—the priesthood of the "sons of Aaron." Nowhere does the Chronicler discuss the genealogy of the "sons of Zadok." Nowhere does the Chronicler discuss the institutional organization of the "sons of Zadok." Instead we see a continual focus on the Aaronites. Zadok is presented in Chronicles as part of that structure.

Knoppers rightly acknowledges the Chronicler's efforts at establishing an Aaronite priesthood in contrast to a common assumption that the Chronicler seeks to glorify only the Levites. Most importantly, Knoppers notes the Aaronite (as opposed to Zadokite) emphasis of the Chronicler. Although the Chronicler's History is sometimes said to reflect Zadokite dominance in postexilic Judah, the sons of Zadok appear within a larger Aaronide lineage (1 Chr 5:29–41; 6:34–45). To be sure, Zadok plays a role during the Chronicler's discussions of united monarchy (1 Chr 12:28; 15:11; 16:39; 18:16; 24:3, 6, 31; 27:17; 29:22). Nevertheless, the Chronicler characteristically speaks of the priests as the sons of Aaron (1 Chr 5:29–33; 9:20; 11:12; 23:21, 22; 24:1–6, 28) and the sons of Ithamar (1 Chr 5:29; 24:1–6). Hence, the Chronicler's presentation differs from that of the temple vision in Ezekiel, which gives pride of place to the Zadokites (Ezek 40:46; 43:19; 44:15; 48:11).[160] As Knoppers says,

> The Chronicler's work is sometimes said to reflect Zadoqite dominance in postexilic Judah, but the situation is more complicated. The stance cannot be construed as a passive acquiescence to the emergence of a new status quo, because as the evidence provided by Malachi...suggests, it is unlikely that any one stand on the priesthood won unanimous acceptance in the Persian period. It is more likely that the authors of Chronicles attempt to mediate among a variety of positions. The sons of Zadoq are related to Aaron (5:29) and appear within the context of a larger Qohathite genealogy (5:27–41; 6:34–45).[161]

160. Knoppers (*1 Chronicles 23–27*, 791) agrees with Japhet and others that the Chronicler is responsible for the material. His conclusion becomes important when considering the provenance of a Zadokite priesthood. Knoppers correctly notes that the "focus of the authors of Chronicles is on the First Temple and not the Second." He further concludes that "the writers validate contemporary sacerdotal arrangements and aspirations by recourse native precedents in Israel's past. Institutions of the Second Temple period are authorized by their creation during the First Temple. Major families living in postexilic Jerusalem could argue that their positions were established by no less an authority than David himself" (p. 797). As we will see in Chapter 7, this type of legitimation was crucial given the social, political, and cultural dynamics of the Second Temple period.

161. Knoppers, *1 Chronicles 1–9*, 406. He continues, "Over the course of the centuries it has become a commonplace to refer to 1 Chr 5:27–31 as a high-priestly

It is in discussing this list that, contrary to her usual careful analysis, Japhet falls prey to prevailing traditional presuppositions. She says, "Since the main priestly line was that of Zadok, it was he who was to be affiliated with Eleazar; for the sake of symmetry the other priestly house, that of Abiathar, had to be traced to Ithamar."[162] One might argue that the "sons of Eleazar" are given twelve courses as opposed to the six courses assigned to the "sons of Ithamaar" thus favoring Zadokites.[163] In fact, this favors "Eleazarites." To her credit, she notes clearly, and on the same page, "The affiliation of Zadok, the prominent priest of the time of David and Solomon, to the branch of Eleazar, is repeated in several biblical sources, all of them late." Of course, Zadok is mentioned, but as part of the sons of Aaron. It is not a Zadokite dynasty that is being created; it is an Aaronite dynasty; and clearly a postexilic Aaronite dynasty.

1 Chronicles 27

First Chronicles 27:16–22 provides a list that includes Zadok. This list names the heads of the tribes of Israel as part of an overall listing of the administrators over the people of Israel:

genealogy. The Chronicler or a later editor traced a postexilic institution all the way back to the time of Israel's origins. In this calculation, Aaron is but the first of a long line of high priests. The list ends with Jehozadaq, but by implication the pattern of high-priestly succession extends into the Persian period. A variation of this line of interpretation calls special attention to the position of Zadoq. The Chronicler or a later editor attempts to document Zadoqite claims to the high priesthood in Persian period Yehud by providing Zadoq with an Aaronide priestly ancestry. In spite of the immense popularity of both of these views, one needs to be questioned and the other needs to be qualified..." (p. 412).

162. Japhet, *I & II Chronicles*, 427; L. Dequeker, "I Chronicles XXIV and the Royal Priesthood of the Hasmoneans," in *Crisis and Perspectives: Studies in Ancient Near Eastern Polytheism, Biblical Theology, Palestinian Archaeology and Intertestamental Literature* (OtSt; Leiden: Brill, 1986), 94–106, falls prey to these assumptions even further. He begins his examination of 1 Chr 24 with "My purpose is to investigate the Zadokite claims which arise from this list. Which of the priestly families mentioned claimed to have a right to the office of high priest in the temple because of their Zadokite lineage?" (p. 96). He even goes so far as to say "Zadok, however, is one of the most prominent figures in Chronicles...he occupies the centre of a long genealogical list of high priests" (pp. 96–97).

Cross, *Canaanite Myth and Hebrew Epic*, 207, does not want to find an association of Abiathar (his house of Eli) to Ithamaar and so points out that the reference here "was based on a reordering of the genealogies and cannot be taken at face value."

163. And thus providing parallel reasoning for why Ahimelech is associated with Ithamaar. Zadok is connected elsewhere to the Eleazar branch of the Aaronites (Ezra 7:1–5; 1 Chr 5:30–41; 6:35–38). The pericope simply cannot be seen as elevating Zadokites. The text is about the Aaronites.

> Over the tribes of Israel, for the Reubenites Eliezer son of Zichri was chief officer; for the Simeonites, Shephatiah son of Maacah; for Levi, Hashabiah son of Kemuel; for Aaron, *Zadok*; for Judah, Elihu, one of David's brothers; for Issachar, Omri son of Michael; for Zebulun, Ishmaiah son of Obadiah; for Naphtali, Jeremoth son of Azriel; for the Ephraimites, Hoshea son of Azaziah; for the half-tribe of Manasseh, Joel son of Pedaiah; for the half-tribe of Manasseh in Gilead, Iddo son of Zechariah; for Benjamin, Jaasiel son of Abner; for Dan, Azarel son of Jeroham. These were the leaders of the tribes of Israel. (1 Chr 27:16-22)

As part of a description of David's kingdom, ch. 27 is often seen as secondary.[164] Zadok's inclusion, and Aaron's as well for that matter, are curious. The list claims to present the administrators for each tribe; the tribes are listed, and Aaron is included in the middle. The insertion of Aaron and Zadok follows directly after the naming of Hashabiah the son of Kemuel as head over the tribe of Levi. Williamson notes this unique addition to the list of tribes, but does not discuss the implications.[165] Perhaps the list was modified to include a reference to Zadok as an Aaronite. The interesting question to ask is when and why a redactor might have found it necessary or desirable to insert into the Chronicler's material references to Zadok. The absence of a lineage for Zadok is yet another anomaly in this list. Possibly due to an uncertainty about Zadok's lineage, the absence could also be indicative of the secondary nature of the phrase.

2 Chronicles 31

The final reference in Chronicles to Zadok appears in 2 Chr 31:10 and provides the only reference in the biblical material to a "house of Zadok." This section of the Chronicler's work continues a description of Hezekiah's reign. The reference to Zadok appears in a section (vv. 3–19) detailing fiscal provision for the priesthood:

> And the people of Israel and Judah who lived in the cities of Judah also brought in the tithe of cattle and sheep and the tithe of the dedicated things to YHWH their God, and laid them in heaps. In the third month they began to pile up the heaps. They finished them in the seventh month. When Hezekiah and the princes came and saw the heaps, they blessed YHWH and his people Israel. Then Hezekiah questioned the priests and

164. Japhet, *I & II Chronicles*, 468; Noth, *The Chronicler's History*; Rudolph, *Chronikbücher*; Willi, "Late Persian Judaism and Its Conception of an Integral Israel According to Chronicles"; Williamson, *1 and 2 Chronicles*, 174.

165. Williamson, *1 and 2 Chronicles*, 176; Knoppers (*1 Chronicles 10–29*, 897) thinks "The inclusion of Aaron and Zadok…testifies to the prominence of both in the Chronistic perspective."

> the Levites about the heaps. Azariah the chief priest who was of the house of *Zadok*, answered him, 'Since they began to bring the contributions into the house of the Lord we have eaten and had enough and have plenty left; for YHWH has blessed his people so that we have this great store left. Then Hezekiah commanded them to prepare chambers in the house of YHWH. They prepared them and faithfully brought in the contributions, the tithes and the dedicated things. The chief officer in charge of them was Conaniah the Levite with Shimei his brother as second; while Jehiel, Azaziah, Nahath, Asahel, Jerimoth, Jozabad, Eliel, Ismachiah, Mahath, and Benaiah were overseers assisting Conaniah and Shimei his brother by the appointment of Hezekiah the king and Azariah the chief officer of the house of God. (2 Chr 31:6–13)

Unlike the other genealogical references to Zadok in Chronicles, this text mentions (the house of) Zadok in the context of a narrative. Does this narrative reflect the social context extant at the time of its writing? The text discusses temple economics, a topic not yet broached in Chronicles.[166] Japhet wonders if it reflects the situation of the referent period or the situation as experienced by the Chronicler. Preferring the context of the writer, Japhet suggests that the portrait of responsibility shared between the ruler and the people provided by the chapter reflects more consistently the fiscal support of the temple found in Darius' decree and in Ezekiel's temple vision than that found in the guidelines for temple maintenance resting solely with the people found in Neh 10:33–40 (ET 10:32–39).[167]

A noticeable feature of the text, of course, is the reference to Azariah as the chief officer of the *house of Zadok*. Japhet, in commenting on this *hapax legomenon*, says,

> Uniquely, however, Azariahu is defined as "who was of the house of Zadok." Although descent of the high priests from "Zadok" is presupposed by the constitutive genealogy of the priests (I Chron. 6.1ff. [MT 5.27ff.]), this is never explicitly stated for any high priest. This unusual reference brings to mind another person by a similar name: "Azariah(u) the son of Zadok…the priest" [*sic*] of Solomon's time (I Kings 4.2). One may take this lead in regarding this person as a literary rather than a historical figure; or one may claim simply that the name was common in the house of Zadok.[168]

As this study seeks to assert, this presupposition of an extant "house of Zadok" must be questioned. If, as one of Japhet's possible explanations

166. Japhet, *I & II Chronicles*, 960.

167. Ibid., 960–61. What does that imply about the historical context of both Chronicles and Nehemiah?

168. Ibid., 966.

suggests, this "Azariah,[169] chief officer of the house of Zadok" is a literary construct, we should consider that this text reflects a context when the legitimation of priests associated with Zadok became important. Japhet's other possible explanation, that Azariah was inserted because it was a common name within the house of Zadok, cannot answer questions about the text because we have insufficient evidence that there was a house of Zadok during Hezekiah's reign. Japhet is not consistently confined by the presupposition regarding the prominence of a "house of Zadok"; for example, when discussing 1 Chr 5:30–41, she correctly notes the implicit legitimation of the house of Aaron.[170] We may conclude that the "house of Zadok" was not presupposed, but was imposed at some critical point in time.

Summary of References in Chronicles

What can we conclude from the references in Chronicles to Zadok? Almost certainly there was a figure named Zadok in Israel's collective memory. Given the apparent obsessions with genealogy, there was likely some general confusion about lineage. There had not necessarily been a Zadokite priesthood prior to this time, during either the monarchic period or the exile. In fact, if there had been a Zadokite priesthood, and certainly if there had been a dominant Zadokite priesthood, that same Zadokite priesthood would be more apparent in the biblical material. It is not. At some point, and at the earliest in the late Persian period, someone found it necessary to legitimate a group of priests by creating a "house of Zadok."

169. Williamson, *1 and 2 Chronicles*, 375, briefly discusses the difficulties in identifying this Azariah historically.

170. Japhet, *I & II Chronicles*, 142–56, as opposed to a "house of Zadok."

Chapter 5

Biblical Evidence of the Zadokites

Ezekiel

Introduction

בני צדוק are found in the book of Ezekiel four times, the only references to the Zadokites. The first issue to be addressed is the historical context of Ezek 40–48 and its inclusion in the book of Ezekiel. Scholarship over the last century has taken almost every possible stance. Most early critical scholarship touted the unity of the book as marked by style and language; G. B. Gray concludes, "no other book of the Old Testament is distinguished by such decisive marks of unity of authorship and integrity as this."[1] A few dissenting voices began to rise in the 1920s and 1930s. G. Hölscher concludes that a vast majority of the Ezekielian material (over 1000 of the 1273 verses) should be attributed to later additions, so that questions began to rise about the historical context of the book. In 1936, C. C. Torrey sets the entire book in the Seleucid period.[2]

Beginning in the late 1930s, scholars favored situating the book in Babylonia.[3] Disparate views on the unity of the book continued with

1. George Buchanan Gray, *A Critical Introduction to the Old Testament* (New York: Scribner's, 1913), 198. Also see Driver, *An Introduction to the Literature of the Old Testament*, 279; J. E. McFadyen, *Introduction to the Old Testament* (New York: Armstrong, 1906), 162; H. A. Redpath, *The Book of the Prophet Ezekiel* (London: Methuen, 1907), xiv. Even as late as 1950, S. Fisch, *Ezekiel* (Soncino Books of the Bible 7; London: Soncino, 1950), xiv, says there could be no question about the unity of the book of Ezekiel.

2. Gustav Hölscher, *Hesekiel, Der Dichter und das Buch* (BZAW 39; Giessen: Töpelmann, 1924), 113–18. In 1943, William Irwin (*The Problem of Ezekiel: An Inductive Study* [Chicago: University of Chicago Press, 1943], 283) allowed 251 verses out of a total of 1273 to the original prophet (as opposed to Hölscher's 170). C. C. Torrey, *Pseudo-Ezekiel and the Original Prophecy* (YOSR 18; New Haven: Yale University Press, 1930).

3. Alfred Bertholet, *Hesekiel* (HAT; Tübingen: Mohr, 1936); G. A. Cooke, *A Critical and Exegetical Commentary on the Book of Ezekiel* (ICC; Edinburgh:

some scholars suggesting numerous redactions.[4] Many scholars adopted an exilic, and often multi-layered, point of view in dating the book.[5] Basically, an argument for almost every point of view could be found. A prominent scholar on Ezekiel, H. H. Rowley, identified three "collections" of material contained in the book, dating the compilation to the postexilic period (sometime in the fifth or fourth century B.C.E.).[6] Still, Rowley and others see frequent evidence of a "single mind" throughout the book and concluded that the final compiler/editor probably offered little in the way of composition. Of the sections in the book, chs. 40–48 are most easily regarded as separate.

Ezekiel 40–48

Debates about chs. 40–48 continued in the 1950s and 1960s, focusing on the unity and the context of the material.[7] Almost every conclusion was endorsed by a number of scholars ranging from an insistence on complete unity and an early date, as described above, to the Seleucid dating of Torrey and the proposal by Ronald Hals that "Neither in genre nor in context, neither in literary-critical analysis nor in structural continuity as literature, does some impression of a positive sense of completeness emerge."[8] Eichrodt saw the book as coincident with the exile. He discussed the wide variety of varying opinions:

> This unsatisfactory fluctuation in the theories is no mere matter of change; it is the necessary result of all the difficulties encountered by any attempt to work out such a fundamental theory on the basis of a text

T. & T. Clark, 1936); Carl Gordon Howie, *The Date and Composition of Ezekiel* (JBL Monograph Series 4; Philadelphia: Society of Biblical Literature, 1950).

4. Bertholet, *Hesekiel*; Cooke, *A Critical and Exegetical Commentary on the Book of Ezekiel*; W. O. E. Oesterley and T. Robinson, *Introduction to the Books of The Old Testament* (New York: Macmillan, 1934), 318–25, 328–29.

5. Robert H. Pfeiffer, *Introduction to the Old Testament* (New York: Harper, 1941); H. Wheeler Robinson, *Two Hebrew Prophets: Studies in Hosea and Ezekiel* (London: Lutterworth, 1948); Carl G. Howie, *The Date and Composition of Ezekiel*; G. Fohrer, *Die Hauptprobleme des Buches Ezechiel* (BZAW 72; Berlin: Töpelmann, 1952).

6. Rowley, "The Book of Ezekiel in Modern Study."

7. Of particular concern were the references to sacred vessels and calendar issues which seemed to be later rather than earlier. See Samuel Sandmel, *The Hebrew Scriptures: An Introduction to Their Literature and Religious Ideas* (New York: Knopf, 1963). Carl G. Howie's focus on language led him to accept the historical context as described in *The Date and Composition of Ezekiel*. (For chs. 40–48, he acknowledged that it was written down by a writer other than the prophet but in complete harmony with the prophet's vision.)

8. Ronald M. Hals, *Ezekiel* (FOTL 19; Grand Rapids: Eerdmans, 1989), 287–89.

> which states the exact opposite… All these widely divergent theories serve to illustrate the danger of throwing away what this book testifies to in regard to itself, because it only leads to fleeting speculations which, in spite of all their cleverness, cannot arouse any confidence in their results.[9]

However, just because it is causes a problem for us does not mean we should ignore it. In fact, the problem should encourage us to look for new answers or to further develop the ones we have. Gese's tradition history of Ezekiel focused more carefully on the composition of the material. He sees ideological treatises layered over Ezekiel's original presentation. For Gese, these layers, in their chronological order, include material about נשיא, division of the land, and the authority and rights of the sons of Zadok.[10] The next major work on Ezek 40–48, that of Zimmerli, follows Gese with regard to נשיא but questions a full and intentional treatise regarding the "sons of Zadok." For Zimmerli, Ezek 44:6–16 and 44:28–30a represent a unit, while the remainder of Gese's Zadokite layer (44:17–21, 31 and 45:13–15) are "expansions which, from the point of view of substance, also partly point in a quite different direction."[11] In adherence to Wellhausen's synthesis of the history of priests and Levites and the subsequent adoption of this as an assumption, Zimmerli chooses to align himself with Gunneweg[12] in recognition of a "Zadokite section in 44:6ff and of its 'metastases' in the corrective additions"[13] made by an Ezekielian school of disciples. He is willing to consider, with George Berry, a Hasmonean context for the material, but prefers a postexilic placement.[14]

Jon Levenson sees Ezek 40–48 as presenting a moral ideal, whether the work of the prophet or his school. Ezekiel takes on the mantle of Moses, ascending the mountain to proclaim legislation. "Ezek 40–48 is the only corpus of legislation of the Hebrew Bible which is not placed in the mouth of Moses."[15] While Levenson follows a traditional view that the text refers to apostasy of the Levites and the general assumption of a dominant Zadokite priesthood, he acknowledges this, "The high-priesthood being a shadowy office for which we have little direct evidence, we

9. Eichrodt, *Ezekiel*, 8.

10. Gese, *Der Verfassungsentwurf des Ezechiel*, 110–15.

11. Zimmerli, *Ezekiel 2*, 452–53.

12. A. H. J. Gunneweg, *Leviten und Priester* (FRLANT 89; Gottingen: Vandenhoeck & Ruprecht, 1965), 191–220.

13. Zimmerli, *Ezekiel 2*, 458.

14. George R. Berry, "The Authorship of Ezekiel 40–48," *JBL* 34 (1915): 17–40; idem, "The Date of Ezekiel 45:1–8a and 47:13–48:35," *JBL* 40 (1921): 70–75; Zimmerli, *Ezekiel 2*, 463.

15. Levenson, *Theology of the Program of Restoration of Ezekiel 40–48*, 7–15, 39.

search eagerly in Ezek 40–48 for materials to flesh out our conception of it and especially of its self-understanding. The office, however, does not appear."[16] Albertz sees a second generation of Ezekielian disciples as responsible for the mostly unrealized temple vision found in Ezek 40–48.[17]

McConville, in his 1983 "Priests and Levites in Ezekiel: A Crux in the Interpretation of Israel's History," raises the issue of the relationship between Ezek 40–48 and P, especially as discussed by Wellhausen, Gese, and Zimmerli. He argues for continuity and unity of the material and sees the unit as a later reflection on the entire Pentateuch.[18]

By 1984, Aelred Cody emphatically states that "All agree that Ezekiel did not write everything in the book bearing his name."[19] He accepts the multi-layer notion and dates the completion of Ezek 40–48 to some time "before the arrival of Zerubbabel the civil governor and Joshua the high priest who were in Jerusalem by 520."[20] His conclusions about the בני צדוק material in Ezek 40–48 are clearly formed by pre-existing assumptions. For example, in discussing the distinction between priests and Levites, Cody states, "The priests intended [in ch. 44] are those of the group whose members had the priestly establishment in Jerusalem firmly in their hands before the Exile."[21]

In a work also in 1984, Moshe Greenberg sees Ezek 40–48 as unified by the prophet himself with the rest of the book and sets it in Babylon

16. Ibid., 140. Note that here Levenson also says, "The Zadokite party was aboriginally the party of the high-priest, and so it was to be in the post-Exilic era as well."

17. Albertz, *Israel in Exile*, 367–76. For Albertz, "Still unresolved is the relationship between the priestly party inspired by the prophetic tradition responsible for the book of Ezeiel and the leaders of the Jerusalem priesthood, the Hilkiads, presumed to be among the proponents of the Deuteronomistic History. Probably both were of the ancient Jerusalemite Zadokite lineage. Nevertheless, the language and theology of the former distinguish them clearly from the priestly party with Deuteronomistic leanings. The latter probably included the first high priest after the return, Joshua ben Jehozadak. Soon, however, there must have been a shift of power between the priestly parties: by the fifth century at the latest, the dominant representatives of the priesthood exhibit clear linguistic and theological affinities with the disciples of Ezekiel. The indictment of Joshua during the rebuilding of the temple (cf. Zech 3) may be associated with an attempt by the reforming priesthood to challenge his office. It would seem that Joshua's opponents accused him of not meeting their criteria of holiness, which were clearly much more strict (3:3)" (p. 376).

18. McConville, "Priests and Levites in Ezekiel," 16–28.

19. Cody, *Ezekiel*, 13.

20. Ibid., 20.

21. Ibid., 23.

where it seems to encourage those in exile.[22] He offers explanations based on comparative ancient Near Eastern data for Gese's "disintegrating" analyses. Greenberg prefers to opt for an assumption of unity without conclusive evidence to the contrary. He succinctly names a dilemma facing historians of priesthoods in ancient Israel, "The background of the desecration scenes [in 40–48] must be the paganization [*sic*] of Judah under the reign of Manasseh, and the only way to dissociate the Zadokites from the cultic crimes of that age is to assume they were out of office during Manasseh's reign."[23]

Susan Niditch sees some layering of an Ezekielian "cosmogenic" vision as "a later Zadokite extension of the ordering process tailored to the Zadokite worldview" which serves as a guideline for "models of an almost bourgeois moderation…the essence of establishment behaviour… [in] the late sixth-century B.C. restoration of Zechariah and Haggai with its essential conservatism."[24] In essence, she recognizes ideological issues in Ezek 40–48 that bear similarity to those in Ezra–Nehemiah, especially in becoming increasingly exclusive about inclusion in the true Israel. For Niditch, "later Zadokite editors" busily draw those boundaries. Paul Hanson must see the book as a single unit set in the exile or very early postexilic period because he sees the book as supplying the basic theological framework for the postexilic prophets Haggai and Zechariah.[25]

As Ronald Hals points out, "The search by past scholarly generations for some means of literary-critical stratification was rooted in the desire to uncover the historical situation in which the positive intentions of the material would make sense, and to which time the stratum could then be

22. Moshe Greenberg, "The Design and Themes of Ezekiel's Program of Restoration," *Int* 38 (1984): 181–208 (183). Haran ("The Law-Code of Ezekiel XL–XLVIII," 61–65), on the other hand, places the distinction between the Zadokites and other priests in pre-exilic times. Jacob Milgrom, *Leviticus 1–16: A New Translation with Introduction and Commentary* (AB 3; New York: Doubleday, 1991), also dates P to the pre-exilic period and sees Ezek 44 as midrash on P (passim, e.g., pp. 8, 452). Milgrom sets the Zadokites in the lineage of Phinehas and makes note of Jeremiah's rejection of "the Zadokite monopoly" resulting in Jeremiah's usage of the term "levitical priests" (p. 722).

23. Greenberg, "The Design and Themes of Ezekiel's Program of Restoration," 195–96. Actually, that is not the "only way" to dissociate the Zadokites from the "cultic crimes." The "age" is the critical factor in determining the crimes, as I will discuss below.

24. Susan Niditch, "Ezekiel 40–48 in a Visionary Context," *CBQ* 48 (1986): 208–24 (216–19).

25. Paul D. Hanson, "Israelite Religion in the Early Postexilic Period," in *Ancient Israelite Religion: Essays in Honor of Frank Moore Cross* (ed. P. Hanson, P. D. Miller, and S. Dean McBride; Philadelphia: Fortress, 1987), 485–508.

dated."[26] Using this approach, however, necessitates solipsistic assumptions. Hals notes one obvious but often neglected point:

> Here, alas, our lack of historical background information makes dating more difficult, but at least the absence of any references in the book of Ezekiel to a high priest would make it certain that all the material about priests must antedate the community of 520 B.C. in which the high priest figures so prominently. This would mean, however, that the connection between Ezekiel and the Pentateuch as sources for the history of the priesthood now becomes an area of considerable complexity.[27]

He further correctly comments that traditional literary-critical and historical reconstruction approaches have not yielded decisive results in the study of Ezek 40–48.

Steven Tuell follows in the same vein as Jon Levenson, suggesting "a final, purposive unity" for "the religious polity of the Judean Restoration.[28] Tuell's analysis falls somewhere between the multiple strands of Gese and Zimmerli and the single unified authorship concept of Clement, Haran, and Greenberg. Tuell sees the text as presenting descriptions of Persian period institutions. He suggests the Persians set the Zadokites in place of the Levites.[29] Andrew Mein concludes that the text is primarily exilic and predominantly focuses on ritual, serving as a vision for some future point in time.[30] Joseph Blenkinsopp places chs. 40–48 in the exilic period as well.[31]

Still today, no scholarly consensus offers conclusions about the composition and historical setting of Ezek 40–48; neither is there consensus

26. Hals, *Ezekiel*, 287.

27. Ibid., 287–88. Interestingly, Hals recommends a focus on the negative aura of the text as opposed to the typical concentration on positive aspects (p. 289).

28. Tuell, *The Law of the Temple in Ezekiel 40–48*, 13, 14. He calls this "polity" a "present-tense description of the authors's self-conception and their conception of God" (p. 14).

29. Ibid., 78–102.

30. Andrew Mein, *Ezekiel and the Ethics of Exile* (Oxford Theological Monographs; Oxford: Oxford University Press, 2001), 142–43. According to mean, "It is likely that the prophet's words have been supplemented by later editors, but, as is the case elsewhere in the book, there is such a degree of homogeneity both of theme and language that it is very difficult to judge what is original and what is not… It seems likely, given this considerable continuity, that the bulk of the material in these chapters, along with the rest of the book, was completed by the time of the return or, at the latest, during the early post-exilic period. It is appropriate, therefore, to treat 40–48 as an 'exilic' phenomenon" (p. 143 n. 21).

31. Joseph Blenkinsopp, "Bethel in the Neo-Babylonian Period," in *Judah and the Judeans in the Neo-Babylonian Period* (ed. Oded Lipschitz and Joseph Blenkinsopp; Winona Lake, Ind.: Eisenbrauns, 2003), 93–108 (104).

regarding authorship and the intention of the writer(s).[32] The traditional idea regarding Ezek 40–48, prevalent since Wellhausen's synthesis of ancient Israel's history and serving as a pillar in reconstructing both a history of ancient Israel and a history of priesthood in ancient Israel, fails on several and often noted counts. Perhaps application of these analyses to broaden historical reconstruction has not disturbed mainstream biblical scholarship because the book of Ezekiel and particularly the "vision" material of chs. 40–48 are viewed as beyond the biblical period, as post-monarchic. Yet, several factors make Ezek 40–48 critical for the whole of biblical scholarship. It contains the only (four) biblical references to בני צדוק (Ezek 40:45–46; 43:18–19; 44:6–16; 48:9–11), and four of five possible biblical references to Zadokites, the other being the reference to לבית צודק in 2 Chr 31:10. The four Ezekiel texts read as follows:

> Ezek 40:45–46: And he said to me, this is the chamber that faces south for the priests who have charge of the temple. And the chamber that faces north is for the priests who have charge of the altar, these are the *sons of Zadok*, from the sons of Levi, who may come near to YHWH to serve him.
>
> Ezek 43:18–19: And he said to me, son of man, thus says the Lord YHWH, These are the guidelines for the altar on the day when it is built, for offering burnt offerings on it and for throwing blood against it. You will give to the Levite priests, they who are the *sons of Zadok*, the ones who draw near to me, says the Lord YHWH, to serve me (to them you will give) a bull, a son of a cow, as a sin offering.
>
> Ezek 44:6–16: And you will say to the rebellious house of Israel, thus says the Lord YHWH, enough of you—of all your abominations, O house of Israel, in admitting foreigners, uncircumcised in heart and uncircumcised in flesh, to be in my sanctuary, profaning my temple when you offer my food, the fat and the blood. They have broken my covenant with all your abominations. You have not kept charge of my holy things but have established to keep my charge in my sanctuary for yourself. Thus says the Lord YHWH—any foreigner—of all the foreigners who are among the people of Israel, uncircumcised in heart and flesh—shall not enter my sanctuary. But the Levites, who went far from me when Israel went astray, going astray from me after their idols, they will bear their punishment: they will be ministers in my sanctuary, having oversight at the gates of the temple and serving in the temple. They will slay the burnt offering and the sacrifice for the people and they will stand before them to serve them because they ministered to them before their idols so that the house of Israel became a stumbling block of iniquity. Therefore I have sworn concerning them, says the Lord YHWH, that they shall bear their punishment: they will not come near to me to serve me as priest and they will

32. Scholars describe the situation as "baffling" (Cook, "Innerbiblical Interpretation in Ezekiel 44," 193).

not come near any of my sacred things—the things that are most sacred. They will bear their shame because of the abominations which they have committed. Still I will appoint them to keep charge of the temple to do all its service and all that is to be done in it. But the Levitical priests, the *sons of Zadok*, who kept the charge of my sanctuary when the people of Israel went astray from me, they will come near to me to minister to me and they will attend to me—to offer me the fat and the blood, says the Lord YHWH. They will enter into my sanctuary and they will approach my table to minister to me. They will keep my charge.

Ezek 48:9–11: The amount which you will set aside for YHWH will be twenty-five thousand cubits in length and ten thousand cubits in width. These will be the amount of the holy portion which will be given to the priests, twenty-five thousand on the northern side and ten thousand on the western side in width and on the eastern side ten thousand and on the southern side twenty-five thousand in length, with the sanctuary of YHWH in its midst. For the consecrated priests, the *sons of Zadok*, who kept my guidelines, who did not go astray when the people of Israel went astray, as did the Levites.

Ezekiel 40–48 formed a critical component in Wellhausen's synthesis of Israel's history which still informs biblical scholarship today, informing his tripartite system. Even though this component of Wellhausen's work has been challenged, the implications of the challenges have not been fully applied to an understanding of Israel's history. Finally and perhaps most importantly, this pericope serves as a pillar in paraphrased reconstructions of both the religion of ancient Israel and the history of priesthood in ancient Israel. Traditionally, as discussed above, these references have been seen as a way to justify Zadokite control of a Jerusalem temple in the restoration period, a way to discount the role of the priests currently in power, the Levites. One difficulty for this traditional reading, as shown in the discussion above of First Chronicles, is that the Aaronites were likely the priestly group establishing their control during the restoration period. We are left to find a referent for the sons of Zadok mentioned in Ezek 40–48.

Two recent efforts, those of Joseph Blenkinsopp and Stephen Cook, note some of the major problems facing contemporary studies of Ezekiel and attempt to re-examine the material with different methodologies—both recognizing the difficulties facing the interpretation of the Zadokite passages in Ezek 40–48 and both seeking a new referent for the text.[33]

33. Joseph Blenkinsopp, "The Judaean Priesthood During the Neo-Babylonian and Achaemenid Periods: A Hypothetical Reconstruction," *CBQ* 60 (1998): 25–43; Cook, "Innerbiblical Interpretation in Ezekiel 44."

Blenkinsopp and a Referent for Ezekiel 40–48

Joseph Blenkinsopp finds a referent for Ezek 40–48 even though the text is not the direct target of his study. In his 1998 *Catholic Bible Quarterly* article, "The Judaean Priesthood during the Neo-Babylonian and Achaemenid Periods: A Hypothetical Reconstruction," Blenkinsopp argues for a sanctuary of YHWH in or near Mizpah (Tell en-Naṣbeh) during the period of neo-Babylonian rule after the fall of Jerusalem.[34] In this sanctuary that later existed between Mizpah and Bethel or that eventually moved to Bethel, the administering clergy claimed the name of Aaron.[35] Through questioning underlying assumptions of previous biblical scholarship and through lucid readings of Second Temple prophetic texts such as Zech 7:1–3 (MT), Blenkinsopp establishes the plausibility of an official sanctuary, probably sanctioned by imperial Babylon, at Bethel.[36]

Blenkinsopp notes that Deuteronomy and the deuteronomistic history do not mention Aaronite priests and concludes that the Aaronite priesthood rose later than the pre-exilic period in Israelite history. He further notes that extant material from the early Persian period does not refer to Aaronite priests, leaving Aaron and Aaronite priests to P and the Chronicler. Even Ezra–Nehemiah, "which has a great deal to say about priests past and contemporary, is almost completely silent about Aaron and Aaronite priests."[37] Blenkinsopp then sets about to create a scenario for

34. Blenkinsopp, "The Judaean Priesthood During the Neo-Babylonian and Achaemenid Periods," 27. Also see idem, "Bethel in the Neo-Babylonian Period."

35. Blenkinsopp, "The Judaean Priesthood During the Neo-Babylonian and Achaemenid Periods," 36.

36. Because traditional scholarship assumed that some kind of sanctuary remained in Jerusalem, complicated textual explanations have been used to incorporate Bethel into a reading. Thus Blenkinsopp translates the MT of Zech 7:1–3 as: "In the fourth year of King Darius, the word of Yahweh came to Zechariah on the fourth of the ninth month, in Chislev, Sareser, Regemmelech and his men had sent to Bethel to entreat the favor of Yahweh and to ask the priests who belonged to the house of Yahweh Sebaoth and the prophets, 'Should I mourn [weep] in the fifth month and practice abstinence as I have been doing for these many years?' " as opposed to the NRSV: "In the fourth year of King Darius, the word of the Lord came to Zechariah on the fourth day of the ninth month, which is Chislev. Now the people of Bethel had sent Sharezer and Regem-melech and their men, to entreat the favor of the Lord, and to ask the priests of the house of the Lord of hosts and the prophets, 'Should I mourn and practice abstinence in the fifth month, as I have done for so many years?' " Jer 41:5 and Hag 2:14 also read differently with new underlying assumptions.

37. Blenkinsopp, "The Judaean Priesthood During the Neo-Babylonian and Achaemenid Periods," 38. The existing references in Ezra–Nehemiah—Ezra 7:1–5; Neh 10:39–40; 12:47—are all commonly thought to originate from a later period (pp. 38–39).

the "rise of the Aaronite branch of the priesthood to a position of power in the temple community of Jerusalem" late in the Persian period.[38]

The priesthood functioning at Bethel claimed Aaronic descent. Zadokites, with no connection to Aaronites, functioned as the priesthood in exile and later returned with Ezra to Jerusalem. Although Blenkinsopp does not speculate on any impetus for the development, he argues that the Aaronites gradually rose to prominence in Jerusalem, a journey marked by struggle and compromise with the Zadokites. Ezekiel 40–48 is a remnant of Zadokite polemics against an Aaronite "Levitical" priesthood at Bethel, a priesthood that went astray (Ezek 44:10–16; 48:11).

Blenkinsopp's hypothesis answers questions about the Ezekiel texts that previously have been problematic for the reigning consensus which stemmed from the prominence of Wellhausen's synthesis and its consequential conclusion that the apostasy and talk of *bamot* refer to Josiah's reform. Blenkinsopp recalls several reasons why Josiah's reform cannot be the referent for Ezek 40–48, including the problem of "the aberrant tendencies" of the dominant priesthood at the official sanctuary and the inconsistency between the idea that Ezekiel was uplifting the dominant priests of Jerusalem in chs. 40–48, while he condemned the Jerusalemite priesthood earlier (Ezek 7:26; 8:1–18).[39]

He suggests instead that the referents of the "Zadokite" complaints in Ezek 40–48 are the priests performing "unacceptable cultic practice" in Judah, particularly at the sanctuary at Mizpah/Bethel.[40] His hypothesis regarding an official, exilic Aaronite sanctuary at Bethel is tantalizing and certainly plausible. His notion that Ezek 40–48 is a Zadokite response to the rising Aaronites is more problematic. Blenkinsopp rightly questions assumptions and, at the same time, makes one of his own that affects his argument. He, like many others, assumes that Zadokites were the dominant priesthood in Jerusalem and certainly in the exile:

> Though we cannot be sure that an unbroken Zadokite succession extended from the time of David to the Babylonian exile, we do know that the Zadokite branch of the priesthood represented by the priest Joshua maintained exclusive title to the high priestly office in the Babylonian diaspora.[41]

38. Ibid., 39.
39. Ibid., 41–42.
40. He also hints of a Persian period association between Bethel and Samaria. Also see Levenson, *Theology of the Program of Restoration of Ezekiel 40–48*, 136–51, and Kennett, "The Origin of the Aaronite Priesthood."
41. Blenkinsopp, "The Judaean Priesthood During the Neo-Babylonian and Achaemenid Periods," 40–41.

As discussed throughout this study, there is no warrant to substantiate this assumption. Perhaps Blenkinsopp's Aaronites of Bethel *are* the referents of Ezek 44:10–15 and 48:11, but we cannot necessarily assume this because of supposed dominance of priesthood in Jerusalem and in exile.[42] Still, he raises important questions for the study of the history of Israel's priesthood. Why do we assume that a sanctuary/shrine existed in Jerusalem after the destruction? And why do we assume that it was administered by Levites?[43] Could there have been an official sanctuary elsewhere? How can we explain that the Aaronites are not mentioned until the late Persian period? What are the implications of this for any history of priesthood in ancient Israel?

Cook and a Referent for Ezekiel 40–48

In 1995, Stephen L. Cook took a fresh look at the material as well. He sees Ezek 40–48 as an idealized "restoration program," a blueprint among others, that was never implemented—a blueprint formulated by Zadokites seeking to connect with the community's pre-exilic heritage.[44] Cook, following and extending the work of Levenson, reverses Wellhausen's idea that Ezekiel served as referent for P by suggesting that the "principal referent" of chs. 40–48, and ch. 44 in particular, "must be identified as a P tradition or a P text."[45] Specifically, Cook posits a direct relationship between the "P story of Korah's rebellion" and Ezek 44:6–16, the primary reference in the book of Ezekiel to the sons of Zadok.[46] For Cook, Ezek 44 "refers not to a historical development in Israel's priesthood but to a story of conflict in the wilderness." He uses textual, lexical, and syntactical studies to compare the two pericopes, arguing that Ezek 44 interprets the Num 16–18 story of "conflict in the wilderness," before seeking to identify the purpose of the interpretation.[47] He suggests that the authors of the Ezek 44 text saw the Numbers story as metaphorically

42. Furthermore, if Aaronite priests at Bethel are the referents for Ezek 40–48, why does 40–48 discuss Levites instead of Aaronites? Who then are the foreigners established over the sanctuary?

43. Blenkinsopp, "The Judaean Priesthood During the Neo-Babylonian and Achaemenid Periods," 25.

44. Cook, "Innerbiblical Interpretation in Ezekiel 44," 195.

45. Ibid., 196.

46. Ibid., 197–201. Cook credits Fishbane, Milgrom, Gunneweg, and McConville for previously noting a connection. This connection goes further back, even to Gese (*Der Verfassungsentwurf des Ezechiel*, 66), who noted the relationship and stated that we are unable to discern which came first (p. 197 n. 13).

47. Cook, "Innerbiblical Interpretation in Ezekiel 44," 201.

"embodying and explaining abuses in the post-settlement Temple" and as a means to discuss both the nature of holiness and the position of foreigners.[48] In Zadokite understanding, the Korah rebellion is a metaphor for Israel's cultic history. Cook sees the writer(s) of Ezek 44 as engaging in an ideological discussion, he calls them "priestly debates," with the writers of Isa 56–66 as an example of interaction between groups of priests in the postexilic period over "normative religions traditions shared in common."[49]

Cook offers an intriguing proposition and helps scholarship move toward new discussions and approaches—particularly in seeking the referent given the information available. He also addresses the questions remaining from traditional scholarship. He offers a constructive proposition in answer to the challenges to Wellhausenian notions. He further offers textual evidence and a partial historical context for his position.

Several textual connections help make his argument. The addressee of Ezek 44:6–16 is מרי, "the rebellious" (house of Israel), a term which occurs only twice as a noun in the Pentateuch—in Num 17:25 (ET 17:10) and Num 20:10.[50] רב־לכם provides another connection between the texts; the messenger formula in Ezek 44:6b begins with an exclamation —רב־לכם, "enough" of Israel's abominations. In the Pentateuch, רב־לכם is found in Moses' response to Korah's rebellion (Num 16:7).[51] Furthermore, Ezek 44:7–8 decries Israel for failing to fulfill the משמרת ("obligation/duty") to YHWH's holy things; in Num 18:4–5, the Levites and Aaronites were to fulfill these משמרות, they were to keep charge of the tent and sanctuary, and in so doing, keep out strangers (זור).[52]

Key for Cook's argument is Ezek 44:10, which raises again the rebellion of Levites; a factor which has caused considerable difficulties for interpretations based on Wellhausen's synthesis—a factor that "considerably narrows the field" for possible referents for the Ezek 44 text. This criterion, found specifically in the Ezekiel text, further supports Cook's association of the text with the Korah story in Num 16–18 because Korah is a descendant of Levi. Cook's clenching argument comes with the occurrence of the idiom נשאו עונם, "they shall bear their iniquities,"

48. Ibid., 203.

49. Ibid., 208. A similar argument to that of Hanson, although Cook (p. 205) tries to differentiate from Hanson, *The Dawn of Apocalyptic*, 220–69.

50. But frequently in Ezekiel (15 times): 5 in ch. 2, 5 in ch. 12. Cook says the 17:25 reference is the only one in the Pentateuch; perhaps he is referring to that particular form.

51. As well as Num 16:3; Deut 1:6; 2:3.

52. This Hebrew term presents a difficulty for Cook as Ezek 44 uses נכר.

which, when referring to a Levitical rebellion, is found only in Num 18:23 and this Ezekiel text.[53]

Cook willingly raises the difficulties with his hypothesis: a key word, the word for outsider, is different between the texts and there is no mention of a key issue, idol worship, in Numbers as there is in Ezek 44:10. Most important for this study is the difficulty Cook identifies with את־ביתי. Cook explains that the "epexegetical" reference in Ezek 44:7 to לחללו את־ביתי is less easy to interpret as a reference to Korah's rebellion and thus complicates his reading.[54] And rightly so. Cook suggests that ביתי could refer to the reconstructed temple or to a tent of worship as found in Judg 18:31; 1 Sam 1:7, 24; 2 Sam 12:20. In a footnote he tries to demonstrate how את־ביתי "seems to specify the Temple," found in 1 Kgs 7:12 and thereafter, based on a text-critical discussion by Gese.[55] But the wording in 1 Kgs 7:12 says בית יהוה, which is different. It is in fact the reference to ביתי that points to another potential referent for the Ezek 44 text—a referent located within the book of Ezekiel.

The only references to ביתי that even have the potential for referring to the house of YHWH are clearly late—Isa 56:7; Hag 1:19; Zech 1:16; 1 Chr 28:6; Isa 56:5; Jer 23:11; and perhaps Mal 3:10 and 1 Chr 7:14—these out of the 41 occurrences in the Hebrew Bible to ביתי. None of the references to ביתי is found in the Pentateuchal material. So, while Cook's hypothesis is certainly plausible, issues with his hypothesis remain to be resolved.

Another Plausible Referent for Ezekiel 40–48

Blenkinsopp and Cook both offer helpful readings of the Ezek 44 text particularly as they pertain to the straying of the Levites and their causing Israel to stumble. I would like to suggest an additional reading of Ezek 44, one that focuses primarily on the introductory section of the pericope:

> And you will say to the rebellious house of Israel, thus says the Lord YHWH, enough of you—of all your abominations, O house of Israel, in admitting foreigners, uncircumcised in heart and uncircumcised in flesh, to be in my sanctuary, profaning my temple when you offer my food, the fat and the blood. They have broken my covenant with all your abominations. You have not kept charge of my holy things but have established to keep my charge in my sanctuary for yourself. Thus says the Lord YHWH—any foreigner—of all the foreigners who are among the people of Israel, uncircumcised in heart and flesh—shall not enter my sanctuary.

53. But found frequently elsewhere—Exod 28:38; 34:7; Num 5:31; 14:18; 30:16; Hos 14:3; Mic 7:18; Pss 32:5; 85:3; Lev 5:1, 17; 10:17; 17:16.

54. Cook, "Innerbiblical Interpretation in Ezekiel 44," 198.

55. Ibid., 198 n. 18; Gese, *Der Verfassungsentwurf des Ezechiel*, 57 n. 3.

> But the Levites, who went far from me when Israel went astray, going astray from me after their idols, they will bear their punishment: they will be ministers in my sanctuary, having oversight at the gates of the temple and serving in the temple. They will slay the burnt offering and the sacrifice for the people and they will stand before them to serve them because they ministered to them before their idols so that the house of Israel became a stumbling block of iniquity. Therefore I have sworn concerning them, says the Lord YHWH, that they shall bear their punishment: they will not come near to me to serve me as priest and they will not come near any of my sacred things—the things that are most sacred. They will bear their shame because of the abominations which they have committed. Still I will appoint them to keep charge of the temple to do all its service and all that is to be done in it. But the Levitical priests, the Zadokites, who kept the charge of my sanctuary when the people of Israel went astray from me, they will come near to me to minister to me and they will attend to me—to offer me the fat and the blood, says the Lord YHWH. They will enter into my sanctuary and they will approach my table to minister to me. They will keep my charge. (Ezek 44:6–16)

In his commentary on the book, Blenkinsopp correctly points out the progression of the text: foreigners, Levites, Zadokites.[56] Cook and Blenkinsopp both correctly make an association between this text and the pro-foreigner rhetoric of Isa 56–66.[57] Could it be that this text demonstrates additional innerbiblical interpretation? Could it be that the authors of Ezek 44 were commenting on earlier Ezekielian material found in Ezek 23? Ezekiel 16 may also function in this way.[58] As with many other Ezekiel texts, this Ezekielian material is difficult to interpret and difficult to place in socio-historical contexts. Among the most violent texts in the Hebrew Bible,[59] with rape, pornography, raging anger, threats, abuse of

56. Blenkinsopp, *Ezekiel*, 217–18.

57. Cook, "Innerbiblical Interpretation in Ezekiel 44," 208; Blenkinsopp, *Ezekiel*, 218–22.

58. Blenkinsopp, *Ezekiel*, 98, calls Ezek 16 the "story of the nymphomaniac bride," 76–79. Ezek 23 is "taking up from the story of the nymphomaniac bride."

59. Renita J. Weems, *Battered Love: Marriage, Sex, and Violence in the Hebrew Prophets*, *Overtures to Biblical Theology* (Minneapolis: Fortress, 1995), 96. See also on Ezek 23: Jacqueline E. Lapsley, "Shame and Self-Knowledge: The Positive Role of Shame in Ezekiel's View of the Moral Self," in *Book of Ezekiel: Theological and Anthropological Perspectives* (ed. Margaret S. Odell and John T. Strong; Atlanta: Society of Biblical Literature, 2000), 143–73; Corrine L. Patton, "'Should Our Sister Be Treated Like a Whore?': A Response to Feminist Critiques of Ezekiel 23," in *Book of Ezekiel* (Atlanta: Society of Biblical Literature, 2000), 221–38; Robert Carroll, "Whorusalamin: A Tale of Three Cities as Three Sisters," in *On Reading Prophetic Texts: Gender-Specific and Related Studies in Memory of Fokkelien van Dijk-Hemmes* (ed. Bob Becking and Meindert Dijkstral; Leiden: Brill, 1996), 67–82;

power, *lex talionis*, and "images of dread, chaos, anarchy, and evil,"[60] this text uses the marriage metaphor to describe the relationship of God to the people.

An examination of Ezek 23 proves helpful:

> The word of YHWH came to me saying, son of man, there were two women, daughters of one mother. They were prostitutes in Egypt. In their youth, they were prostitutes. There their breasts were pressed and there the bosoms of their virginity were handled. Their names were Oholah, the older one, and Oholibah, her sister. They became mine and they bore sons and daughters. As for their names, Samaria is Oholah and Jerusalem is Oholibah. Oholah was a prostitute while she was mine. She doted on her lovers, the Assyrians, who were near. They were clothed in purple, governors and commanders, desirable young men they all were. They were horsemen riding on horses. She bestowed upon them, the choicest of the men of Assyria, all of them, her whoredom. And on everyone of them on whom she doted, she defiled herself with all the idols. She did not give up her prostitution (which she had been doing) from Egypt. For men had lain with her in her youth and had handled the bosoms of her virginity. They had poured out their lust upon her. Therefore I delivered her into the hands of her lovers, into the hands of the Assyrians upon whom she

Fokkelien van Dijk-Hemmes, "The Metaphorization of Woman in Prophetic Speech: An Analysis of Ezekiel 23," in *On Gendering Texts: Female and Male Voices in the Hebrew Bible* (ed. Athalya Brenner and F. van Dijk-Hemmes; BibInt Series 1; Leiden: Brill, 1993), 167–76; J. Cheryl Exum, "The Ethics of Biblical Violence Against Women," in *The Bible in Ethics: The Second Sheffield Colloquium* (ed. John W. Rogerson et al.; JSOTSup 207; Sheffield: Sheffield Academic Press, 1995), 248–71; Katheryn Pfisterer Darr, "Ezekiel's Justifications of God: Teaching Troubling Texts," *JSOT* 55 (1992): 97–117. And on Ezek 16: Moshe Greenberg, "Ezekiel 16: A Panorama of Passions," in *Love and Death in the Ancient Near East: Essays in Honor of Marvin H. Pope* (ed. John H. Marks and Robert M. Good; Guilford, Conn.: Four Quarters, 1987), 143–50; Margaret S. Odell, "The Inversion of Shame and Forgiveness in Ezekiel 16.59–63," *JSOT* 56 (1992): 101–12; Marvin H. Pope, "Mixed Marriage Metaphor in Ezekiel 16," in *Fortunate the Eyes That See: Essays in Honor of David Noel Freedman in Celebration of His Seventieth Birthday* (ed. Astrid B. Beck et al.; Grand Rapids: Eerdmans, 1995), 384–99; Carol J. Dempsey, "The 'Whore' of Ezekiel 16: The Impact and Ramifications of Gender-Specific Metaphors in Light of Biblical Law and Divine Judgment," in *Gender and Law in the Hebrew Bible and the Ancient Near East* (ed. Victor Matthews, Bernard Levinson, and Tikva Frymer-Kensky; JSOTSup 262; Sheffield: Sheffield Academic Press, 1998), 57–78; Linda Day, "Rhetoric and Domestic Violence in Ezekiel 16," *BibInt* 8 (2000): 205–30; Peggy L. Day, "The Bitch Had It Coming to Her: Rhetoric and Interpretation in Ezekiel 16," *BibInt* 8 (2000): 231–54, and idem, "Adulterous Jerusalem's Imagined Demise: Death of a Metaphor in Ezekiel xvi," *VT* 50 (2000): 285–309.

60. Weems, *Battered Love*, 61.

doted. These are the ones who uncovered her nakedness. They seized her sons and her daughters. And as for her, they slew her with a sword. And she was there among women when (this) judgment was done to her. Oholibah, her sister, saw (this). And yet she was more depraved in her lust and her prostitution than the lust and prostitutions of her sister. She doted upon the Assyrians, governors and commanders, nearby, clothed in full armor. They were horsemen riding on horses. They were desirable young men, all of them. And I saw that she was defiled, one way to the two of them. But she added to her prostitution. She saw portraits of men, images of the Chaldeans, upon the wall, pictured in vermillion. They were girded with belts upon their loins. They had flowing turbans on their heads. They were looking like officers, all of them were a picture of Babylonians (in) Chaldea, the land of their birth. Then she doted upon them to the sight of her eyes and she sent messengers to them in Chaldea. And the Babylonians, they came to her, into the bed of love and they defile her with their lust. After she was defiled by them she turned herself in disgust from them. When she went out (in) her prostitution and flaunted her nakedness, then I myself turned from her as I myself had turned from her sister. Still she increased her prostitution, remembering the days of her youth when she had prostituted herself in the land of Egypt, when she lusted for her lovers, those who had bodies like donkeys and whose see was like that of stallions. Thus you wished for the wickedness of your youth when the Egyptians pressed your bosom, the breasts of your youth. Therefore, Oholibah, thus says the Lord YHWH, behold, I will arouse your lovers against you, the ones you yourself turned from in disgust and I will bring them against you from every side, the Babylonians and all the Chaldeans, Pekod and Shoa and Koa and all the Assyrians with them, desirable young men, governors and commanders, all of them, officers, called ones, riding on horses, all of them. And they will come against you from the north with chariots and a wheeled war chariot and an assembly of peoples. (With) buckler and shield and helmet, they shall set themselves against you on every side and I will give to them the judgment and they will judge you by these judgments. And I will place my indignation against you, that they may work with you in fury. They will cut off your nose and your ears. Your survivors will fall by the sword. They will seize your sons and your daughters and your survivors will be devoured by fire. They will strip you of your clothes and take away all of your beauty. This is how I will put to rest your corruption from you and your prostitution from the land of Egypt so that you will not carry your eyes to them and the Egyptians will not remember you any more. For thus says the Lord YHWH, Behold, I will give you into the hands of those you hate, into the hands of those from whom you turned in disgust. They will deal with you in hatred and will take away all the fruit of your labor. They will leave you naked and bare and the nakedness, the corruption and the prostitution of your prostitution will be uncovered. You have done this to yourself because you were a prostitute with the nations, because you defiled yourself with their idols. You have gone in

> the path of your sister. Therefore I will give her cup into your hand. Thus says the Lord YHWH, you will drink the deep and large cup of your sister. You will be laughed at and scorned for this cup holds drunkenness and sorrow. The cup will be filled with horror and desolation, it is the cup of your sister, Samaria. You will drink it and drain it completely. You will break its sherd and you will tear your breasts. For I have spoken says the Lord YHWH. Therefore thus says the Lord YHWH, because you have forgotten me and thrown me behind your back, therefore (you) will carry the consequences of your corruption and your prostitution. This YHWH said to me, son of man, will you judge Oholah and Oholibah? Then tell them (about) their abominations, for they have committed adultery. Blood is upon their hands. With their idols they have committed adultery. They have even offered their sons, whom they bore to me, up to the idols for food. Furthermore they have done (this) to me, they have defiled my sanctuary on the same day and they have profaned my sabbaths. For when they sacrificed their children to their idols, they came into my sanctuary on the same day to defile it and behold, this is what they did in my house. They even sent for men to come from far away, a messenger was sent to them and behold, they came. For them you bathed yourself and painted your eyes and adorned yourself in ornaments. You perched on a formal couch with a table spread before it. You placed my incense and my oil on it. The sound of a loud group of people was with her. And men, from a multitude of men, were brought in drunk from the wilderness and they put bracelets upon their (her) hands and beautiful crowns upon their (her) head(s). Then I said about this woman of prostitution, they are prostituting and she is prostituting. For they had gone in to her as men go into a prostitute. This is how they went in to Oholah and to Oholibah, those loose women. But righteous men will judge them with the judgment of adultery and with the judgment of women that shed blood because they are adulteresses and blood is upon their hands. For thus says the Lord YHWH, Bring up an assembly against them and make them the object of terror and booty. The assembly will stone them with stones. They will dispense with their sons and their daughters with swords. They will destroy their houses with fire. Thus I will put a rest to the corruption in the land so that all women shall be warned, so that they will not perform in corruption as you have done. And your corruption shall be given back upon you and you will bear the consequences of your idolatry; and you will know that I am the Lord YHWH. (Ezek 23)

The prophet focuses on two sisters, Ohalah ("She who has her own tent") and Oholibah ("my tent [is] in her"[61]) in reference to the worship centers Samaria and Jerusalem respectively. They are accused of playing whores (v. 2) in Egypt where their breasts were caressed and their virgin bosoms were fondled. Oholah lusted after her foreign lovers (vv. 5–6), bestowed

61. Eichrodt, *Ezekiel*, 322.

her favors on these foreigners (v. 7), defiled herself with idols of everyone for whom she lusted (v. 7), did not give up her whoring (v. 8), and allowed men to lay with her in her youth when they poured out their lust upon her (v. 8). Her sister, Oholibah, was even more corrupt (v. 11). She also lusted after the foreigners; she was defiled; she carried her whorings further (v. 14); she saw foreign male figures carved on the wall and lusted after them (vv. 15–16); she sent messengers after them; they came to her and defiled her with their lust; she defiled herself with them and then turned from them in disgust; she carried on her whorings in the open, flaunting her nakedness; she increased her whorings; she lusted after the paramours of her youth from Egypt whose members were like those of donkeys and whose emission was like that of stallions (v. 20); she longed for the lewdness of her youth. As a consequence, foreigners will be raised against her from every side (v. 22); YHWH's judgment will be in their hands (v. 24) and she will be judged according to the laws of the foreigners (v. 24); they will mutilate her and sacrifice her children (vv. 25, 47); they will sexually exploit and mutilate her (v. 26); YHWH will deliver her into the hands of those she hates and they will treat her in their hate (v. 28).

Of particular interest for understanding Ezek 44 is the text in Ezek 23:38–39:

> Furthermore they have done (this) to me, they have defiled my sanctuary on the same day and they have profaned my sabbaths. For when they sacrificed their children to their idols, they came into my sanctuary on the same day to defile it and behold, this is what they did in my house.

In Ezek 44:6–7 we find:

> And you will say to the rebellious house of Israel, says the Lord YHWH, Enough of you—of all your abominations, O house of Israel, in admitting foreigners, uncircumcised in heart and uncircumcised in flesh, to be in my sanctuary, profaning my temple when you offer my food, the fat and the blood. They have broken my covenant with all your abominations. You have not kept charge of my holy things but have established to keep my charge in my sanctuary for yourself. Thus says the Lord YHWH—any foreigner—of all the foreigners who are among the people of Israel, uncircumcised in heart and flesh—shall not enter my sanctuary.

I would suggest we might reflect on Ezek 44 as midrash upon Ezek 23.[62] Consider the following parallels: the sanctuary defiled (23:38–39; 44:6–7); sabbath as an issue (23:28; 44:24); idols (23:7, 30, 37, 39; 44:10); and,

62. And Ezek 16 as well. Fishbane (*Biblical Interpretation in Ancient Israel*, 138) discusses Ezek 44:9–16 as an "exegetical oracle."

of course, ביתי (23:39; 44:7); concern with foreigners (16; 23; 44:6–7); covenant (16:61, 62; 44:6–7) abominations (23:36–49; 44:7); heart (16:30; 44:6–7); and blood (23:37, 48; 44:7).[63]

So, another possible reading of Ezek 44 is as an interpretation of Ezek 23. I would like to suggest that the foreigners were the driving impetus for the writers of the Ezek 44 text—Israel defiled itself first with the Assyrians (23:7) and then with the Babylonians (23:15–18). Whenever "now" may be, Israel is defiled by the admittance of foreigners—uncircumcised in heart and flesh, into the sanctuary. Purity is of paramount importance and the sanctuary is defiled by the offering of food—fat and blood—in the presence of foreigners. The foreigners broke (ויפרו) the covenant by the abominations of the house of Israel. The transgression prompting the entire "sons of Zadok" section in Ezek 44 is the impurity caused by the admittance of foreigners. Worse yet is the establishment of these foreigners to keep charge of the sanctuary.

Immediately, the rhetoric and concerns of Ezra–Nehemiah come to mind so that a case for the provenance of the Ezekiel text is possible. The chief question to be answered in that case would concern the establishment of foreigners to keep charge of the sanctuary. Why does this not say "temple" as in היכל? Why sanctuary? היכל is used eight times in chs. 40–48 while מקדש is used 17 times. The foreigners are the key issue. When were foreigners set over YHWH's sanctuary?[64] Certainly there could have been a struggle over who should control the temple in the late restoration period. Concomitant with this evidence is the focus on priestly genealogies in Chronicles. The question becomes, then, for the biblical scholar: Is late restoration the best setting to place this material? Is this the only option? The question must remain open at the time.

Summary of Ezekiel Material

Thus, this provides another plausible reading for the Ezek 44 pericope, a reading that discourages the traditional reading of Ezek 40–48 as it relates to the Zadokites. The historical context of the authorship of Ezek 40–48 provides the critical and missing piece. Whether we place it in the late sixth century B.C.E. or the Hasmonean period, we must conclude that at the time of writing there was some discussion of the duties and rights of priests and that the author of the material considered priests called "sons of Zadok" as central to service of YHWH.

63. Mein (*Ezekiel and the Ethics of Exile*, 160–75) provides an interesting discussion of Ezekiel's references to blood.

64. נכר is a clear foreign/alien meaning.

Summary of Biblical Evidence

As stated at the outset of this chapter, biblical evidence regarding the Zadokites is scarce. צדוק is mentioned fifty-three times, most often in reference to David's priest, Zadok. At least twenty-two of the twenty-six occurrences in Samuel/Kings refer to a priest named Zadok. The other four refer to Ahimaaz son of Zadok (three times) or Jerusha daughter of Zadok. Chronicles has seventeen references to someone named "Zadok" (of these, eight seem to refer to a priest). Ezra–Nehemiah contains six references to persons named "Zadok." The Zadokites, בני צדוק, are mentioned only four times in the biblical material, all within Ezek 40–48. Second Chronicles 31:10 refers to בית צדוק. These represent the entirety of biblical references to Zadok or the Zadokites.

Samuel–Kings provides evidence that the author had a memory of Zadok as first David's, then Solomon's, priest. His sons are mentioned as well. We find no evidence in Samuel–Kings for a Zadokite priestly dynasty. Ezra–Nehemiah does not demonstrate that Zadokite priests returned from exile or even that there was a Zadokite priesthood. Nor does it give any evidence that Ezra was a Zadokite priest. The Ezra 7:1–5 list provides Ezra a genealogy. Most likely it is an attempt to provide a genealogical legitimation for an Aaronite priesthood. The genealogical lists of priests in Chronicles serve to legitimize the institution of priesthood. The writer of the lists in Chronicles may have sought to integrate Zadok and a few other priests into previously existing Aaronite genealogical lists, and even this attempt could have been less an effort to establish a particular priestly person or group and more of an effort to hearken back to a favored figure in the lore of the Davidic monarchy. At best, Zadok is incorporated into a continued focus on Aaronites. Certainly, a Zadokite priestly dynasty had not existed prior to this time. The Chronicles lists are clumsy and self-contradictory and, as demonstrated several times in this study, cannot be taken as a historically accurate lists of priests.

From Ezekiel, we can conclude that the historical context of the authorship of Ezek 40–48 provides the critical and missing piece. Whether we place it in the late sixth century B.C.E. or the Hasmonean period, we must conclude that, at the time of writing, there was some discussion of the duties and rights of priests and that the author of the material considered priests called "sons of Zadok" as central to service of YHWH.

The paucity of biblical evidence makes it nearly impossible to draw credible conclusions about Zadokites or a Zadokite priesthood.

Chapter 6

Extrabiblical Evidence of the Zadokites

Introduction

Extrabiblical references to בני צדוק are as obscure as the biblical references. They are mentioned once in one of six Hebrew manuscripts of Ben Sira and several times in various Dead Sea Scrolls found near Qumran. Josephus mentions Zadok and speaks at length about priestly lineage, but does not mention Zadokites. Zadok is also mentioned in 1 Esd 8:2 and 2 Esd 1:1. Clearly, we have a paucity of evidence regarding Zadokites.[1] This chapter seeks to address these few references to Zadokites (and Zadok).

1 Esdras

First Esdras, found in the standard texts of the Septuagint, presents a portrait of legendary religious leaders in a history from Josiah's reign to the time of Ezra and is often understood as a parallel to the work of the Chronicler.[2] R. Pfeiffer suggests that First Esdras is a fragment of a

1. And certainly a paucity considering how much is made of them in histories of ancient Israel.

2. With the exception of 1 Esd 3:1–5:6. Grabbe, *Ezra–Nehemiah*, 69–81, notes the many questions still surrounding the relationship between Ezra–Nehemiah and 1 Esdras; also see Blenkinsopp, *Ezra–Nehemiah*, 70–77. Although Blenkinsopp sees it as "A very different account of the origins of the Second Commonwealth… This Greek version of events from Josiah to Ezra differs in two important respects from the canonical book: it omits entirely the Nehemiah narrative and adds a long novelistic account of how Zerubbabel obtained permission from Darius to return and rebuild both the city and the temple (chs. 3–4)… On the assumption that 1 Esdras is a tendentious rewriting of the last section of C's history, its intent appears to be to elevate Zerubbabel and Ezra as the founding fathers at the expense of Nehemiah. And in that case it could be plausibly read as countering the kind of pro-Hasmonean propaganda represented vby the letter" (p. 57).

refashioned Chronicler's work with the intent of valorizing both Zerubbabel and Ezra in their efforts to rebuild the temple and establish religious reforms.[3]

Regarding Zadok, the First Esdras text bears remarkable similarity to Ezra 7:

> After these things, when Artaxerxes, the king of the Persians, was reigning, Ezra came, the son of Seraiah, son of Azariah, son of Hilkiah, son of Shallum, son of *Zadok*, son of Ahitub, son of Amariah, son of Uzzi, son of Bukki, son of Abishua, son of Phinehas, son of Eleazar, son of Aaron, the high priest. This Ezra came up from Babylon as a scribe practiced in the law of Moses, that which was given by the God of Israel; and the king honored him, for he found favor before the king in all his requests. (1 Esd 8:1–4)

> Now after these matters, in the reign of Artaxerxes, king of Persia, Ezra, son of Seraiah, son of Azariah, son of Hilkiah, son of Shallum, son of *Zadok*, son of Ahitub, son of Amariah, son of Azariah, son of Meraioth, son of Zerhiah, son of Uzzi, son of Bukki, son of Abishua, son of Phinehas, son of Eleazar, son of Aaron, the chief priest, this Ezra went up from Babylonia and he was a skilled scribe in the torah of Moses which YHWH, God of Israel, had given. The king gave to him all that he asked because the hand of YHWH, his God, was on him. (Ezra 7:1–6)

The two texts are basically the same except that the Ezra priest list contains three more names than the 1 Esdras list; following Amariah, the Ezra pericope lists Azariah, Meraioth, and Zerhiah. Bartlett emphatically assumes that the 1 Esdras list was based upon the Ezra 7 list[4] (which is discussed in Chapter 4). That a relationship between the two exists is clear.[5] Bartlett sees the purpose of this list as an attempt to connect Ezra to Aaron.[6] Nothing about this list in particular provides additional information about Zadokites. The conclusions remain the same as those in the analysis of Ezra–Nehemiah; there is considerable discussion about whether the Ezra 7:1–5 list provides a historically credible list of high priests and about how this list relates to other lists of priests. We cannot detect any prominence for Zadokites in this list.

3. R. Pfeiffer, *History of New Testament Times with an Introduction to the Apocrypha* (New York: Harper, 1949).
4. Bartlett, "Zadok and His Successors at Jerusalem," 5.
5. See the discussions of Grabbe, *Judaism from Cyrus to Hadrian*, vol. 1; Jacob M. Myers, *I and II Esdras* (AB 42; Garden City, N.Y.: Doubleday, 1974); Cross, "A Reconstruction of the Judean Restoration."
6. Bartlett, "Zadok and His Successors at Jerusalem," 6.

2 Esdras

Also known as the Apocalypse of Ezra or 4 Ezra, 2 Esdras was apparently written in Hebrew or Aramaic near the end of the first century B.C.E. Studies of 2 Esdras generally focus on the apocalyptic nature of the book; chs. 1–2, where Zadok is mentioned, are not central to the readings of this apocalyptic material. Zadok is listed in the opening paragraph of the book:

> The book of the prophet Ezra, son of Seraiah, son of Azariah, son of Hilkiah, son of Shallum, son of *Zadok*, son of Ahitub, son of Ahijah, son of Phinehas, son of Eli, son of Amariah, son ofAzariah, son of Meraimoth, son of Arna, son of Uzzi, son of Borith, son of Abishua, son of Phinehas, son of Eleazar, son of Aaron, of the tribe of Levi, who was a captive in the country of the Medes in the reign of Artaxerxes, king of the Persians. (2 Esd 1:1–3)

As in most of the other lineages of Ezra, this one seeks to establish Ezra as descendant of Aaron; Zadok, son of Ahitub, is part of that lineage. Here Ezra is named a prophet instead of a priest.

Josephus

Flavius Josephus, born around 37 C.E., wrote over thirty volumes in four works, yielding a portrait of the ancient world during the Roman period and broadening our understanding of history of ancient Israel with his biblical paraphrases and interpretations. Many questions about Josephus' writings remain unanswered. His use as a source is both standard and questionable, raising issues about both modern and ancient historiography. As H. Moehring writes,

> The writings of Flavius Josephus have at times achieved semi-canonical status, but there exists no orthodox line of interpretation, at least apart from…the unscrupulousness with which everybody exploits his writings for whatever purpose may at the moment be in mind. Josephus has truly been all things to all men… There certainly is a great amount of pseudo-history present: the use of Josephus for contemporary apologetic purposes without regard for the intentions of his writings.[7]

Josephus opens *The Jewish Antiquities* with the promise that he will present the details of the scriptures, "without adding anything to what is

7. Horst R. Moehring, "The *Acta Pro Judaeis* in the *Antiquities* of Flavius Josephus," in *Christianity, Judaism and Other Greco-Roman Cults: Studies for Morton Smith at Sixty* (ed. Jacob Neusner; SJLA 12; Leiden: Brill, 1975): 124–58 (124).

therein contained, or taking away anything there from" (*Ant.* 1.3.17), confounding modern historians since Josephus clearly revises the septuagintal biblical material as we have it. In historiographic ambivalence, then, Josephus is regarded as a primary source for information about "post-biblical" times. Some suggest that the phrase was rhetorically expected in Josephus' day and time. Others suggest that Josephus incorporated midrash into the biblical material.[8] As Steve Mason correctly states,

> Josephus claims that he is following the precedent provided by the Greek (Septuagint) translation of the Torah. He says that this translation (made in the third century BC) proves both Jewish willingness to publicize their laws and Greek readiness to hear. But a new translation is necessary because the older one was limited to the laws of Moses (1.5, 9–13). So he will render the whole of the scriptures into Greek without adding or omitting anything (1.17).[9]

Josephus has been misused and abused by both ancient and modern scholars, theologians, and historians. Mason reminds us that, in the ancient world and "in the absence of paper, printing presses, and photocopiers, it was not a foregone conclusion that any given book would live beyond its author's own generation."[10] Probably we have access to Josephus' works today because of their institutionalization in Rome's imperial library. After the fall of the Roman empire, the Christian church under the leadership of both Origin and Eusebius incorporated Josephus' works into their writings. Early Christian writers were attracted to Josephus' works because of the wealth of background information they provided. They yielded references to important figures for Christianity; they provided a model for apologetics; they lent a certain historic legitimation for Christianity which was often viewed as an oxymoron—a "new religion."[11] Considering themselves to be the rightful heirs of the biblical tradition, early Christians used Josephus' presentation of Israel's history to substantiate their position.

Ironically, Josephus' primary purpose served to fuel the greatest abuse of his works. Josephus sought to legitimize Judaism by presenting the ancient, glorious, noble, upright history of his people and their religious faith. He presented the Jews as having consistently been a peace-loving people who fit perfectly into Roman societal mores of order and harmonious living. For Josephus, those "Jews" who revolted were abominations;

8. Louis H. Feldman, "Josephus," *ABD* 3:981–98.

9. Steve Mason, *Josephus and the New Testament* (Peabody: Hendrickson, 1992), 71.

10. Ibid., 7.

11. Ibid., 9–19.

they veered from their ancestral laws as maintained and presented by the priests as religious leaders and by the temple. The Romans, in destroying Jerusalem, were God's agents of divine retribution—bringing just punishment as a consequence of the actions of the few rebels. Josephus provided extensive details of the horrors resulting from the rebellious revolt against Rome and the subsequent destruction of the temple.[12]

The abuse of Josephus by the early Christian writers came in the outright dismissal of Judaism. Using Josephus' notion of divine retribution as a guiding principle, these writers reinterpreted the destruction of Jerusalem as God's divine destruction of Judaism in favor of the new, true faith—Christianity.[13] The most flagrant misuse of Josephus—using his works as raw data to be pieced together as facts—was operative in early historical work and continues. His work has been, and continues to be, removed from its socio-historical and literary context. For example, Josephus served as a primary source for Emil Schürer's *The History of the Jewish People in the Age of Jesus Christ*.[14] Per Mason,

> He (Schürer) regularly cited Josephus' isolated statements as if they were "facts," which could be combined with other facts (i.e. statements of other writers or archaeological evidence) to produce a whole picture. For example, Schürer opens his discussion of the Pharisees with a collection of passages from Josephus, combined with fragments from other sources, and then proceeds to weld these together into a coherent whole. He fails to take into account, however, that Josephus' remarks can be understood only in the context that Josephus gave them, for words have meaning only in context.[15]

Mason calls this the "scissors-and-paste" style of history—a style often recognized and criticized in hindsight but just as often difficult for historians to avoid. Mason's main point is well taken—in order to appreciate Josephus fully and in order to use his work within today's scholarship, we must recognize him as an individual author of literature which was written for his purposes and within his context. His perspective, his assumptions, and his intentions feed his literary product.

Josephus' presentation of his own genealogy is an interesting case in point. He claims secular and sacred heritage in the line of the Hasmoneans and as evidenced in official archives. He traces his royal lineage through his mother (*Life* 2) and then provides the lineage list through his

12. Ibid., 27.

13. Furthermore, Josephus was used to blame Jesus' death on Jews, see ibid., 19.

14. Emil Schürer, *A History of the Jewish People in the Time of Jesus Christ* (Edinburgh: T. & T. Clark, 1890).

15. Mason, *Josephus and the New Testament*, 27.

father's family line—his great-great-great grandfather married into the Hasmonean family (*Life* 4). Further fogging his genealogical picture, in *Ant* 13.301 he notes that the Hasmoneans only took on the title of "king" under Aristobulus (ca. 103 B.C.E.), well after the marriage of his great-great-great grandfather into the Hasmonean family. Furthermore, his ancestral arithmetic[16] raises questions. Josephus claims that his great-grandfather was born in 135 B.C.E.; his grandfather in 70 B.C.E.; and his father in 6 B.C.E. While not entirely out of the question, given our contemporary understanding of ancient life-spans and fertility potentiality, the numbers seem questionable at best. Nonetheless, most scholars agree, based on the priestly and pro-Hasmonean biases clearly present in Josephus' works, that he was a priest and had some connection to the Hasmonean line.

Another well-known example concerns his presentation of his own philosophical training. Even if he was a precocious child as he claims,[17] it seems impossible that he would have completed the rigorous training of not one but three major Jewish schools, the Pharisees, the Sadducees, and the Essenes, before abandoning them for three years with the strict teacher, Bannus, in the wilderness—all in the short span of three years. We understand more clearly when we view the rhetoric within the context of elite Roman society whose ideal called for a successful young man to focus on public life, moving from military to governmental positions. Roman youth typically studied philosophy as part of their gymnasium training in order to gain a broad philosophical perspective. Given Josephus' desire to represent Judaism in a favorable light to his Roman readership, his self-portrait is readily understood.

As pointed out by Lester Grabbe, "Josephus is—or is not—reliable. He is—or is not—a good historian. He is—or is not—this, that, and the other thing. Frequently, however, no such evaluation is possible… [T]he dominant conclusion is that each section of his history must be examined on its own merit."[18] Grabbe recommends the following in contemporary use of Josephus: (1) comparison of parallel accounts without either synthesizing or selecting the most preferred account, (2) consideration of Josephus' underlying sources, (3) consideration of ancient historiography, (4) mindfulness of apologetic purposes, and (5) utilization of as many other sources as possible.

16. Arithmetic is often an issue when reading Josephus.

17. And as is claimed by many other ancient authors and biographers (such as Pythagoras, Apollonius of Tyana, Moses, and Jesus).

18. Grabbe, *Judaism from Cyrus to Hadrian*, 1:11.

Steve Mason builds upon his previous studies as well as the extensive work of Tessa Rajak, Per Bilde, Louis Feldman, and Gohei Hata, suggesting the only appropriate reading of Josephus is a holistic reading with the understanding that Josephus' representation "allows him both to remain loyal to his patrons and to speak as a committed Jew."[19] Josephus' intent was to contradict existing misinformation about Jews and to legitimize Judaism by assuring his readers that a mere handful of misguided Jews caused the revolt and that these aberrant Jews did not represent Jews as a whole, Jews whose origin story showed a noble history. He sought to portray Jews as "exemplary citizens of the empire…committed to the bedrock values of Greco-Roman civilization: piety toward God, justice toward humanity, and a firm belief in divine retribution."[20] Throughout his work, Josephus spends considerable time on Moses, establishing him as "the Jews' founding philosopher," the one who handed down his teachings to the high priests who preserved them intact throughout the ages in exact harmony with preferred Roman practices. He loftily describes the priests:

> And where shall we find a better or more righteous constitution than ours, while this makes us esteem God to be the governor of the universe, and permits the priests in general to be the administrators of the principal affairs, and withal intrusts the government over the other priests to the chief high priest himself! Which priests our legislator, at their first

19. Mason, *Josephus and the New Testament*, 60. Idem, "Introduction," in *Understanding Josephus: Seven Perspectives* (ed. Steve Mason; JSOTSup 32; Sheffield: JSOT Press, 1998), advises, "It is because doing history with Josephus requires, unavoidably, that one reckon first and last with the nature of the evidence. Since the past no longer exists, and historians must reconstruct if from the literary and physical traces that survive, making an effort to understand the evidence is obviously crucial. All responsible history, therefore, must involve at least three stages—whether it makes them explicit or not: understanding the evidence in some plausible and comprehensive way (while admitting disagreement among interpreters); *hypothesizing* about the underlying reality in which the historian is interested; and then returning to explain how the extant evidence came into being if hypothesis X is valid. In the case of Josephus, one needs to show how any hypothesis concerning Herod, the Temple, the rebel leaders' motives, Pontius Pilate, the Sadducees, or whatever, explains what we have in Josephus. This does not mean that hypotheses need to agree with Josephus: one expects that they will not in most cases. But the historian must provide a plausible account of the way in which Josephus came to his views, for such explanations are the only controls on historical reconstruction in the absence of empirical evidence. Such explanations are mainly lacking in contemporary scholarship, however, when they are given, they tend to be arbitrary and sometimes they are demonstrably false" (pp. 11–12).

20. Mason, *Josephus and the New Testament*, 66.

> appointment, did not advance to that dignity for their riches, or any abundance of other possessions, or any plenty they had as the gifts of fortune, but he intrusted the principal management of divine worship to those that exceeded others in an ability to persuade men, and in prudence of conduct. These men had the main care of the law and of the other parts of the people's conduct committed to them; for they were the priests who were ordained to be the inspectors of all." (*Ag. Ap.* 2.185–87)

For Josephus, Judaism fit the contemporary standards for a "national religion": "it had an ethnic and geographical center, with temple, priesthood, and sacrificial system."[21]

Most interesting for this project is Josephus' treatment of priesthood. He presents himself as a priest at the outset of his work. Josephus' concern is an appropriate representation of priesthood and Judaism in the social-religious context of the day. He is faced with the challenge of exalting priesthood as an institution while explaining the deviant behavior of various individual high priests. Most effectively in *War*, Josephus represents the priesthood as the traditional, mainstream, establishment-oriented core[22] of Judaism which stood in opposition to the radical revolt. For Josephus, the priests involved in the revolt violated tradition, the temple, and the priestly institution.

Given Josephus' environment and purpose, then, his references to Zadok (*Ant.* 7.2.56; 7.5.110; 7.10.245; 7.11.8; 7.14.4; 8.1.3; 10.8.6) can be more effectively analyzed. Immediately noticeable is the lack of any references to Zadokites or the sons of Zadok. Such a lacuna raises the question: Were there even Zadokites around? If the Zadokites were important, why are they not mentioned at all by Josephus. Was it that they opposed the Hasmoneans? Even if that were the case, Josephus might be expected to discount the Zadokites somehow instead of not mentioning them. Given this lingering concern, Josephus' mentions of Zadok are as follows.

Josephus, Antiquities *7.2.56*

> There came also seven thousand and one hundred out of the tribe of Simeon. Out of the tribe of Levi came four thousand and seven hundred, having Jehoiada for their leader. After these came *Zadok* the high priest, with twenty-two captains of his kindred. Out of the tribe of Benjamin the armed men were four thousand; but the rest of the tribe continued, still expecting that someone of the house of Saul should reign over them.

21. Ibid., 69.
22. Ibid., 118, 199, 127.

Apparently Josephus used some version of 1 Chr 12:24–29 (ET 12:23–28)[23] for his source material here, simply providing a reference to Zadok as high priest.

Josephus, Antiquities, *7.5.110*

> Now David was in his nature just, and made his determination with regard to truth. He had for the general of his whole army Joab; and he made Jehoshaphat, the son of Ahilud, recorder; he also appointed *Zadok*, of the family of Phinehas, to be high priest, together with Abiathar, for he was his friend; he also made Seisan the scribe; and committed the command over the guards of his body to Benaiah, the son of Jehoiada. His elder sons were near his body, and had the care of it also.

Similar to 2 Sam 8:15–18 and 1 Chr 18:14–17, this text lists David's chief officers. (The three lists are compared below.)

1 Chronicles 18	*2 Samuel 8*	Antiquities *7.5.110*
Joab son of Zeruiah over the army	Joab, son of Zeruiah over the army	Joab general of his whole army
Jehoshaphat son of Ahilud recorder	Jehoshaphat son of Ahilud recorder	Jehoshaphat son of Ahilud recorder
Zadok son of Ahitub Abimelech son of Abiathar priests	Zadok son of Ahitub Ahimelech son of Abiathar priests	Zadok of the family of Phinehas together with Abiathar (a friend) high priest
Shavsha secretary	Seraiah secretary	Seisan scribe
Benaiah son of Jehoiada over the Cherethites and the Pelethites	Benaiah son of Jehoiada	Benaiah son of Jehoiada over the guards of his body
David's sons priests	David's sons chief officials in service of the king	David's elder sons had the care of his body

Notably at this point, Josephus fails to mention Ahitub and sets Zadok in the family of Phinehas;[24] Abiathar is clearly secondary, and Zadok and Abiathar are mentioned as high priests instead of priests as found in the Chronicles and Samuel texts. *Antiquities* 5.1.119 names Phinehas, son of Eleazar, as high priest upon the death of Eleazar.

23. As discussed earlier.

24. David Bernat, "Josephus's Portrayal of Phinehas," *JSP* 13 (2002): 137–49, suggests that Josephus remakes Phinehas over in his (Josephus') own image.

Josephus, Antiquities, *7.10.245, 249*

> *Ant.*: But now Ahimaaz, the son of *Zadok* the high priest, went to Joab, and desired he would permit him to go and tell David of this victory, and to bring him the good news that God had afforded his assistance and his providence to him…
>
> …but when the watchman saw Ahimaaz, and that he was already very near, he gave the king notice, that it was the son of *Zadok* the high priest, who came running. So David was very glad, and said he was a messenger of good tidings, and brought him some such news from the battle as he desired to hear.

Similar to the account in 2 Sam 18, and not found in Chronicles, this text mentions Ahimaaz as son of Zadok the high priest.[25]

Josephus, Antiquities, *7.11.292*

> So she prevailed with them, and they cut off the head of Sheba, and threw it into Joab's army. When this was done, the king's general sounded a retreat, and raised the siege. And when he was come to Jerusalem, he was again appointed to be general of all the people. The king also constituted Benaiah captain of the guards, and of the six hundred men. He also set Adoram over the tribute, and Sabathes and Achilaus over the records. He made Sheva the scribe; and appointed *Zadok* and Abiathar the high priests.

Similar to 2 Sam 20:23–26, this text names Zadok and Abiathar high priests, as opposed to priests in the Samuel account. This text does not mention Ira, the Jairite, who is named a priest of David in the Samuel account.

Josephus, Antiquities, *7.14.345–46*

> Now the fourth son of David was a beautiful young man, and tall, born to him of Haggith his wife. He was named Adonijah, and was in his disposition like to Absalom; and exalted himself as hoping to be king, and told his friends that he ought to take the government upon him… When his father saw this, he did not reprove him, nor restrain him from his purpose… Now Adonijah had for his assistants Joab, the captain of the army, and Abiathar, the high priest; and the only person that opposed him were *Zadok* the high priest, and the prophet Nathan, and Benaiah, who was the captain of the guards, and Shimei, David's friend, with all the other most mighty men…but had not invited to this feast either *Zadok* the high priest, or Nathan the prophet, or Benaiah, the captain of the guards, nor any of those of the contrary party.

25. Perhaps Josephus did not use Chronicles as his source after all. See the earlier discussion on biblical evidence for an examination of the Samuel text.

Bearing some similarity to material in 1 Kgs 1 and 2, this text again names Abiathar and Zadok as high priests, demonstrating Abiathar's allegiance to Adonijah and laying the foundation for the transference of the priesthood to Zadok seen in the next text.

Josephus, Antiquities, *8.1.9*

> So he [Solomon] called for Benaiah, the captain of the guards, and ordered him to slay his brother Adonijah; he also called for Abiathar, the priest, and said to him, "I will not put thee to death, because of those other hardships which thou hast endured with my father, and because of the ark which thou hast borne along with him; but I inflict this following punishment upon thee, because thou wast among Adonijah's followers, and wast of his party. Do not thou continue here, nor come any more into my sight..." For the forementioned cause, therefore, it was that the house of Ithamar was deprived of the sacerdotal dignity, as God had foretold to Eli the grandfather of Abiathar. So it was transferred to the family of Phinehas to *Zadok*. Now those that were of the family of Phinehas, but lived privately during the time that the high priesthood was transferred to the house of Ithamar (of which family Eli was the first that received it) were these that follow: Bukki, the son of Abishua the high priest; his son was Joathan; Joatham's son was Meraioth; Meraioth's son was Arophaeus; Arophaeus's son was Ahitub; and Ahitub's son was *Zadok*, who was first made high priest in the reign of David.

Thus this text provides a connection to ancestral traditions as well as an etiology for Zadok's priestly significance.

Josephus, Antiquities, *10.8.151*

> *Ant.* 10.8.151: And now, because we have enumerated the succession of the kings, and who they were, and how long they reigned, I think it necessary to set down the names of the high priests, and who they were that succeeded one another in the high priesthood under the kings. The first high priest then at the temple which Solomon built was *Zadok*; after him his son Achimas received that dignity; after Achimas was Azarias; his son was Joram, and Joram's son was Isus; after him was Axioramus; his son was Phideas, and Phideas's son was Sudeas, and Sudeas's son was Juelus, and Juelus's son was Jotham, and Jotham's son was Urias, and Urias's son was Merias, and Nerias's son was Odeas, and his son was Sallumus, and Sallumus's son was Elcias, and his son was Sareas, and his son was Josedec, who was carried captive to Babylon. All these received the high priesthood by succession, the sons from their father. When the king was come to Babylon, he kept Zedekiah in prison until he died, and buried him magnificently, and dedicated the vessels he had pillaged out of the temple of Jerusalem to his own gods, and planted the people in the country of Babylon, but freed the high priest from his bonds.

Josephus delineates the patronymic lineage of the high priesthood from the time of Solomon with Zadok as high priest to Josedec who was taken captive to Babylon.[26]

Josephus presents priesthood as it exists in his social milieu and projects into the past, even placing a high priest in the pre-monarchical period. Josephus presents the legitimate priesthood as stemming from the line of Phinehas. He makes some effort to establish Zadok in that line, probably because Zadok was well accepted in oral tradition as David's high priest. We gain little understanding of pre-exilic, exilic, or early postexilic priesthood from Josephus. Neither do we gain any understanding of a Zadokite priesthood except that we might ponder that Zadokites were not a dominant priesthood in the Hasmonean and Roman periods since they do not appear in Josephus' works.

Ben Sira

Although the Wisdom of Ben Sira was likely written during the early second century B.C.E., the hymnal section containing a reference to the Zadokites is almost certainly much later. It reads:

> Give thanks to YHWH, for he is good, for his mercy endures forever. Give thanks to the God of praises, for his mercy endures forever. Give thanks to the guardian of Israel, for his mercy endures forever. Give thanks to the one who formed all things, for his mercy endures forever. Give thanks to the redeemer of Israel, for his mercy endures forever. Give thanks to the one who gathers the dispersed of Israel, for his mercy endures forever. Give thanks to the one who rebuilt his city and his sanctuary, for his mercy endures forever. Give thanks to the one who makes a horn to sprout for the house of David, for his mercy endures forever. Give thanks to the one who has chosen the sons of *Zadok* to be priest, for his mercy endures forever. Give thanks to the shield of Abraham, for his mercy endures forever. Give thanks to the rock of Isaac, for his mercy endures forever. Give thanks to the mighty one of Jacob, for his mercy endures forever. Give thanks to the one who has chosen Zion, for his mercy endures forever. Give thanks to the king of the kings of king, for his mercy endures forever; He has raised up a horn for his people, let this be his praise for all his loyal ones; for the children of Israel, the people close to him. Praise YHWH. (Ben Sira 51:1–16)

Various scholars suggest the possibility that the hymn indeed might have been part of the original book and that it was subsequently removed by Ben Sira's grandson, who wrote the prologue, in case the hymn

26. For a discussion of Josephus and priestly lineage, see Stephen N. Mason, "Priesthood in Josephus and the 'Pharisaic Revolution,'" *JBL* 107 (1988): 657–61.

proved offensive to the non-Zadokite Hasmonean priests.[27] Several factors discount this possibility. Saul Olyan, in his 1987 article, "Ben Sira's Relationship to the Priesthood," correctly characterizes Ben Sira as intensely pro-priesthood and additionally pro-Aaronite. In honoring the priesthood, it is Aaron that he extols (45:6–22, 25); it is Aaron's grandson, Phinehas, who is further honored (45:23–24). He further convincingly notes the absence of Zadokite references throughout the work. For Olyan, "Zadok is conspicuously absent."[28] Olyan, like many others, assumes that the Oniads were Zadokite and that Zadokites controlled the priesthood until the time of the Hasmoneans.[29] Still, he correctly emphasizes the non-Zadokite nature of the Wisdom of Ben Sira.

Often thought to be modeled on Ps 136, this hymn of praise is only found in one of the six Hebrew manuscripts of Ben Sira. Scholars almost universally agree that the hymn is a later addition.[30] Di Lella convincingly

27. This is often used in dating Ben Sira; see Alexander A. Di Lella, *The Hebrew Text of Sirach: A Text-Critical and Historical Study* (Studies in Classical Literature 1; The Hague: Mouton, 1966), 277, for example, although Di Lella says it is more likely an addition from Qumran.

28. Olyan, "Ben Sira's Relationship to the Priesthood," 275. Olyan's suggestion of the non-Zadokite nature of Ben Sira's work stands in contrast to R. H. Lehmann, "Ben Sira and the Qumran Literature," *RevQ* 3 (1961): 103–16 (114).

29. Olyan, "Ben Sira's Relationship to the Priesthood," 267 n. 23, 270, 270 n. 31, 275–77. He, perhaps inadvertently, raises an interesting issue. In ch. 44, Ben Sira begins a litany of praise for famous ancestors. Near the beginning is Aaron: YHWH "made an everlasting covenant with him, and gave him the priesthood of the people" (NRSV Ben Sira 45:7a). Phinehas follows Aaron: "Phinehas son of Eleazar ranks third in glory for being zealous in the fear of the Lord, and standing firm, when the people turned away, in the noble courage of his soul; and he made atonement for Israel. Therefore a covenant of friendship was established with him, that he should be leader of the sanctuary and of his people, that he and his descendants should have the dignity of the priesthood forever. Just as a covenant was established with David son of Jesse of the tribe of Judah, that the king's heritage passes only from son to son, so the heritage of Aaron is for his descendants along" (NRSV Ben Sira 45:23–25). Most frequently, the story of Phinehas found in Num 25 is used to explain how *the* priesthood passed from the family of Eli to the Zadokites. Perhaps Num 25 speaks of the perpetual covenant of priesthood with Aaronites (into which Zadok was incorporated at a later period). I agree with Olyan (pp. 270–71 n. 31), that Ben Sira is asserting the (high) priesthood for the entire Phinehas line, he would have specified Zadokites, if he had meant Zadokites.

30. Pancratius C. Beentjes, ed., *The Book of Ben Sira in Modern Research: Proceedings of the First International Ben Sira Conference 28—31 July 1996 Soesterberg, Netherlands* (BZAW 255; Berlin: de Gruyter, 1997); Box and Oesterley, "The Book of Sirach"; Olyan, "Ben Sira's Relationship to the Priesthood"; Stefan C. Reif, "The Discovery of the Cambridge Genizah Fragments of Ben Sira: Scholars and Texts," in Beentjes, ed., *The Book of Ben Sira in Modern Research*, 1–22; Patrick

concludes that a copy of the Wisdom of Ben Sira, including the hymn of praise, was hidden in a cave near Jericho and subsequently found around 800 C.E. by Karaites. A copy of this book was found in the Cairo Synagogue Genizah. Di Lella suggests that this particular manuscript, labeled Manuscript B, is a Zadokite recension, placed in the Jericho cave by Qumranites of the Dead Sea Scroll fame. His idea is certainly plausible but questions remain. While no copy of this hymn has been found in the Qumran caves, a copy of the second appendix, 51:13–30, is part of the acrostic poem in 11QPs[a], *The Psalms Scroll of Qumran Cave 11*. Skehan and Di Lella further note that "Evidence for a Qumran origin of the psalm can be seen in the use of the phrase *lĕʾēl hattešbŏḥôt*, 'to the God of [our] praises' (51:12 ii); the reverse of that expression, *tešbŏḥôtʾēl*, 'the praises of God,' is found in one of the standards in the War Scroll (1QM iv 8)."[31] One would think that a copy of the "Zadokite" hymn would also be found in the Qumran caves. Still, the idea has merit. As will be discussed in the following Dead Sea Scrolls section, some group claiming Zadok functioned in the Qumran community for part of its history. This group could have easily placed a "Zadokite" copy of Ben Sira's book in a Jericho cave. Thus, we have available several texts formed in a "Zadokite trajectory":[32] Ezek 40–48 (as discussed in the previous chapter); Ben Sira 51:12 i–xvi; and references in the Dead Sea Scrolls (to be discussed below).

Dead Sea Scrolls

Introduction

The Dead Sea Scrolls, Qumran, and the Zadokites will be discussed contextually in the following chapter. Here the task is to examine the Dead Sea Scroll textual references to Zadok (as found in Damascus Document [hereafter CD] 5.5 and Copper Scroll) and sons of Zadok (as found in CD 3.21–4.3; 1QS/Rule of the Community 5.2, 9; 9.14; 1QS[a]/Rule of

W. Skehan and Alexander A. Di Lella, *The Wisdom of Ben Sira: A New Translation with Notes; Introduction and Commentary* (AB 39; New York: Doubleday, 1987); Stern, "Aspects of Jewish Society"; Benjamin G. Wright, "'Fear the Lord and Honor the Priest': Ben Sira as Defender of the Jerusalem Priesthood," in Beentjes, ed., *The Book of Ben Sira in Modern Research*, 189–222, but contra Lehmann, "Ben Sira and the Qumran Literature"; S. Schechter, "Introduction," in *The Wisdom of Ben Sira: Portions of the Book Ecclesiasticus from Hebrew Manuscripts in the Cairo Genizah Collection Presented to the University of Cambridge by the Editors* (ed. S. Schecther and C. Taylor; Cambridge: Cambridge University Press, 1899), 35.

31. Skehan and Di Lella, *The Wisdom of Ben Sira*, 569.
32. Olyan, "Ben Sira's Relationship to the Priesthood," 274.

the Congregation 1.2, 24; 2.3; 1QS^{b}/Rule of the Blessing 3.22; 4QFlor/Florilegium 1–3.1.17 and perhaps 4QIsaPesher^{c} 22.3).[33] For traditional understandings of Qumran, the Dead Sea Scrolls, and the Zadokites (as discussed in the following chapter), the sons of Zadok are mentioned relatively few times in the scroll collection. If indeed they founded the community, we would expect references to them in the Temple Scroll, the War Scroll, the *pesharim*, 4QMMT (the *halakhic* letter), and the descriptions of the new Jerusalem, to name just a few. The evidence does not support the notion that any Qumran community regarded itself as Zadokite.

References to Zadok
CD 5.1b–6a.

> And about the prince it is written, "He will not multiply wives for himself." But, David did not read the sealed book of the Torah which was in the ark, for it had not been opened in Israel since the day of the death of Eleazar and Joshua and the elders. They worshipped Ashtaroth and had hidden it until *Zadok* arose. So David's works were acceptable, except for Uriah's blood, and God forgave them for him.

Some suggest that the cited Zadok is the founder of the Qumran community.[34] Others see him as some historical priestly figure. Both Philip Davies and James VanderKam correctly note Zadok, the priest of David, as the most likely referent for the Zadok cited here and dispense with any suggestion that this Zadok is somehow the founder of the community.[35]

Copper Scroll 10.15–11.8.

> In the pond of the latrines of Siloam, underneath the water outlet: seventeen talents. In the four corners, gold and offering vessels. Nearby, under

33. The fragmentary nature of the Pesher Isaiah text prevents it from being useful to the discussion. References to בני צדק in 1QS 3.20, 22; 4Q502 Ritual of Marriage, and 4Q503 Daily Prayers may or may not be related to "sons of Zadok," if only as word-play; see Philip R. Davies, "Sons of Zadok," in Schiffman and VanderKam, eds., *Encyclopedia of the Dead Sea Scrolls*, 2:1005–7.

34. I. Leví, "Un écrit sadducéen antérieur à la destruction du temple," *REJ* 61–62 (1911): 180–85; P. Wernberg-Møller, "צדך, צדיך and צודך in the Zadokite Fragments (CDC), the Manual of Discipline (DSD) and the Habakkuk-Commentary (DSH)," *VT* 3 (1953): 310–15.

35. See Philip R. Davies, *Behind the Essenes: History and Ideology in the Dead Sea Scrolls* (BJS 94; Atlanta: Scholars Press, 1987), 55–56, and J. C. VanderKam, "Zadok and the SPR HTWRH HHTWM in Dam. Doc. V, 2–5," *Rev Q 44* (1984): 561–70, for a full discussion.

> the southern corner of the portico, in *Zadok*'s tomb, underneath the column of the covered hall, offering vessels of pine resin and offering of senna. Near there, in the (?) at the top of the rock facing towards the west, near *Zadok*'s garden, under the large slab which covers the water outlet: a special offering.

Milik suggests Zadok in the Copper Scroll makes reference to Zadok, priest of David, and offers little insight into a Qumran community.[36]

References to Sons of Zadok
CD 3.20–4.3.

> Those who remained steadfast will have eternal life, and all the human glory is theirs. As God set for them by the hands of Ezekiel the prophet, saying "The priests and the levites and the *sons of Zadok* who kept the watch of my sanctuary when the children of Israel strayed from me, they will offer the fat and the blood to me." The priests, they are the converts of Israel who left the land of Judah. The levites are those who went with them. The *sons of Zadok* are the chosen ones of Israel, those called by name, who stand in the end of days.

Even in CD, one of the documents delineating the internal and hierarchical structure of the group, we find the sons of Zadok only twice, both in midrash on Ezek 44:15:

> But the Levitical priests, the sons of *Zadok*, who kept the charge of my sanctuary when the people of Israel went astray from me, they will come near to me to minister to me and they will attend to me.

Note particularly the differences between the MT text and the quote cited in CD. While the ending does not substantially change the connotation of the material, the reference to "the priests and the levites and the sons of Zadok" raises ideological questions.[37] In this Dead Sea Scroll midrash, Zadokites are not the only priests, they stand with others in offering the fat and the blood.

As for the three groups found in this CD text—the priests, the Levites, and the sons of Zadok—Philip Davies suggests that these three categories, the converts of Israel who left the land of Judah, the Levites who joined them, and the sons of Zadok who are the chosen of Israel, might describe the history of the community in stages and concludes that the

36. M. Baillet, J. T. Milik, and R. de Vaux, *Les "Petites Grottes" de Qumran: Exploration de la falaise, les grottes 2q, 3q, 5q, 7q à 10q, le rouleau de cuivre* (DJD 3; Oxford: Clarendon, 1962), 214, 271.

37. See the discussion in Davies, *Behind the Essenes*, 53.

community cannot be "identified as 'sons of Zadok' any more than it can with 'levites,'" also present in the Ezekiel text and equally applied.[38]

1QS 5.1–10b.

> This is the rule for the men of the Community who give themselves to turn away from all evil and to hold steadfast in all he has commanded as being in compliance with his will. They should separate themselves from the congregation of the men of deceit, in order to constitute a Community with Torah and possessions, and answering to the authority of the *sons of Zadok*, the priests, who guard the covenant according to the multitude of the men of the Community, those who hold steadfastly in the covenant. By its authority, decisions shall be made by lot in everything involving the Torah, property, and judgment, to do together truth and humility, righteousness, justice, and compassionate love—behold walking properly in all their ways. No one should wander in the stubbornness of his heart in order to go astray following his heart and his eyes and the plan of his tendency. Instead he should circumcise in the Community the foreskin of his tendency and of his stiff neck. They should lay a foundation of truth for Israel, for the Community of the eternal covenant. They should atone for all who give themselves for holiness in Aaron and for the house of truth in Israel and for those who join together for the Community. In lawsuit and the judgment, they should proclaim as guilty all those who transgress the decree. These are the regulations of their ways according to all these statutes when they are gathered in the Community. Whoever enters the council of the Community enters the covenant of God in the presence of all who freely give themselves. He shall swear upon his soul a binding oath to return to the Torah of Moses according to all its statutes, with all his heart and with all his soul, according to all that has been revealed concerning it to the *sons of Zadok*, the priests who keep the covenant and seek his will and according to the multitude of the men of the covenant who give themselves to his truth and to walking according to his will.

In this text and the previous text, the "sons of Zadok" are not the only members of the community, the founding members of the community, or the sole authority within the community.[39] The "sons of Zadok" are the priests in the community.

38. Ibid., 54.

39. Note also in 1QS 9.7–11, "only the sons of Aaron shall rule in judgment." In other words, there the sons of Aaron hold sole authority. This understanding of authority at Qumran stands in contradiction to Liver, "The 'Sons of Zadok the Priest' in the Dead Sea Sect," and Geza Vermes, "The Leadership of the Qumran Community: Sons of Zadok–Priests–Congregation," in *Geschichte–Tradition–Reflexion: Festschrift für Martin Hengel zum 70. Geburtstag* (ed. Hubert Cancik, Hermann Lichtenberger, and Peter Schäfer; Tübingen: J. C. B. Mohr, 1996), 375–84.

1QS 9.12–16a.

> These are the statutes by which the master shall walk with every living being according to the ways of every period and the worth of each man: he shall do the will of God according to everything that has been revealed for every period. He shall learn all the understanding that has been gained according to the periods and the statute of the endtime. He shall separate and weigh the *sons of Zadok* according to their spirits. He shall keep hold of the chosen ones of the endtime according to his will, as he has commanded. And according to a man's spirit, judgment of him should be carried out. According to the purity of his hands, he may approach and according to the authority of his insights, he may draw near. And thus shall establish his love and his hatred.

Most scholars suggest this reference to "sons of Zadok" should be read "sons of righteousness" as a reference to all members of the community.[40] The parallel text in 4QS^{e} reads "sons of righteousness." Robert Kugler's analysis of the text concludes that there should be no emendation, that the text does read "sons of Zadok," and again demonstrates the various stages in the development of documents. He concurs with Sarianna Metso's suggestion that 1QS might never have served as a rulebook but instead as a history of the community for new initiates.[41]

1QS^{a} 1.1–5.

> And this is the rule of the congregation of Israel in the final days, when they gather in community to walk continuously in accordance with the regulation of the *sons of Zadok*, the priests, and the men of the covenant who have turned away from walking in the way of the people. These are the men of his counsel who have kept his covenant in the midst of wickedness to atone for the land. When they come, they shall assemble all those who enter, including children and women, and they shall read into their ears all the regulations of the covenant, and shall instruct them in all their judgments, so that they do not stray.

1QS^{a} 1.19–2.5a.

> And as the years of a man increase, according to his ability, they shall assign him duties in the service of the congregation. And every man who is mentally impaired shall not enter the lot to take a stand in the congregation of Israel to decide a dispute or judgment, or to perform a task of the congregation, or to go out in battle to subdue the nations. Rather, his family shall inscribe him in the register of the army, and he will do his

40. Davies, *Behind the Essenes*, 57–58.

41. Robert A. Kugler, "A Note on 1QS 9:14: The Sons of Righteousness or the Sons of Zadok?," *DSD* 3 (1996): 315–20.

> service in tasks to the extent of his ability. The sons of Levi shall each stay in his post, according to the authority of the sons of Aaron, to make all the congregation come in and go out, each one in his rank, at the hand of the chiefs of the clans of the congregation, as rulers, judges and officers, according to the number of all their armies, under the authority of the *sons of Zadok*, the priests and of all the chiefs of the clans of the congregation. And if there is a convocation of all the assembly for a judgment, or for the community council, or for a convocation of war, they shall sanctify themselves for three days, so that every one who comes is prepared for the council. These are the men who have been invited to the community council: all the sages of the congregation, the discerning ones and those of knowledge, those perfect of the way, and the men of valour, together with the chiefs of the tribes and all their judges and their officers, and the chiefs of thousands, the chiefs of hundreds, of fifties and of tens, and the levites, among the division of his service. These are the famous men, those invited for the appointed time, those who are gathered for the council of the Community in Israel before the *sons of Zadok*, the priests. But any man who is afflicted with impurities shall not enter into the assembly of God. And anyone who is defiled shall not be established in his office among the congregation.

While this text has sometimes been regarded as the only reference to "sons of Zadok" that gives them sole authority over the community, this cannot be substantiated by the text.[42] As in the other Dead Sea Scroll texts referring to authority, the sons of Aaron and Levites are also mentioned.

1QS^b 3.22–27.

> Words of blessing of the master to bless the *sons of Zadok*, the priests whom God chose to restore his covenant, forever to distribute all his judgments in the midst of his people, to instruct them in accordance with his commandment. They rose up in truth…and in righteousness watched over all his commandments and walked in accordance with what he choose. May the Lord bless you from his holy dwelling. May he set you as a perfected ornament in the midst of the holy ones. May he renew for you the covenant of eternal priesthood. May he grant you a place… May he judge all the noble ones by your works and from the flowing source of your lips, all the…people. May he give you as inheritance the first fruits… May he bless the counsel of all flesh by your hand.

42. Charlotte Hempel, "The Earthly Essene Nucleus of 1QSA," *DSD* 3 (1996): 253–69. Hempel argues that the original 1QS^a document did not contain 1.1–5; 2.11b–22 or the reference to Zadokites in 1.24. She suggests that these references reflect a later stage of redaction/development.

The text gives no reference to the sons of Zadok in relationship to authority and therefore yields no insight into the power structure within the community or the formation of the community.

4QFlorilegium (4Q174) 1.14–17.

> Midrash of "How blessed is the man who does not walk in the counsel of the wicked." Interpreted: this saying concerns those who turn aside from the way of the people, as it is written in the book of Isaiah the prophet concerning the last days: "And it came to pass that with a mighty hand he turned me aside from walking on the path of this people." And this refers to those about whom it is written in the book of Ezekiel the prophet that "they should not defile themselves any more with all their filth." This refers to the *sons of Zadok* and to the men of his council, those who seek justice eagerly, who will come after them to the council of the community.

Likewise, this text, a midrash on Ezek 44:10, has no relationship to the structure of the community. The translation of this text is the point of much discussion. Allegro translates it "they are the sons of Zadok and the men of their community...after them to the counsel of the community."[43] George Brooke translates it "they are the sons of Zadok and the men of their council who keep far from evil and after them...a community."[44] Geza Vermes translates it as "the Sons of Zadok who seek their own counsel and follow their own inclinations apart from the Council of the community."[45] This translation speaks for itself as a negative appraisal. No conclusion can be reached about the overall signification of this reference at present.

Priestly ideas play an important role at Qumran. כהן appears about 300 times in the Dead Sea Scrolls; הכהן הגדול is seen almost twenty times. בני צדוק appears relatively few times, as discussed above, while בני אהרון appear about thirty times and בני לוי appear almost 100 times. Priests in the Dead Sea Scrolls wielded authority, led worship, and community ceremonies, interpreted laws, served as judges, appeared as eschatological figures, and governed community property.[46]

43. John Allegro, *QUMRÂN CAVE 4: I (4Q158–4Q186)* (DJD 5; Oxford: Clarendon, 1968), 53–57 (54).

44. George J. Brooke, *Exegesis at Qumran: QFlorilegium in Its Jewish Context* (JSOTSup 29; Sheffield: JSOT Press, 1985), 83–129 (92–93).

45. Geza Vermes, *The Dead Sea Scrolls in English* (4th ed.; London: Penguin, 1995), 354.

46. For a complete discussion of these ideas, see Robert A. Kugler, "Priesthood at Qumran," in *The Dead Sea Scrolls after Fifty Years: A Comprehensive Assessment* (ed. Peter W. Flint and James C. VanderKam; Leiden: Brill, 1999), 93–116.

Analysis of the textual references to "sons of Zadok" leaves the conclusion that the "sons of Zadok" are not the only members of the community, neither are they the founding members of the community, or the sole authority within the community. Anything more that can be said must be based on evidence other than textual analysis.

Other Texts

Finally, if the Zadokites had been prominent in the Hellenistic period, they would likely appear in the literature of the period. With the exceptions noted above, the Zadokites are not mentioned. While absence of evidence cannot be equated with evidence of absence, the paucity of references is noteworthy. No mention is made in Hecataeus of Abdera of Zadokites, Aaronites, priestly dynasties, or high priesthood. First Enoch refers to Aaron but does not discuss priesthood and does not mention Zadokites. Tobit mentions the Aaronites but not the Zadokites. *Jubilees* mentions neither the Aaronites nor the Zadokites. First Maccabees name priests and makes some reference to Aaronites but never mentions Zadokites. Second Maccabees names priests but does not mention Zadokites. The Letter of (Pseudo-)Aristeas names priests but does not mention Zadokites. Judith refers to priests and to high priests by name but never mentions Zadokites. The New Testament refers to a number of priests, most notably, Aaron and Melchizedek but does not refer to Zadok or Zadokites.[47]

Summary of Extrabiblical Evidence

The references to Zadok in 1 Esdras bring us no closer to understanding the Zadokites than did the reference to Zadok in the Ezra 7:1–5 genealogical list. There is considerable discussion about whether the Ezra 7:1–5 list provides a historically credible list of high priests and about how this list relates to other lists of priests. We cannot detect any prominence for Zadokites in this list. The reference in 2 Esdras offers little more than that Ezra is named as a prophet instead of a priest.

As with all historians, Josephus presents a historical portrait based on available evidence interpreted through his own experience and context. Regarding the priestly lines, his concern is to establish firmly the line of Phinehas. Josephus does not mention the sons of Zadok or a Zadokite line. Seemingly we are faced with at least two choices: either Josephus

47. Grabbe, "Were the Pre-Maccabean High Priests 'Zadokites'?"

was unaware of any existence of a Zadokite line of priests or he wanted to diminish their importance and so excluded them. Since Zadokites are mentioned so infrequently elsewhere, it is reasonable to conclude that Josephus was unaware of a priestly line called the Zadokites. All in all, the works of Josephus give little help in a study of the Zadokites.

The mention of "sons of Zadok" in Ben Sira promotes ambivalence regarding the station of Zadokites during the time when the material was written. As the book focuses on and promotes priesthood, one would expect a prominent priesthood to be mentioned more than once. Perhaps, as found in the Ezra–Nehemiah material, the Aaronites were exalted, while the mention of Zadokites was secondary.

The Dead Sea Scrolls provide more references to the Zadokites than are available elsewhere and so it is here that we may find our first plausible setting for the prominence of a Zadokite priesthood. The final chapter will provide a socio-historical scenario for this historical possibility.

Chapter 7

ZADOKITES IN SOCIAL CONTEXT

Introduction

A Zadokite priesthood? Conventional scholarship acknowledges David had a priest named Zadok. Zadok was the father of an extensive priestly dynasty. He and his descendants controlled the centralized priesthood throughout biblical history. In fact, the Zadokites were *the high* priests for centuries; they continued through the monarchic period, the exile, the return, the restoration, and the Ptolemies and the Seleucids—they lasted until the Maccabees bought and assumed the high priesthood at which time the Zadokites retreated to Qumran and planned for the future.

There are, however, problems with this view. We do not have evidence of an institution of the priesthood in pre-exilic times. We do not have evidence of a Zadokite dynasty. We do not have evidence of an exilic Zadokite priesthood. We do not have evidence of a Zadokite priesthood in the early postexilic period. We have mention of sons of Zadok in a portion of Ezekiel that is particularly difficult to date. We have mention of Zadok in Ezra, Nehemiah, and Chronicles and have concluded that these references were inserted late to serve as tools of legitimation. We have mention of sons of Zadok in a portion of the Hebrew version of Ben Sira which is also difficult to date. We have mention of sons of Zadok in the Dead Sea Scroll literature, the insertion of which almost certainly comes well after the formation of any community at Khirbet Qumran. This chapter, then, examines the Zadokites of Qumran.

Historical Context of Understanding the Zadokites in Qumran

Schechter and the Cairo Genizah

Association of "Zadokite" with Qumran and the Dead Sea Scrolls was in many ways preordained by a discovery made about half a century before the initial Qumran findings. In 1896, Solomon Schechter collected fragments of certain medieval manuscripts from the genizah of the Ben Ezra

Synagogue in Old Cairo. He published these fragments in 1910 and called them *Fragments of a Zadokite Work*, basing his decision on the prominence of 'sons of Zadok' in the work and a linguistic association of צדוק with Sadducees.[1] He noticed the prominence of "sons of Zadok" in the work and made a linguistic association of צדוק with Sadducees. For Schechter, these Sadducees were a Jewish group which used a sun calendar and stood in opposition to rabbinical Judaism and were possibly the group mentioned by the Kararite Khirkisani, who referred to a group led by someone named Zadok.[2] This began an on-going discussion of the "sons of Zadok" as found in these fragments, an on-going discussion maintaining and even promoting the Zadokite label. Discovery of the Dead Sea Scrolls solidified the link. The "sons of Zadok" appeared in both Cairo Genizah fragments *and* Dead Sea Scrolls documents, sealing the eventual connection between the initial, Cairo Genizah label "Zadokite" and the Dead Sea Scrolls. A priestly theme along with dualistic notions readily found in the Dead Sea Scrolls sectarian documents only added fuel to the Zadokite association, contributing to the formation of an initial consensus establishing the Zadokites, disenfranchised by the Hasmoneans, as central figures in the formation of a Qumran community.

The Consensus: F. M. Cross

Frank Moore Cross in his 1969 article, "The Early History of the Qumran Community," builds on the work of many scholars to furnish a tantalizing summary that is somewhat representative of this consensus.[3] For Cross, two decades after the discovery of the Dead Sea Scrolls marked a mature and refined phase for Qumran studies. "Certain coherent patterns of fact and meaning have emerged" so that "the scrolls and the people of the scrolls can be placed within a broad historical framework with relative certitude."[4] Cross lays out his "broad historical framework" based on his analysis of archaeological data and artifacts, paleography, and literary studies. He constructs a picture of a large group forced by "powerful motivations" to withdraw into the "desolate environment" of a "wasteland" where their daily activities occurred in communal buildings before they retired for the night to surrounding caves.[5] For Cross, this could "only" have happened in the second half of the second century B.C.E.[6] He uses Josephus to dispense with the association of the inhabitants of

1. Schechter, *Documents of Jewish Sectaries*.
2. Ibid., ix–lxix, 1–20.
3. Cross, "The Early History of the Qumran Community."
4. Ibid., 63.
5. Ibid., 65.
6. Ibid., 65.

Qumran with any other group than the Essenes, fortifying his point with phrases like "There is no reason to belabor the point"; "...virtually decisive in view of the absence of strong counter arguments..."; "...establishes the identification, in my opinion, beyond cavil."[7]

While acknowledging three archaeological phases for Khirbet Qumran, Cross nevertheless conflates any stages of a community there in his literary analysis. The Essenes of Qumran were "a priestly party," led by a priest, a son of Zadok, standing in opposition to another priestly party headed by the Wicked Priest of Jerusalem. The struggle between these priestly groups that eventuated in the formation of this isolated community was based not on doctrine, but on deeper and long-lived socio-political struggles between families of high priests.

The Qumran group, "guided by a party of the ancient Zadokite priests," recognized the futility of re-establishing their "ancient authority in the theocracy of Jerusalem" and withdrew to their wasteland to regroup for the future. With this in mind, Cross has "no difficulty in discovering the general background" of this dire situation. Under the reign of Antiochus Epiphanes, the Zadokites lost control of the high priesthood to "the highest bidder." The ensuing chaos paved the way for the entrance of the Maccabees so that "in this fashion the ancient Zadokite house gave way to the lusty, if illegitimate, Hasmonean dynasty." For Cross, "Essene origins are to be discovered precisely in the struggle between these priestly houses and their adherents."[8]

Hence a general summary of the consensus theory: the Zadokites, long the dominant priesthood, were suddenly faced with the topsy-turvy hellenized world of the Hasmoneans. The controlling empire/overlords betrayed them. Fellow Judeans, corrupted by the world, sought power and bought the position—but not the status—of the priesthood from the empire. The temple, corrupted by the function of these impure priests in its sacred space, became polluted. The Zadokites along with other religious practitioners responded in a variety of ways. Most particularly, the Zadokites, angry and alienated, withdrew and formed a counter-culture community in isolation by the Dead Sea, preserving sacred documents and waiting for the restoration and re-sanctification of the temple.

Crisis with the Consensus: Davies and Baumgarten

Development of this consensus tradition and its trajectory over the last thirty years provides an interesting case study for historiography. As early as 1987, in a series of essays collected in *Behind the Essenes: History*

7. Ibid., 68.
8. Ibid., 72.

and Ideology in the Dead Sea Scrolls, Philip Davies acknowledges the beauty of "scholarly research" as a "communal effort" that refines questions and seeks to offer "a critically plausible account of the texts as relics of the past."[9] He warns that the "prevailing consensus" should re-examine assumptions, particularly regarding the sons of Zadok.[10] Albert Baumgarten, in his critical and unfortunately often ignored study, "Crisis in the Scrollery," calls it the "dying consensus."[11] This study will use the term "Assumed Consensus," because the consensus theory is often presupposed in studies of both the Dead Sea Scrolls and the Second Temple period. Philip Davies' 1992 article, "Prehistory of the Qumran Community," analyzes the historiographic methodology used to create the Assumed Consensus.[12] For Davies, "Hindsight confers a privilege which can too easily be abused, and too vigorous criticism [of the assumed consensus] is uncalled for... We need, however, to be frank about earlier mistakes and to learn not to repeat them." He calls on scholars not to rely so heavily on the harmonizing conclusions of literary criticism and to acknowledge "the extent to which the whole question of origins is now without consensus."[13]

The Assumed Consensus

The consensus theory grew out of the information available at its time and within its context. In a sense, it came out of first-wave settlement theories. Its acceptance and continued/continuing prominence is due in part to the circumstances surrounding the analysis and delayed publication of the scrolls. New questions and new interpretations were inevitable. Today, over thirty years later, we can name at least three presuppositions of this Assumed Consensus: the prominence and long-held dominance of a Zadokite priesthood; the ousting of this prominent and dominant Zadokite priesthood by non-Zadokite Hasmoneans; and

9. Davies, *Behind the Essenes*, 10, 13.

10. Philip R. Davies, "The Prehistory of the Qumran Community," in *The Dead Sea Scrolls: Forty Years of Research* (ed. Devorah Dimant and Uriel Rappaport; Leiden: Brill, 1992), 116–25.

11. Baumgarten, "Crisis in the Scrollery."

12. Davies, "The Prehistory of the Qumran Community." Hartmut Stegemann discusses many challenges to the consensus in his "The Qumran Essenes—Local Members of the Main Jewish Union in Late Second Temple Times," in *The Madrid Qumran Congress: Proceedings of the International Congress on the Dead Sea Scrolls, Madrid 18–21 March, 1991* (ed. Julio Trebolle Barrera and Luis Vegas Montaner; STDJ 11; Leiden: Brill, 1992), 1:83–166. In the end, he seeks to revise the Essene hypothesis, founded upon the Onaid = Zadokite assumption.

13. Ibid., 119.

the ousted Zadokite priesthood retreated and formed a community by the Dead Sea. Occasional questions have been raised regarding at least some of these presuppositions but they have not, for whatever reason, been effective in modifying the Assumed and Applied Consensus.

The presupposition regarding the prominence and long-held dominance of a Zadokite priesthood has been addressed in preceding chapters. That a Zadokite priesthood, or part of a Zadokite priesthood, was disenfranchised by the Hasmoneans and subsequently acted in hostile response to the non-Zadokite Hasmoneans is long-standing and certainly deserves attention in this forum. Legitimation was *the* key issue. Strategies of legitimation were continually at play. Where lineage had previously served as chief legitimizer, money and politics came to prominence. The sacred was displaced by economics and power. That the ensconcement of the Hasmoneans ousted the long-prominent Zadokites and transformed the heretofore religious office into a more political function reaches at least back to 1857 and Abraham Geiger.[14] This general view has been followed and further developed by many, in both Dead Sea Scroll and Second Temple studies, including de Vaux, Vermes, Hauer, Milik, Schiffman, and Stegemann.[15] Challenges to this notion of "radical opposition to the Hasmoneans" have been present but rarely heeded in scholarship. As early as 1967, Joseph Liver finds no evidence for a conflict between the Hasmoneans and the Zadokites as a direct cause prompting the development of the Qumran settlement.[16] In 1992, 4Q448 was published by

14. Abraham Geiger, *Urlchrift und Uebersetzungen der Bibel in Ihrer Abhängigkeit von der Innern Entwickelung des Judenthums* (Breslau: Julius Hainauer, 1857).

15. De Vaux, *Ancient Israel*, 397–405; Lawrence H. Schiffman, *Reclaiming the Dead Sea Scrolls: Their True Meaning for Judaism and Christianity* (New York: Doubleday, 1994), 83–126 (87). For Schiffman, the Sadducees designated themselves as 'sons of Zadok' when they formed the Qumran community out of disappointment at the outcome of the Maccabean situation which removed the Zadokite priestly line; see his "The New Halakhic Letter (4QMMT) and the Origins of the Dead Sea Sect," *BA* 52 (1990): 64–73; Christian E. Hauer, Jr., "The Priests of Qumran" (Ph.D. diss., Vanderbilt University, 1959); Geza Vermes, *Discovery in the Judean Desert* (New York: Desclee, 1956), 74; J. T. Milik, *Ten Years of Discovery in the Wilderness of Judaea* (SBT 26; London: SCM Press, 1959), 44–98; D. R. Schwartz, "On Two Aspects of a Priestly View of Descent at Qumran," in *Archaeology and History in the Dead Sea Scrolls: The New York University Conference in Memory of Yigael Yadin* (JSPSup 8; JSOT/ASOR Monographs 2; Sheffield: JSOT Press, 1990), 157–79. Thanks to Magen Broshi for his kindness and for many hours of discussions about Qumran and the scrolls.

16. Liver, "The 'Sons of Zadok the Priest' in the Dead Sea Sect," 27–30. Also see Timothy H. Lim, "The Wicked Priests of the Groningen Hypothesis," *JBL* 112 (1993): 415–25.

Esther Eshel, Hanan Eshel, and Ada Yardeni, "A Qumran Composition Containing Part of Psalms 154 and a Prayer for the Welfare of King Jonathan and His Kingdom."[17] As others have asked before, why would a community formed in opposition to the Hellenistic Hasmoneans keep a prayer for the welfare of Jonathan with their (authoritative) literature?[18] The semicursive script of the text is difficult to read, allowing for numerous readings and interpretations—often harmonized with the Assumed Consensus. Harrington and Strugnell suggest the prayer is, in actuality, a curse.[19] Eshel, Eshel, and Yardeni are sure the fragment demonstrates Hasmonean propaganda. Other explanations suggest the Qumranites could not read the difficult text and therefore did not realize that it praised a hated Hasmonean or that they so loved the psalm at the end of the document that they kept it. If praise of a Hasmonean were the only serious challenge to the Assumed Consensus tradition, these explanations might be useful. Still, we should recognize that there was more ambiguity about the Hasmoneans, even within the scrolls, than the Assumed Consensus allows.

Perhaps the presupposition of the Assumed Consensus most requiring (re)visitation concerns the idea that a disenfranchised Zadokite priesthood initially formed a Qumran community in response to circumstances at the temple in Jerusalem.[20] Interesting from a historiographical point of view, even before the information that is available today, some scholars raised relevant questions. In 1967 Liver and in 1987 Davies questioned whether Zadokites were even involved in the creation of this wasteland hideaway. In addition to adding fuel to the notion of "radical opposition to the Hasmoneans" issue, the publication of 4QMMT raised several questions about the impetus for the formation of a Qumran community.[21] Most scholars see this letter as foundational for the formation of

17. Esther Eshel, Hanan Eshel, and Ada Yardeni, "A Qumran Composition Containing Part of Ps. 154 and a Prayer for the Welfare of King Jonathan and His Kingdom," *IEJ* 42 (1992): 192–229.

18. Baumgarten, "Crisis in the Scrollery," notes that not only should the Zadokites be prominent in the letter (4QMMT), opposition to the Hasmoneans should be apparent, and yet the last section of the letter seems to indicate the letter may have been written *to* a Hasmonean leader by someone who held that leader in favour; see pp. 404–5 n. 27.

19. Daniel J. Harrington and John Strugnell, "Qumran Cave 4 Texts: A New Publication," *JBL* 112 (1993): 491–99.

20. The appropriateness of "Qumran community" is questioned by some.

21. Baumgarten, "Crisis in the Scrollery," 404–5 n. 27. Not only should the Zadokites be prominent in the letter, opposition to the Hasmoneans should be apparent, and yet the last section of the letter seems to indicate that the letter may have been written to a Hasmonean leader by someone who held that leader in favor.

a Qumran community and date the work to an early period in the community's history.[22] Naming differences, particularly the legal differences, between the community and the *status quo*, the letter calls for a change of behavior on the part of the opposition. Elisha Qimron and John Strugnell, publishing the document in 1994 after years of delay, noted the absence of the "sons of Zadok" in the document—an absence which, coming from such a basic document, raises the question of a viable role for Zadokites as the impetus for the formation of a Dead Sea Scroll sect.[23] Perhaps insufficient in and of itself to draw conclusions about the Zadokites, 4QMMT provides another piece to the puzzle, stimulating concerns about the Assumed Consensus.

Geza Vermes' publication of fragments in 1991 provided the final whisper that started an avalanche onto the Assumed Consensus concept. Even when Vermes initially brought to light the fragments found in cave 4 of *Serek Ha-Yahad*, scholars seemed to avoid engagement with the consequential issues.[24] Vermes offered "Preliminary Remarks on Unpublished Fragments of the Community Rule from Qumran Cave 4," commenting on the absence of references to the sons of Zadok in key portions referring to the establishment of the community as seen in *Serek Ha-Yahad*.[25] Where 1QS column 5 begins with "As this is the rule for the men of the community"—the parallel fragments in 4QS^b and ^{d} begin with: "Teaching for the master concerning the men of the Law." Of particular interest, from line 2, 1QS states,

> They shall separate from the congregation of the men of falsehood and shall unite with respect to the Torah and possessions, and they shall be under the authority of the sons of Zadok, the priests, who keep the Covenant, and of the multitude of the men of the Community, who hold fast to the Covenant. Every decision shall be determined by them concerning all matters of Torah, property and justice. They shall practice truth in common and humility.

The parallel fragments 4QS^b and ^{d} from cave 4 produce:

> And they shall separate from the congregation of the men of falsehood and shall unite with respect to the Torah and possessions, and they shall be under the authority of the Congregation concerning all matters of Torah and property. They shall practice humility… [Vermes]

22. Ibid., 404; see also Schiffman, "The New Halakhic Letter," 64, and *Reclaiming the Dead Sea Scrolls*, 87–95.

23. Elisha Qimron and John Strugnell, *Qumran Cave 4: V: Miqṣat Maᶜaśe ha-Torah* (DJD 10; Oxford: Clarendon, 1994), 113.

24. Baumgarten, "Crisis in the Scrollery," 412 n. 21.

25. Geza Vermes, "Preliminary Remarks on Unpublished Fragments of the Community Rule From Qumran Cave 4," *JJS* 42 (1991): 250–55.

And a few lines down, when talking about new entrants into the community, 1QS reads:

> Whoever approaches the council of the men of the community will undertake by a binding oath to return with all his heart and soul to every commandment of the Law of Moses, in accordance with all revealed of it to the sons of Zadok, the keepers of the covenant and seekers of His will, and to the multitude of the men of their covenant who together have pledged themselves to His truth. (1QS 5.7–10)

Alternatively, 4QS[b] and [d] both have the entrant swearing an oath "to return to the Torah of Moses with all heart and all soul, to everything revealed from the Torah to the multitude of the council of the men of the Community and to separate from all the men of deceit." The Cave 4 fragments have no reference to the sons of Zadok.

Sarianna Metso completed a comprehensive study of the textual tradition of *Serek Ha-Yahad*.[26] Her extensive and careful study clearly establishes 4QS[b] and 4QS[d] as products of an early stage in the recensional history of the document, confirming the early suspicions of Milik and Vermes.[27] She correctly raises questions about the role of the document in the community. Her literary- and redaction-critical analyses offer several conclusions, although she cautions against "linking a particular practice with an actual historical period of time."[28]

Although tentative due to the delay in the appearance of yet to be published texts, Metso posits ideas about the *sitz im leben* of *Serek Ha-Yahad*. She correctly raises questions about the role of the document in the community. Her literary and redaction-critical analyses offer several

26. Sarianna Metso, *The Textual Development of the Qumran Community Rule* (STDJ 21; Leiden: Brill, 1996).

27. J. T. Milik, "Numérotation des feuilles des rouleaux dans le scriptorium de Qumran (Planches X et XI)," *Semeia* 27 (1977): 75–81; Vermes, "Preliminary Remarks."

28. Sarianna Metso, "In Search of the *Sitz Im Leben* of the *Community Rule*," in *The Provo International Conference on the Dead Sea Scrolls: Technological Innovations, New Texts, and Reformulated Issues* (ed. Donald W. Parry and Eugene Ulrich; STDJ 30; Leiden: Brill, 1999), 306–15 (309). Also, thanks to several comments by Philip Davies, we should note that we cannot draw conclusions about community practice based on a document because "the" community maintained several copies at one time. Davies further notes that we see only some elements of "historical reality" in this "literary tradition of utopianism"; see Philip R. Davies, "Redaction and Sectarianism in the Qumran Scrolls," in *The Scriptures and the Scrolls: Studies in Honour of A. S. Van Der Woude on the Occasion of His 65th Birthday* (ed. F. García Martínez, A. Hilhorst, and C. J. Labuschagne; Leiden: Brill, 1992), 152–63 (157–60).

conclusions although she cautions against "linking a particular practice with an actual historical period of time."[29]

Metso concludes that redaction of the document reflects changes in the "life and practices of the community."[30] For Metso, the addition of phrases and words demonstrates an effort to infuse the community with enthusiasm for its self-understanding. She notes that מבקר (community official in 1QS and CD, not in 1QDS[a]) and פקיד (a title unique in 1QS, פקד in CD) do not occur in 1QS 1–4 and that at one stage of redaction, הרבים is replaced by a reference to the sons of Zadok and the men of the community. Instead of 1QS 5.9–10's sons of Zadok and men of the congregation, 4QS[b, d] have עצה אנשי היחד. Metso assumes a "theological" reason for the change from "council of the men of the community" to "sons of Zadok, the keepers of the covenant and seekers of His will" since these particular texts focus on the "duty of the priests and the men of the community to keep the covenant and point out the Zadokite lineage of the leaders of the community."[31] She suggests care should be taken in interpreting these, as well as other, texts from the period, referring to the concise conclusions of J. M. Baumgarten and Jacob Weingreen stating such texts provide primarily information about circulation and transmission.[32] She cautions against VanderKam's notion that *Serek Ha-Yahad* provides a "constitution for the Qumran Community."[33] Metso concludes that the Zadokites became actors in the texts only at a later date, well after the initial formation of a community, and had a 'restricted' range. Zadokite priests did not establish, form, or create the Qumran community. For such actors, we must look elsewhere. Some Zadokite group, however, was involved at some point in the community's history.

If, as is apparent, we cannot maintain some of the underlying assumptions of the Assumed Consensus, how might we locate a "Zadokite" "priesthood" in the socio-historical context of ancient Israel—particularly in the Second Temple period. There must have been a group of people functioning as part of the social, religious, and political milieu of the Hellenistic period who referred to themselves as sons of Zadok. If they were functioning in the sectarian environment of the late Hellenistic

29. Metso, "In Search of the *Sitz Im Leben* of the *Community Rule*," 308, 310.

30. Ibid., 310.

31. Ibid., 312 n. 14. She also makes a disclaimer—noting methodologically—"we cannot postulate a separate group whenever discrepancies occur between thematically parallel passages."

32. Ibid., 313; Joseph M. Baumgarten, "The Unwritten Law in the Pre-Rabbinic Period," *JSJ* 72 (1972): 7–29; Jacob Weingreen, *From Bible to Mishna: The Continuity of Tradition* (Manchester: Manchester University Press, 1976), 76–99.

33. VanderKam, *The Dead Sea Scrolls Today*, 57.

period as evidenced by their inclusion in the third recensional stage of 1QS, what else, if anything, can be said about the Zadokites? Given the paucity of primary source material, we must turn to other means for determining their socio-historical context, one of the positive results of interest in social-scientific studies.

If we use the insertion in the third stage of the Dead Sea Scrolls documents as the *terminus a quo* for the existence of a group designated Zadokites, we can assume this group functioned after the assumption of the Hasmoneans.

Chapter 8

CONCLUSIONS: STARTING TO PLACE THE ZADOKITES

Social-Scientific Portrait: A New Starting Point

The Socio-Politico-Religious Setting: Sectarianism

Today almost no one disputes the religious pluralism of the Judean Hellenistic period.[1] Over a decade ago, prominent scholars (such as Gabriel Boccaccini and Lawrence Schiffman) acknowledged the flourishing of traditions that would later become known as Judaisms. While some scholarship argues that the restoration in the Persian period and the following century invited sectarianism, other scholars (such as Shaye Cohen and Albert Baumgarten) see that earlier period as setting the stage for sectarianism—a period of "proto-sectarianism" from whence came such works as *Jubilees* and 1 Enoch. By contrast, from the mid-second century B.C.E. until the destruction of the temple, we see a time of prominence for sectarian notions—a time when the seedlings of dissent planted earlier reached full maturity. Baumgarten argues, somewhat effectively,

1. Albert I. Baumgarten, *The Flourishing of Jewish Sects in the Maccabean Era: An Interpretation* (JSJSup 55; Leiden: Brill, 1997). He defines a sect "as a voluntary association of protest, which utilizes boundary marking mechanisms—the social means of differentiating between insiders and outsiders—to distinguish between its own members and those otherwise normally regarded as belonging to the same national or religious entity" (p. 7). (Baumgarten concludes from his research that there were apparently not many terms available to groups of the period so that self-appellations of various groups often overlapped [pp. 141–46].) Baumgarten emphasizes voluntary association, while S. J. D. Cohen (*From the Maccabees to the Mishnah* [Philadelphia: Westminster, 1987], 125) stresses absolute truth claim in appropriate understanding of God's will. For Cohen, law, temple and scripture serve as the focal points for sectarian dissent (pp. 128–35). Baumgarten notes, following J. Katz ("In Clarification of the Term 'Forerunners of Zionism,'" in *Jewish Emancipation and Self-Emancipation* [Philadelphia: The Jewish Publication Society of America, 1986], 104–15), that, for the existence of sectarianism, "there must be more than one group" and "at least one group must have taken its own position seriously enough to secede from the mainline institutions."

that the Maccabean period provided fertile ground for the flourishing of sectarian groups. Traditional scholarship places full-fledged sectarianism as the outcome of experiences from the mid-fifth century B.C.E.[2] Baumgarten argues that, prior to this period, conditions were not ripe for the full maturity of the seedlings of dissent.[3] Other literature portraying a period foretelling a fully sectarian environment includes early portions of 1 Enoch, the book of *Jubilees* (both of which Baumgarten sees as being written in response to the encroachment of Hellenism) and early parts of CD, which portrays members seeing themselves as not "properly fulfilling the law but still seeing the 'right path.'"[4] Fully mature sectarianism required "one further transformation" and that took place during the "rapid social change" which coincided with the ascension of the Maccabees and included (1) encounters with Hellenism; (2) persecutions of Antiochus IV which changed "the terms of close to four hundred years of

2. Baumgarten notes the work of Joseph Blenkinsopp, "A Jewish Sect of the Persian Period," *CBQ* 52 (1990): 5–20; Hanson, *The Dawn of Apocalyptic*; and A. Rofé, "The Beginnings of Sects in Post-Exilic Judaism," *Cathedra* 49 (1988): 13–22. Also see Shemaryahu Talmon, "The Internal Diversification of Judaism in the Early Second Temple Period," in *Jewish Civilization in the Hellenistic-Roman Period* (ed. S. Talmon; Philadelphia: Trinity, 1991), 16–43, and idem, "The Emergence of Jewish Sectarianism in the Early Second Temple Period," in Miller, Hanson, and McBride, eds., *Ancient Israelite Religion*, 587–616. Blenkinsopp ("A Jewish Sect of the Persian Period," 20) argues, but not so convincingly, for a late emergence of mature sectarianism (not convincingly because he uses historicity of Ezra–Nehemiah and Josephus). More convincing is his focus on the flourishing of a community at Qumran as evidenced by archaeological evidence. He places a fully flourishing sect there during the time of Janneus. (He also acknowledges that there must have been a long pre-history to the development of this group [p. 21].)

So the roots came from elsewhere: the Groningen Hypothesis sets them in third century B.C.E. (F. García Martínez and J. Trebolle Barrera, *The People of the Dead Sea Scrolls* [trans. W. G. E. Watson; Leiden: Brill, 1995]; F. García Martínez and A. S. van der Woude, "A Groningen Hypothesis of the Qumran Origins and Early History," *RevQ* 14 [1990]: 521–41), while P. R. Davies sets them in Babylon (see his *Sects and Scrolls: Essays on Qumran and Related Topics* [South Florida Studies in the History of Judaism 134; Atlanta: Scholars Press, 1996]; "The Prehistory of the Qumran Community"; *Behind the Essenes*).

3. Baumgarten, *The Flourishing of Jewish Sects in the Maccabean Era*, 25. Cohen (*From the Maccabees to the Mishnah*, 137) names the earlier period a time of "Proto-sectarianism." Where Baumgarten says sectarianism was in full maturity in the Hasmonean period, Cohen says it was the "Heyday of Jewish sectarianism" which he dates from the mid-second century B.C.E. to the destruction of the temple in 70 C.E. For Baumgarten, the conditions that allowed for this flourishing at this time provoke a "significant historical question, worthy of extended consideration" (p. 19).

4. Baumgarten, *The Flourishing of Jewish Sects in the Maccabean Era*, 25.

control of Jews and Judaism by different world empires"; (3) "the cooperation of at least some of the traditions leaders with those persecutions"; (4) the successful revolt against Antiochus IV and his decrees; and (5) the rise of a new dynasty [*sic*] of high priests, soon to be followed by (6) the achievement of political independence.[5] Given these characteristics, the most prominent sectarians during this period, then, were the Sadducees, Pharisees, Essenes, Qumran, Fourth Philosophy, and followers of John the Baptist or Bannus.[6] The Hasmonean period provided fertile ground for the full flourishing of sectarian groups. Factors promoting this included: rapid social change; the persecutions of Antiochus IV; the complicity of some religious and/or political leaders in the persecutions; a successful revolt against the Seleucid overlords; the installation of the new rulers as the priests; and a new state of political independence.

The socio-politico-religious issues of the day included calendar, synagogue, apocalypticism, law, sabbath, temple, and land.[7] This portrait assumes the existence of numerous sectarian groups and further assumes the sects were in full and ripe bloom during the second and first centuries B.C.E. Where can and do Zadokites fit into this picture? It was in this socio-political and religious milieu that we find the sons of Zadok as one of several groups struggling with religious identity. By definition, the sectarians acted in response to the contemporary *status quo*. Evidence shows a group calling themselves Zadokites existed around this time. Ancient texts show at least some self-proclaimed Zadokites stood outside the mainstream.[8] The Dead Sea Scrolls reveal at least some were connected to Qumran.

5. Ibid., 26.
6. Ibid., 11.
7. Grabbe, *Judaism from Cyrus to Hadrian*, 1:309–10; Cohen, *From the Maccabees to the Mishnah*; Talmon, "The Internal Diversification of Judaism," and idem, "The Emergence of Jewish Sectarianism."
8. Early scholarship considered the Zadokites the precursors of the Sadducees. A story from *ʾAbot R. Nat.* A.5 derives "Sadducees" from Zadok of Antigonus of Soco, of the second century B.C.E. M. Mansoor ("Sadducees," *EncJud* 14:620–22), associates Sadducees with "anyone who is a sympathizer with the Zadokites." Schiffman (*Reclaiming the Dead Sea Scrolls*) still advocates the older association based on his analysis of 4QMMT, but the idea has since been discredited in most circles, mostly on ideological grounds. The association no longer holds for most scholars today. For more information, see James C. VanderKam, "The People of the Dead Sea Scrolls: Essenes or Sadducees?," *BR* (April 1991): 42–47; Daniel R. Schwartz, "Law and Truth: On Qumran-Sadducean and Rabbinic Views of Law," in Dimant and Rappaport, eds., *The Dead Sea Scrolls*, 229–40.

The association between Zadok and Sadducees is predicated on the dominance of the Zadokites, particularly through the majority of the Second Temple period. Also

A Social-Scientific Approach: Lenski's Macro-Sociological Model

Sociological modeling provides us a certain access to that ancient world.[9] For quite some time, Gerhard Lenski, in his comparative studies of human societies, has been working to synthesize the best of functional and conflict theories in an effort to answer the question: Who gets what and why? He develops a descriptive framework which allows us to approach the historical context and to create a plausible scenario for our Zadokites.

necessary for that contention is that the Oniads were Zadokites. In light of this study, both concepts are problematic.

9. Questions have been raised concerning the viability of socio-scientific criticism and modeling for historical reconstruction of ancient worlds. George Mendenhall's essay, "The Hebrew Conquest of Palestine," *BA* 25 (1962): 66–87, set the sociological wheels in motion. Mendenhall states, "This paper represents a conscious attempt to substitute a quite different 'ideal model' for that which has so long been held; the purpose of hypothesis is not to give dogmatic answers to historical problems, but rather to suggest further fruitful lines of inquiry, and to suggest relationships between seemingly unrelated bits of information" (pp. 66–67).

Then in 1988, Halpern (*The First Historians*, 5), a scholar who often, and in this context ironically, makes use of socio-scientific studies denounced sociological modeling, proposing that these models "call on models extrinsic not just to the text, but to the culture as a whole. They apply universal, unhistorical schematics, like those of the natural sciences, yet deal, like the human sciences, in variables (e.g. forms of society) whose components, whose atoms, are never isolated. Such tools cannot usher in a revolution in historical certainty. Their promise, like that of the positivist program of the nineteenth century, is an eschatological one."

While Halpern's comments could equally apply to most methodological approaches in writing history and while socio-scientific methodology *can* be misused, investigation of historical periods via sociological models offers a means of broadening the historical portrait. As Frank S. Frick ("'Second Wave' Social-Scientific Criticism," in *Tracking "The Tribes of Yahweh": On the Trail of a Classic* [ed. Roland Boer; JSOTSup 351; Sheffield: Sheffield Academic Press, 2001], 17–34), states, "Socially informed studies, however, have alerted us to other issues such as differences in the social locations not only between ourselves and our ancient Israelite sisters and brothers, but also within ancient Israel itself" (pp. 32–33). Lester Grabbe says it well in his article, "Sup-urbs or Only Hyp-urbs? Prophets and Populations in Ancient Israel and Socio-Historical Method," in *"Every City Shall be Forsaken": Urbanism and Prophecy in Ancient Israel and the Near East* (ed. Lester L. Grabbe and Robert D. Haak; JSOTSup 330; Sheffield: Sheffield Academic Press, 2001), 95–123, "Social theories are simply analogies based on one or more cultures. They are not 'facts' that can then be taken as givens by biblical scholars. They are interpretations and, like the usual suspects, to be rounded up and given the third degree—to be subjected to a bit of the rubber hose just to test their metal. They are, in short, simply ways of interrogating the textual or other data. They are templates of interpretation, not tablets from Sinai" (p. 121).

Lenski, in *Power and Privilege: A Theory of Social Stratification*, offers sociological models for hunting and gathering, horticultural, agrarian, and industrial societies.[10] This study applies his model of agrarian states to Hasmonean Judea in an effort to examine the social- scientific context of the Zadokites during that time. Lenski operates on several assumptions. People are social beings; they live as members of society and are shaped by that society. Further, people tend to act habitually; this defines customs. Most actions are motivated by self-interest. Most objects are in short supply. Groups of people relate on an intra- and inter-group basis. Members of groups will almost always choose their own interests, or that of their group, over the interests of others.

Power serves as the foundational variable within the system. Privilege is primarily a function of power. Similarly, prestige is largely a function of power and privilege. Lenski posits that any given political regime goes through an observable cycle which begins with the forcible seizure of power, typically by violent means whereby organized resistance is destroyed or suppressed.[11] While force enables the seizing of power, as time passes, it becomes obvious that force is not the most effective means of retaining and exploiting power; it is inefficient and costly (and without honor—which is a basic human value). As Gaetano Mosca states, "Ruling classes do not justify their power exclusively by de facto possession of it, but try to find a moral and legal basis for it, representing it as the logical and necessary consequence of doctrines and beliefs that are generally recognized and accepted."[12] Therefore a need increases to reduce the use of force and to solidify power (and privilege and prestige) through techniques of legitimization which will institutionalize the power. A shift ensues from the "rule of might" to "the rule of right." Of course, this rule of right may be halted or reversed if those in power are challenged severely—as it affects their image of invincibility. When having

10. A strength of Lenski's macrosociological approach, providing generalized models, is simultaneously a weakness in his approach. Thus, not every aspect of any model is equally applicable across specific settings. Mein (*Ezekiel and the Ethics of Exile*, p. 27) raises a pertinent question about using Lenski's theoretical model: "However, we must question whether this is really enough to explain the complex society of ancient Israel." As I have suggested elsewhere, application of this model enhances the historical portrait rather than offering a complete portrait.

11. "Political regime" is defined as "members of a particular political elite who come to power by force and to all their successors who come to power by legitimate means. Thus, a regime governs from the time of its victory in one revolution until its defeat or overthrow in a subsequent war or revolution" (Lenski, *Power and Privilege*, 59).

12. Gaetano Mosca, *The Ruling Class* (trans. Hannah Kahn; New York: McGraw–Hill, 1939), 70.

internal difficulties, those in power may subordinate their challengers through successes in war and the annexation of foreign territories. Subsequent distribution of booty often quiets those most able to protest. Those in power may seek legitimization in a variety of ways—most of which use or reshape societal institutions. Those in power may seek legitimization by rewriting the law of the land.[13] They may also cultivate legitimization by the use and reshaping of societal institutions which in turn shape public opinions. Inducements, threats, and manipulation of educational and religious institutions utilized through coercion and consensus serve as instruments for propaganda and create an aura of legitimacy.[14] To attain legitimacy, the seeker must, in some degree, be in accord with commonly accepted notions of justice and morality. In the shift from the rule of might to the rule by institutions, power typically becomes more impersonal and is distinguished by authority and influence. The more the legitimization or institutionalization of power, the less dependent the maintenance of power is on the occupant and the more dependent the maintenance of power is on the role of the one(s) in power. The effectiveness of attempts at legitimization are dependent on (1) the length of the cycle, (2) the ideology behind the seizure of power, (3) the existence of a previous system of legitimization, (4) the number of threats against the regime, (5) the level of productivity, and (6) economic trends during the legitimization period. Note that, after a shift to the rule of right, the interests of one member of society may not safely equate with the interests of those in power. Those who achieved the initial power by means of force eventually will be replaced by others who will form a similar but new form of the powerful (elite). Vilfredo Pareto names this the passing of power from lions to foxes.[15] This shift requires new skills and is sometimes the cause of subsequent upheaval because the individuals in question are vulnerable. Concurrently, as rule of right (institutionalized) power becomes the norm, a decentralization of

13. Lenski's model has been used to address issues in various periods. Douglas A. Knight ("Whose Agony? Whose Ecstasy? The Politics of Deuteronomic Law," in *Shall Not the Judge of All the Earth Do What is Right? Studies on the Nature of God in Tribute to James L. Crenshaw* [ed. David Penchansky and Paul L. Redditt; Winona Lake, Ind.:, Eisenbrauns, 2000], 97–112) uses Lenski's model for agrarian societies to place the documentation of Deuteronomic Law as ideological, established in the economic and political self-interest of powerful, elite members of Persian-period Yehud. For this study, Lenski's model serves well to enhance our understanding of the socio-historical context.

14. The notion of propaganda provides an example of the fruitful nature of combining functional and conflict-oriented approaches.

15. Vilredo Pareto, *The Mind and Society* (trans. A. Bongiorno and Arthur Livingstone; New York: Harcourt, Brace & World, 1935).

power typically occurs, allowing diverse centers of power to develop. Reactions of those not-in-power include (1) competition to serve those in power, (2) a struggle for survival among the offspring of the masses, (3) petty thievery, (4) efforts of middle classes to gain control over power, privileges, and resources of those in power, (5) crimes of violence against those in power, and (6) interaction with religious leaders that may have some measure of influence over political ideologies. Most often these factors work toward eventual legitimation and institutionalization of power. Legitimization, and its consequent maintenance of power, however, may be halted or even reversed if the power of the elite is severely and consistently challenged. The cycle begins again sooner or later when power is seized forcibly by another regime.

The Model on Hasmonean Judea

Hasmonean Judea readily fits into Lenski's model of an agrarian state. Hasmonean Judea was a monarchical conquest state—that is, it was formed as a consequence of one group of people's conquest of another group. In this case, it was formed through a conquest by an external empire and then reformed by a revolt from within. So, in Lenski's terms, it was a monarchical conquest state with productive potential that allowed for the collection of taxes. The Hasmonean legacy left evidence of the substantial growth of the power of the state and control over sizable (and often increasing) territory.[16] Warfare, as a "chronic condition in virtually all (of Lenski's) agrarian states," showed itself particularly in the time of Jannaeus. Perhaps most interesting to this study are the internal struggles that often developed. Lenski credits this phenomenon as "common in [agrarian states] without an institutionalized pattern of succession to the throne."[17] Of more interest to this study is the lack of institutionalized patterns of succession to the high priesthood; or, possibly, a shift in those patterns. Furthermore, religion was a matter of concern to state authorities.[18] With Hasmonean Judea in mind, consider Lenski's statement:

> The nature of this concern varied considerably, ranging from cynical maneuvers by rulers seeking to capitalize on the religious commitments of their subjects, to genuine efforts to act in accordance with deeply held personal commitments. In either case, however, the concern led to efforts to harness the powers of religion in the service of the state. Such efforts

16. Lenski, *Power and Privilege*, 193–205.
17. Ibid., 196–97.
18. Ibid., 209.

> usually met with a favorable response on the part of religious leaders, or at least the leaders of the group enjoying political favor. From their standpoint, much could be gained from an alliance or merger of the powers of church and state. Such a relationship assured the group and its leaders a share in the economic surplus and the defense of their interests by the coercive powers of the state. One of the natural consequences of such developments was the gradual weakening of family and local cults and the simultaneous strengthening of national faiths. These cults seldom disappeared… One other feature of the religious situation which deserves special attention is the appearance of organized conflict between religious groups, sometimes on a major scale. This is virtually absent in simpler societies. The reasons it developed in agrarian societies are many and varied. In part these conflicts reflected a growing cultural pluralism and diversity which resulted in tensions between ethnic groups, between classes, between countryfolk and city people, and last but not least, between uninspired religious functionaries and their charismatic critics and rivals. Frequently several of these factors worked together to generate religious conflict. Because of the intimate relations between church and state in agrarian societies, these conflicts usually involved the state and hence the use of coercive measures.[19]

A variety of ethnic groups dwelled in Hasmonean Judea. Hasmonean Judea showed a development and utilization of trade and commerce. Hasmonean Judea saw the occurrence of urban communities, particularly Jerusalem, whose inhabitants evidenced a diversity of vocations and whose population comprised a small percentage of the total societal population. The urban populations, however, dominated the society politically, economically, religiously, and culturally. Economic surplus created a situation where between five and ten percent of the population consumed up to two-thirds of the state's income, which led to social inequality and subsequent struggles for power. Within this agrarian state, Lenski identifies a class structure divided into the ruling, governing, priestly, retainer, merchant, peasant, artisan, unclean/degraded, and expendable classes.

The Ruling Class

With regard to the Hasmonean period, the ruling class can readily be assigned to the Hasmoneans in concert with their sometime friend, sometime foe, the empire of the Seleucids. They gained power by military means for the purpose of "personal gain" and as a way of protecting their "established interests." Their institutions of government served as the primary source of social inequality—a social inequality that increased "as the economic surplus expands, as military technology advances…and

19. Ibid., 209.

as the powers of the state increase."[20] Lenski describes the distributive process in this society thus:

> It is essential to understand the nature of the state as viewed by the most influential members of these societies. For them, the state was not merely an organization which defined and enforced the rules in the struggle for power and privilege. It was itself one of the objects of the struggle. In fact, because of the great powers vested in it, it was the supreme prize for all who coveted power, privilege, and prestige. To win control of the state was to win control of the most powerful instrument of self-aggrandizement found in agrarian societies. By the skillful exercise of the powers of state, a man or group could gain control over much of the economic surplus, and with it at his disposal, could go on to achieve honor and prestige as well. As a consequence, the one who controlled the state would usually fight to preserve his control, while others would strive either to curry his favor and thus share in his good fortune, or would seek to displace him... In nearly every instance these histories are the record of an almost continuous series of intrigues and struggles for power both within and between states. Furthermore, these struggles were usually between individuals and groups concerned far more with their own partisan advantage than with either the principles of distributive justice or the common good, except in those cases where private advantage and the common good happened to coincide.[21]

The ruling class functioned within the "proprietary theory of the state," which dictated that the state belonged to the owner, and was to be used without clear restrictions at the owner's choosing and for the owner's benefit. The members of this class possessed all the land and administered a profitable taxation system.

To speak specifically of Alexander Jannaeus, note his propensity toward military campaigns. The prize of struggles, external and internal, was "the capture of the machinery of government," which brought "fabulous wealth and immense power to the victor."[22] Alexander Jannaeus levied taxes, heavy taxes (and at times was taxed by the Seleucids), as an "exercise of proprietary rights"—collection of taxes and revenue from tribute and services were his primary source of income, which was supplemented by "booty" and "confiscation," e.g., David's tomb.

The Governing Class

Available information about the governing class of Hasmonean Judea is understandably somewhat less precise. This class was typically a small

20. Ibid., 210.
21. Ibid., 210–11.
22. Ibid., 212.

group, less than 2 per cent of the population, which shared the responsibilities of governing with the ruling class. This governing class included high officers of the state, civil servants, counselors, and advisors to the ruler, some appointed by the present ruler and others through inheritance. As Lenski says, "membership in the governing class guaranteed to every individual certain unique opportunities for self-aggrandizement" which served as "their reward for upholding and enforcing the authority of the existing regime."[23] Josephus identifies a lay council of elders as a prime governing body (*Ant.* 12.3). Given the historiographic concerns that Josephus might be anachronistically placing the social structure of his context upon earlier periods, we cannot presume the existence of an actual lay council of elders, but it is probably safe to assume some type of council, and, given data from literature of the period, this council probably consisted of important priests, old-money aristocracy, landed gentry, and heads of families.[24] The governing class possessed at least one-fourth of the national income. The combination of the governing class and the ruling class possessed no less than one-half of the national income.

The Priestly Class

The priestly class included "religious leaders whose livelihood and status in society were dependent primarily on their leadership role in the religious system"[25] and thus were heavily involved in politics. The "holdings" of the priestly class in agrarian societies were frequently quite substantial although not equally distributed within the class and frequently confiscated by political elites.[26] According to Lenski's model, the ruling class recognized their need to obtain legitimation from the priestly class. Thus the relationship between the governing and priestly classes was symbiotic with the political elite needing legitimation that could only be given by the religious establishment and the priestly class depending on the political elite to assist in the spread and perpetuation of the religion, the defense of "the faith," and the erection of extravagant worship centers. The priestly class and the ruling class supported each other except when their interests collided.

23. Ibid., 219–20.

24. Martin Hengel, *Judaism and Hellenism: Studies in Their Encounter in Palestine During the Early Hellenistic Period* (trans. John Bowden; 2 vols.; Philadelphia: Fortress, 1974), 1:25–29.

25. Lenski, *Power and Privilege*, 256.

26. Ibid., 209, 258. Except that in Hasmonean Judea many members of the priestly class were also members of the political elite.

The Retainer Class

Essential to the governing class was the retainer class. This relatively small segment of the population included officials, soldiers, servants, and personal retainers in service to the ruling and governing classes. Their two important characteristics were their reliance on the elite of society and their performance of the crucial task of mediating relations between the governing class and the common people while improving their socio-economic position and enhancing their rights and privileges.

The Merchant Class

In many cases, the merchant class developed when members of the peasant class found economic opportunities in the developing agrarian society. Lenski cites the merchant class as the most difficult class for the political elite to control. The governing class depended on the merchant class to provide them with material goods to sustain their privileged status. While the merchant class was subject to the political authority of the governing class, they avoided economic subjugation. Members of the merchant class were both enemies and admirers of the governing class. For Judea, hellenization brought increased trade that enhanced the position of the merchant class in relation to the elite.

The Peasant Class

The peasant class in this tributary system, even though they lived at or below subsistence level, served as the basic support unit for the state and the elites of the state. The vast majority of the Hasmonean Judean population formed this group whose lives were dominated by the actions and interactions of the above mentioned classes. The artisan class was usually "recruited from the ranks of the dispossessed peasantry and their non-inheriting sons and was continually replenished from these sources."[27] Many of the artisan class were employed by the merchant class. Of Lenski's unclean/degraded and expendable classes, we know precious little in Hasmonean Judea. The constituency of these classes varied between near zero and fifteen percent depending on circumstances. Lenski stresses that the classes within agrarian societies cannot be thought of simply as a series of layers superimposed on one another. Instead, they contain intraclass distributions that overlap with other classes creating a "continuum of power and privilege."[28]

27. Ibid., 278.
28. Ibid., 283–85.

The Model in Action

Interactions between these classes during the Hasmonean period allow reflection, in light of Lenski's model, on how these relationships might have influenced sectarian processes. Regarding interactions between the ruling class and the governing class, the ruling class attempted to draw a direct connection between the performance of the governing class and their continued "enjoyment of power and privilege." Concurrently, the governing class continually sought to "infringe on the rights of the ruler" in an effort to gain equal footing with the ruling class.[29] Lenski cites numerous factors affecting the relationship between the ruling class and the governing class. These include: development and distribution of economic resources (such as land), the size of the state, involvement in external wars, principles of succession, dissension within the governing class, personality factors, and interaction with the common people.[30] The ruling class depended on the governing class to enforce and carry out its policies in a way that would meet the Hasmonean goals for Judea.

The Judeans had long been accustomed to the rule of foreign overlords. Partisan politics affected power, privilege, and prestige. A system of rewards was in place, a system that was not always comfortable and often controversial. Legitimacy was already an issue with the recent history of the high-priesthood for sale to the highest bidder. In contrast with the rule of the foreign empire which knew it must co-opt the elite of the Judean society by whatever means necessary, the new rulers, Judeans themselves, achieving power through their revolt, had no such awareness. They did not seek to co-opt the *status quo*; they came in to overthrow the *status quo*. The systems of rewards changed. The stage was set by the rule of John Hyrcanus (135–104 B.C.E.). Most likely, by this time—a quarter century after the revolt—the Hasmoneans were, consciously or subconsciously, trying to shift from the rule of might to the rule of right. Hyrcanus was assuming the office of high priest as his right, as part of the process of legitimization. If accepted, he further legitimized his power. We understand, however, from Talmudic accounts and others, that many regarded him as unfit to hold the office and to perform its sacrifices. Plagued from the beginning by the unfinished business of his father with the Ptolemies to the south and the Seleucids to the north, Hyrcanus struggled with internal and external tensions, a difficult position for someone trying to solidify and legitimize his power.

29. Ibid., 231.
30. Ibid., 231–42.

Finding himself at extreme odds with Antiochus VII who tore down the defensive walls of Jerusalem, Hyrcanus worked out a political and economic solution, he agreed to pay tribute for cities. Taking care of a threat on one front, he opened himself to internal strife and almost assuredly diminished his legitimation process when he opened David's tomb for cash (and hired mercenaries). Soon thereafter he had a chance to recover. Seleucid power shifted many times and, in those processes, left Hyrcanus alone, providing him a chance to solidify his power. Hyrcanus expanded his territory; he captured Shechem around 128 B.C.E.[31] Samaria fell even though Antiochus IX tried to help.

After the death of Hyrcanus, the next Hasmonean, Aristobulus (who ruled 104–103 B.C.E.) took the title of king—another apparent step toward legitimation, and one that probably met with some resistance and dissent. Although he probably contributed to building projects in Greek cities and took in additional territory (Iturea—southern Lebanon), one year as ruler gave him little time to institutionalize power. Alexander Janneus came to power in 103. We may assume that, following the Lenski cycle, some decentralization of power occurred, enabling diverse centers of power to develop. One way to counter a loss of legitimation was to expand the territory, increase the popularity ratings, distract from internal politics by fighting a war. Janneus did just that, he went about conquering neighboring areas. "Rulers who were successful at war, and were able to annex foreign territories, could subordinate their governing classes much more effectively."[32] In taking Gadara, Amathus, Raphia, Anthedon, Gaza, Moab, and Galaaditis, Jannaeus made economic and political gains for himself. His "ability to distribute booty was a powerful instrument of control." His ability to redistribute conquered lands had the same effect. In fact, land confiscations redistributed among the governing class often solidified a newly established dynasty, "especially when those whose lands were confiscated had no strong ties of kinship or friendship with the governing class. Under other conditions, however, confiscations tended to unite the governing class against the ruler."[33]

Employment of legitimation strategies does not guarantee success. For example, at the time of the Feast of Tabernacles, Alexander Janneus made a blatant non-violent legitimation claim, participating in an event with potential for solidifying his power, but his attempt failed. Janneus, as high priest, boldly sacrificed at the ceremony. Members of the crowd,

31. What if the Zadokites came from Shechem?
32. Lenski, *Power and Privilege*, 236.
33. Ibid., 236.

many members of the crowd, were clearly unhappy with his assumptions. Per Josephus' recounting of the tale, the "nation rose upon him and pelted him with citrons which they had in their hands because the laws of the Jews required that at the Feast of Tabernacles everyone should have branches of the palm tree and citron tree...*and*...they reviled him as derived from a captive" (*Ant.* 8.8.5). Janneus responded by killing 6000 citizens and isolating himself from the people.

Janneus' image suffered again when Nabatean king Obedas defeated him in battle, paving the way for a civil war that lasted six years and cost over 50,000 lives. Yehudites fought on both sides. Janneus' legitimation struggle came to crisis around 88 B.C.E. when his opponents called for help from Demetrius III of Damascus. Janneus had to resort to the rule of might through the employment of mercenaries in an attempt to contain the revolt. His army was defeated, Demetrius left, and the civil war continued. According to Lenski's model,

> losses in war, of course, had a deleterious effect on the ruler's relation to his governing class...the power of rulers depended in part on the myth of their invincibility. Once a ruler's vincibility was shown, his power was weakened and his rights were more likely to be challenged. In a very real sense he lost something of his charismatic character.[34]

Janneus likely relinquished hope of obtaining granted legitimation, resorting totally to rule of might by brutally crucifying 800 men, slaughtering their families before their eyes while he feasted with his cohorts.[35] Eight thousand of his opponents fled the country.[36] To counter the dismal failure at legitimization, he continued with his conquests, taking Moab and Galaaditis (Gilead). He then attacked the Arab king Obodas I but was severely beaten.

Janneus often fought off attacks from neighbors and at the same time continued his conquering activities, mostly in the area northeast of the Sea of Galilee. Around 86 B.C.E., Antiochus XII Dionysus, on his march through to fight against Arabia, invaded Judea. Antiochus died in the battle. Aretas III, an Arab king, invaded Judah but Janneus came to terms with him. So, Janneus had to continue to employ the rule of might because he could not establish his rule of right. The consequence of this inability to actualize legitimation probably resulted in full-fledged sectarianism. Josephus says that Janneus died after falling into distemper by hard drinking.

34. Lenski, *Power and Privilege*, 236–37.
35. See 4QpNah.
36. Qumran's Nahum Pesher sheds interesting light; see 4QpNah 1.6–7.

Finding a Place for the Zadokites: A Direction

How might the Zadokites be placed in this context? In the end, we must limit our assumptions about Zadokites. The following serves as a starting point: there was a group, at least one and maybe more, that called themselves the "sons of Zadok." This group existed during the time of Alexander Janneus and may have existed prior to that time. This group inserted their midrash of some Ezekiel texts into a Qumran community. Someone, at an undetermined time, but prior to the "Zadokite" insertion in *Serek Ha-Yahad*, inserted material in Ezek 40–48 about the superiority of the "sons of Zadok." Someone, perhaps a member of this group, inserted Zadok, at an undetermined time, in priestly genealogical material in the book of the Chronicler (and perhaps in Ezra–Nehemiah). This group stood in opposition to the *status quo*.

I suggest the Second Temple period brought a need for legitimation and everyone felt the need and realized the expediency of developing lineage for purpose of legitimation. This is what we observe in Ezra–Nehemiah and Chronicles, the claiming of Aaron, and the insertion of Zadok in the lineage for added emphasis. This need for legitimation was brought on by rapid social change, by commercialization and the effects of trade issues, by empire shifts, by the upheaval of life—all these factors generated attempts to create new social order.

I suggest there was never a priestly dynasty until the Oniads and these Oniads were ousted by a new dynasty, one that was both religious and political—the Hasmoneans.

As for the Zadokites, I suggest that, since they turn up at Qumran with some measure of authority in the community during the time of Alexander Janneus, we can conclude that they were one of the sectarian groups that developed during this period. They had some issues with the *status quo*, particularly over calendar, temple, and priesthood. They could not tolerate what was happening in the system. They chose to retreat. That they claimed to be sons of Zadok reconfirms the importance of lineage during this time of rapid social change. After the Maccabean revolt, if the issue of lineage was not already important, it came to be of prime importance as the Maccabean rulers claimed the priesthood as part of their legitimization process. The sons of Zadok claimed their sanctity, power, and legitimacy based on the traditions of their ancestors—they claimed the lauded priest of David named Zadok. Who they were before or after that time remains to be seen.

BIBLIOGRAPHY

Abba, Raymond. "Priests and Levites." *IDB* 876–89.

—"Priests and Levites in Ezekiel." *VT* 28 (1978): 1–9.

Abraham, W. J. *Divine Revelation and the Limits of Historical Criticism*. Oxford: Oxford University Press, 1982.

Ackroyd, Peter R. *I & II Chronicles, Ezra, Nehemiah*. TBC. London: SCM Press, 1973.

—*The Second Book of Samuel*. The Cambridge Bible Commentary on the New English Bible. Cambridge: Cambridge University Press, 1977.

Ahlström, Gösta, with a contribution by Gary O. Rollefson. *The History of Ancient Palestine*. Edited by D. V. Edelman. Sheffield: Sheffield Academic Press. Minneapolis: Fortress, 1993.

Albertz, Rainer. *A History of Israelite Religion in the Old Testament Period*. Translated by John Bowden. 2 vols. OTL. Louisville, Ky.: Westminster John Knox, 1992.

—*Israel in Exile: The History and Literature of the Sixth Century B.C.E.* Studies in Biblical Literature Number 3. Translated by David Green, Atlanta: Society of Biblical Literature, 2003.

Albright, William Foxwell. "The Date and Personality of the Chronicler." *JBL* 40 (1921): 104–24.

—"Notes on Early Hebrew and Aramaic Epigraphy." *Journal of Palestine Oriental Society* 6 (1926): 75–102.

Allan, Nigel. "The Identity of the Jerusalem Priesthood During the Exile." *HeyJ* 23 (1982): 259–69.

Alter, Robert. *The Art of Biblical Narrative*. New York: Basic Books, 1981.

Allegro, John. *QUMRÂN CAVE 4: I (4Q158–4Q186)*. DJD 5. Oxford: Clarendon, 1968.

Anderson, Bernhard W. *Understanding the Old Testament*. 4th ed. Englewood Cliffs: Prentice–Hall, 1986.

Baillet, M., J. T. Milik, and R. de Vaux. *Les "Petites Grottes" de Qumran: Exploration de la falaise, les grottes 2q, 3q, 5q, 7q À 10q, le rouleau de cuivre*. DJD 3. Oxford: Clarendon, 1962.

Barr, James. *The Semantics of Biblical Language*. London: Oxford University Press, 1961.

Barrick, W. Boyd, "Genealogical Notes on the 'House of David' and the 'House of Zadok.'" *JSOT* 96 (2001): 29–58

Bartlett, John Raymond. "Zadok and His Successors at Jerusalem." *JTS* 19 (1968): 1–18.

Batten, Loring Woart. *A Critical and Exegetical Commentary on the Books of Ezra and Nehemiah*. ICC 15. Edinburgh: T. & T. Clark, 1972.

Baudissen, Wolf Wilhelm Grafen. *Die Geschichte des alttestamentlichen Priesterthums*. Leipzig: Hirzel, 1889.

—"Priests and Levites." Pages 67–97 in *A Dictionary of the Bible, Dealing with Its Language, Literature and Contents Including the Biblical Theology*. Edited by James Hastings. New York: Scribner's, 1902.

Baumgarten, Albert. I. "Crisis in the Scrollery: A Dying Consensus." *Judaism* 44 (1995): 399–416.

—*The Flourishing of Jewish Sects in the Maccabean Era: An Interpretation*. JSJSup 55. Leiden: Brill, 1997.

Baumgarten, Joseph M., "The Unwritten Law in the Pre-Rabbinic Period." *JSJ* 72 (1972): 7–29

Beentjes, Pancratius C., ed. *The Book of Ben Sira in Modern Research: Proceedings of the First International Ben Sira Conference 28—31 July 1996 Soesterberg, Netherlands*. BZAW 255. Berlin: de Gruyter, 1997.

Bernat, David. "Josephus's Portrayal of Phinehas." *JSP* 13 (2002): 137–49.

Berquist, Jon L. *Controlling Corporeality: The Body and the Household in Ancient Israel*. New Brunswick: Rutgers University Press, 2002.

—*Judaism in Persia's Shadow: A Social and Historical Approach*. Minneapolis: Fortress, 1995.

Berry, George R. "The Authorship of Ezekiel 40–48." *JBL* 34 (1915): 17–40.

—"The Date of Ezekiel 45:1–8a and 47:13–48:35." *JBL* 40 (1921): 70–75.

Bertholet, Alfred. *Hesekiel*. HAT 1/13. Tübingen: Mohr, 1936.

Bickerman, Elias. *The God of the Maccabees: Studies on the Meaning and Origin of the Maccabean Revolt*. SJLA 32. Leiden: Brill, 1979.

Birch, Bruce C., Walter Brueggemann, Terence E. Fretheim, and David L. Peterson, *A Theological Introduction to the Old Testament*. 2d ed. Nashville: Abingdon, 2005.

Blenkinsopp, Joseph. "Bethel in the Neo-Babylonian Period." Pages 93–108 in *Judah and the Judeans in the Neo-Babylonian Period*. Edited by Oded Lipschitz and Joseph Blenkinsopp. Winona Lake, Ind.: Eisenbrauns, 2003.

—*Ezekiel*. Interpretation. Edited by James Luther Mays. Louisville, Ky.: John Knox, 1990.

—*Ezra–Nehemiah*. OTL. London: SCM Press, 1989.

—"A Jewish Sect of the Persian Period." *CBQ* 52 (1990): 5–20.

—"The Judaean Priesthood During the Neo-Babylonian and Achaemenid Periods: A Hypothetical Reconstruction." *CBQ* 60 (1998): 25–43.

—*The Pentateuch: An Introduction to the First Five Books of the Bible*. ABRL. New York: Doubleday, 1992.

—*Sage, Priest, Prophet: Religious and Intellectual Leadership in Ancient Israel*. Library of Ancient Israel. Louisville, Ky.: Westminster John Knox, 1995.

Bloch-Smith, Elisabeth. "Israelite Ethnicity in Iron I: Archaeology Preserves What is Remembered and What is Forgotten in Israel's History." *JBL* 122 (2003): 401–25.

Bowman, Raymond A. "The Book of Nehemiah." Pages 549–69 and 662–819 in *The Interpreter's Bible*. Edited by George A. Buttrick. New York: Abingdon-Cokesbury, 1954.

Box, George H., and Oesterley, William O. E. "The Book of Sirach." *APOT* 1:268–517.

Boys, Mary C. *Educating in Faith: Maps and Visions*. Kansas City: Sheed & Ward, 1989.

Breasted, James Henry. *Ancient Records of Egypt: Historical Documents from the Earliest Times to the Persian Conquest*. Vol. 4, *The Twentieth to the Twenty-Sixth Dynasties*. Chicago: University of Chicago Press, 1906–1907.

—"The Development of the Priesthood in Israel and Egypt—A Comparison." *The Biblical World* (July–December 1893): 19–28.

Brett, Mark G., ed. *Ethnicity and the Bible*. BibInt Series 19. Leiden: Brill, 1996.

—"Israel's Indigenous Origins: Cultural Hybridity and the Formation of Israel's Ethnicity." *BibInt* 11 (2003): 400–12.

Brettler, Marc Zvi. *The Creation of History in Ancient Israel*. London: Routledge, 1995.

—"The Future of Biblical Studies." *The SBL Forum* (October 2004). No pages. Online: http://www.sbl-site.org/Article.aspx?ArticleId=320.

Briant, Pierre. *Historie de l'empire perse: De Cyrus à Alexandre*. Paris: Fayard, 1996.

Bright, John. *A History of Israel*, Westminster Aids to the Study of the Scriptures. Philadelphia: Westminster, 1960.

Brockington, L. H. *Ezra, Nehemiah, and Esther*. Century Bible New Series. London: Thomas Nelson, 1969.

Brooke, George J. *Exegesis at Qumran: 4QFlorilegium in Its Jewish Context*. JSOTSup 29. Sheffield: JSOT Press, 1985.

Bultmann, Rudolph. "Is Exegesis without Presuppositions Possible?" *Enc* 21 (1960): 194–200.

Calhoun, Craig. "Social Theory and the Public Sphere." Pages 429–70 in *The Blackwell Companion to Social Theory*. Edited by Bryan S. Turner. Cambridge: Blackwell, 1996.

Calmet, Augustin. *Calmet's Dictionary of the Holy Bible as Published by the Late Mr. Charles Taylor*. 8th ed. Boston: Crocker & Brewster, 1837.

Camp, Claudia V. *Wise, Strange, and Holy: The Strange Woman and the Making of the Bible*. JSOTSup 320. Gender, Culture, Theory 9. Sheffield: Sheffield Academic Press, 2000.

Carr, Edward. H. *What Is History?* New York: Knopf, 1962.

Carroll, Robert P. "What Do We Know About the Temple? The Temple in the Prophets." Pages 34–51 in Eskenazi and Richards, eds., *Second Temple Studies*, vol. 2.

—"Whorusalamin: a tale of three cities as three sisters." Pages 67–82 in *On Reading Prophetic Texts: Gender-Specific and Related Studies in Memory of Fokkelien van Dijk-Hemmes*. Edited by Bob Becking and Meindert Dijkstra. Leiden: Brill, 1996.

Charles, R. H. "Fragments of a Zadokite Work." *APOT* 785–834.

Clements, Ronald E. *Ezekiel*. Westminster Bible Companion. Louisville, Ky.: Westminster John Knox, 1996.

Clines, D. J. A. *Ezra, Nehemiah, Esther*. NCB. Grand Rapids: Eerdmans, 1984.

—"Response to Rolf Rendtorff's 'What Happened to the Yahwist: Reflections After Thirty Years.'" *The SBL Forum* 4 no. 5 (August 2006). No pages. Online: http://www.sbl-site.org/Article.aspx?ArticleId=551.

Cody, Aelred. *Ezekiel with an Excursus on Old Testament Priesthood*. Old Testament Message: A Biblical–Theological Commentary 2. Wilmington, Del.: Glazier, 1984.

—*A History of the Old Testament Priesthood*. AnBib: Investigationes Scientificae in Res Biblicas 35. Rome: Pontifical Biblical Institute, 1969.

Cogan, Mordechai, and Hayim Tadmor. *II Kings: A New Translation with Introduction and Commentary*. AB 11. New York: Doubleday, 1988.

Coggins, R. J. *The First and Second Books of the Chronicles*. CBC. Cambridge: Cambridge University Press, 1976.

Cohen, S. J. D. *From the Maccabees to the Mishnah*. Philadelphia: Westminster, 1987.

Collins, John J. *The Bible after Babel: Historical Criticism in a Postmodern Age*. Grand Rapids: Eerdmans, 2005.

—*Introduction to the Hebrew Bible with CD-Rom*. Minneapolis: Fortress, 2004.

Coogan, Michael D. *The Old Testament: A Historical and Literary Introduction to the Hebrew Scriptures*. New York: Oxford University Press, 2006.

Cook, Stephen L. "Innerbiblical Interpretation in Ezekiel 44 and the History of Israel's Priesthood." *JBL* 114 (1995): 193–208.

Cooke, G. A. *A Critical and Exegetical Commentary on the Book of Ezekiel*. ITC. Edinburgh: T. & T. Clark, 1936.

Coote, Robert B., and Mary P. Coote. *Power, Politics, and the Making of the Bible: An Introduction*. Minneapolis: Fortress, 1990.

Coote, Robert B., and David Robert Ord. *In the Beginning: Creation and the Priestly History*. Minneapolis: Fortress, 1991.

Corney, R. W. "Zadok the Priest." *IDB* 928–29.

Cross, Frank Moore. "Aspects of Samaritan and Jewish History in Late Persian and Hellenistic Times." *HTR* 59 (1966): 201–11.

—*Canaanite Myth and Hebrew Epic: Essays in the History of Israel's Priesthood*. Cambridge, Mass.: Harvard University Press, 1973.

—"The Discovery of the Samaria Papyri." *BA* 26 (1963): 110–39.

—"The Early History of the Qumran Community." Pages 63–80 in Freedman and Greenfield, eds., *New Directions in Biblical Archaeology*.

—*From Epic to Canon: History and Literature in Ancient Israel*. Baltimore: The Johns Hopkins University Press, 1998.

—"Papyri of the Fourth Century B.C. From Daliyeh: A Preliminary Report on Their Discovery and Significance." Pages 41–62 in Freedman and Greenfield, eds., *New Directions in Biblical Archaeology*.

—"Priestly Houses of Early Israel." Pages 195–216 in *Canaanite Myth and Hebrew Epic*.

—"A Reconstruction of the Judean Restoration." *JBL* 94 (1975): 4–18.

Cross, Frank Moore, and Shemaryahu Talmon, eds. *Qumran and the History of the Biblical Text*. Cambridge, Mass.: Harvard University Press, 1975.

Curtiss, Samuel Ives. *The Levitical Priests: A Contribution to the Criticism of the Pentateuch*. Edinburgh: T. & T. Clark, 1877.

Dahrendorf, Ralf. "Review Symposium: Gerhard E. Lenski, Power and Privilege: A Theory of Social Stratification." *American Sociological Review* 31 (1966): 714–18.

Darr, Katheryn Pfisterer. "Ezekiel's Justifications of God: Teaching Troubling Texts." *JSOT* 55 (1992): 97–117.

Davies, Philip R. *Behind the Essenes: History and Ideology in the Dead Sea Scrolls*. BJS 94. Atlanta: Scholars Press, 1987.

—*In Search of "Ancient Israel"*. JSOTSup 148. Sheffield: Sheffield Academic Press, 1993.

—"The Prehistory of the Qumran Community." Pages 116–25 in Dimant and Rappaport, eds., *The Dead Sea Scrolls*.

—"Redaction and Sectarianism in the Qumran Scrolls." Pages 152–63 in *The Scriptures and the Scrolls: Studies in Honour of A. S. Van Der Woude on the Occasion of His 65th Birthday*. Edited by F. García Martínez, A. Hilhorst, and C. J. Labuschagne. Leiden: Brill, 1992.

—*Sects and Scrolls: Essays on Qumran and Related Topics*. South Florida Studies in the History of Judaism 134. Atlanta: Scholars Press, 1996.

—ed. *Second Temple Studies*. Vol. 1, *Persian Period*. JSOTSup 117. Sheffield: JSOT Press, 1991.

—"Sons of Zadok." Pages 1005–7 in Schiffman and VanderKam, eds., *Encyclopedia of the Dead Sea Scrolls*, Vol. 2.

—"Taking Up Social Scientific Investigations of the Second Temple Period." Unpublished essay, Sheffield University, 1992.

Day, Linda. "Rhetoric and Domestic Violence in Ezekiel 16." *BibInt* 8 (2000): 205–30.

Day, Peggy L. "Adulterous Jerusalem's Imagined Demise: Death of a Metaphor in Ezekiel xvi." *VT* 50 (2000): 285–309.

—"The Bitch Had It Coming to Her: Rhetoric and Interpretation in Ezekiel 16." *BibInt* 8 (2000): 231–54.

De Vaux, Roland. *Ancient Israel: Its Life and Institutions*. First published in English. London: Darton, Longman & Todd, 1961. Translated by John McHugh. The Biblical Resource Series. Grand Rapids: Eerdmans, 1997.

—*Archaeology and the Dead Sea Scrolls*. Rev. ed. The Schweich Lectures 1959. London: Oxford University Press, 1973.

—*L'archéologie et les manuscrits de la mer morte*. The Schweich Lectures 1959. London: Oxford University Press, 1959.

—*Les institutions de L'ancien Testament*. Paris: Cerf, 1958.

Dempsey, Carol J. "The 'Whore' of Ezekiel 16: The Impact and Ramifications of Gender-Specific Metaphors in Light of Biblical Law and Divine Judgment." Pages 57–78 in *Gender and Law in the Hebrew Bible and the Ancient Near East*. Edited by Victor Matthews, Bernard Levinson, and Tikva Frymer-Kensky. JSOTSup 262. Sheffield: Sheffield Academic Press, 1998.

Dequeker, L. "I Chronicles XXIV and the Royal Priesthood of the Hasmoneans." Pages 94–106 in *Crisis and Perspectives: Studies in Ancient Near Eastern Polytheism, Biblical Theology, Palestinian Archaeology and Intertestamental Literature*. OtSt. Leiden: Brill, 1986.

Dever, William G. "The Death of a Discipline." *BAR* 21 (1995): 50–55, 70.

—"Philology, Theology, and Archaeology: What Kind of History Do We Want, and What Is Possible." Pages 290–310 in *The Archaeology of Israel: Constructing the Past, Interpreting the Present*. Edited by Neil Asher Silberman and David Small. Sheffield: Sheffield Academic Press, 1997.

—"Syro-Palestinian and Biblical Archaeology." Pages 31–74 in Knight and Tucker, eds., *The Hebrew Bible and Its Modern Interpreters*.

—*What Did the Biblical Writers Know, and When Did They Know It? What Archaeology Can Tell Us About the Relaity of Ancient Israel*. Grand Rapids: Eerdmans, 2001.

Di Lella, Alexander A. *The Hebrew Text of Sirach: A Text-Critical and Historical Study*. Studies in Classical Literature 1. The Hague: Mouton, 1966.

Dimant, Devorah, and Uriel Rappaport, eds. *The Dead Sea Scrolls: Forty Years of Research*. Leiden: Brill, 1992.

Driver, Samuel R. *An Introduction to the Literature of the Old Testament*. New York: Meridian, 1957.

Duguid, Iain M. "Putting Priests in their Place: Ezekiel's Contribution to the History of the Old Testament Priesthood." Pages 43–60 in *Ezekiel's Hierarchical World: Wrestling with a Tiered Reality*. Edited by Stephen L. Cook and Corrine L. Patton. SBLSymS 31. Leiden: Brill, 2004.

Edelman, Diana V. "Doing History in Biblical Studies." Pages 13–25 in Edelman, ed., *The Fabric of History*.

—ed., *The Fabric of History: Text, Artifact and Israel's Past*. JSOTSup 127. Sheffield: JSOT Press, 1991.

Eichrodt, Walther. *Ezekiel*. Translated by Cosslett Quin. OTL. London: SCM Press, 1970.

Elias, N. *The Civilizing Process*. Vol. 1, *The History of Manners*. Oxford: Blackwell, 1978.

Elmslie, W. A. L. "The First and Second Books of Chronicles." Pages 341–66 in *The Interpreter's Bible*. Edited by George Arthur Buttrick. Nashville: Abingdon, 1954.

Eshel, Esther, Hanan Eshel, and Ada Yardeni. "A Qumran Composition Containing Part of Ps. 154 and a Prayer for the Welfare of King Jonathan and His Kingdom." *IEJ* 42 (1992): 192–229.

Eskenazi, Tamara C. "Jeshua." *ABD* 3:769–71.

—"Book of Ezra." Pages 449–51 in *Eerdmans Dictionary of the Bible*. Edited by David Noel Freedman and Allen C. Myers. Grand Rapids: Eerdmans, 2000.

Eskenazi, Tamara C., and Kent H. Richards, eds. *Second Temple Studies*. Vol. 2, *Temple Community in the Persian Period*. JSOTSup 175. Sheffield: Sheffield Academic Press, 1994.

Ewald, Heinrich Georg August. *The History of Israel: Introduction and Preliminary History*, vol. 1. Translated by Russell Martineau. London: Longman, Green & Co., 1874.

—*The History of Israel, The Rise and Splendour of the Hebrew Monarchy*, vol. 3. 2d ed. London: Longmans, Green & Co., 1878.

Exum, J. Cheryl. "The Ethics of Biblical Violence Against Women." Pages 248–71 in *The Bible in Ethics: The Second Sheffield Colloquium*. Edited by John W. Rogerson et al. JSOTSup 207. Sheffield: Sheffield Academic Press, 1995.

Falk, Daniel K. "High Priests." Pages 361–64 in Schiffman and VanderKam, eds., *Encyclopedia of the Dead Sea Scrolls*, vol. 1.

Fallers, Lloyd A. "Review Symposium: Gerhard E. Lenski, Power and Privilege: A Theory of Social Stratificaiton." *American Sociological Review* 31 (1966): 718–19.

Fant, Clyde E., Donald W. Musser, and Mitchell G. Reddish. *An Introduction to the Bible: Revised Edition*. Nashville: Abingdon, 2001.

Feldman, Louis H. "Josephus." *ABD* 3: 981–98.

Fensham, F. Charles. *The Books of Ezra and Nehemiah*. Grand Rapids: Eerdmans, 1982.

Finkelstein, Israel. "The Archaeology of the United Monarchy: An Alternative View." *Levant* 28 (1996): 181–91.

Finkelstein, Israel, and Neil Asher Silberman. *The Bible Unearthed: Archaeology's New Vision of Ancient Israel and the Origin of Its Sacred Texts*. New York: Free Press, 2001.

Fisch, S. *Ezekiel*. Soncino Books of the Bible 7. London: Soncino Press, 1950.

Fishbane, M. *Biblical Interpretation in Ancient Israel*. Oxford: Clarendon, 1985.

Flanagan, James. "Ancient Perceptions of Space / Perceptions of Ancient Space." *Semeia* 87 (1999): 15–43

Flanders, Henry J., Robert W. Crapps, and David A. Smith. *People of the Covenant: An Introduction to the Old Testament*. 3d ed. New York: Oxford University Press, 1988.

Fohrer, G. *Die Hauptprobleme des Buches Ezechiel*. BZAW 72. Berlin: Töpelmann, 1952.

Forrester, Frederick C. *First and Second Kings in Old Testament Commentary: A General Introduction to and a Commentary on the Books of the Old Testament*. Edited by Herbert C. Alleman and Elmer E. Flaer. Philadelphia: Muhlenburg Press, 1948.

Fox-Genovese, Elizabeth, and Elisabeth Lasch-Quinn. "Introduction." Pages xiii–xxii in Fox-Genovese and Lasch-Quinn, eds., *Reconstructing History*.

—eds. *Reconstructing History: The Emergence of a New Historical Society*. New York: Routledge, 1999.

Freedman, David Noel, and Jonas C. Greenfield, eds. *New Directions in Biblical Archaeology*. Garden City, N.Y.: Doubleday, 1969.

Frick, Frank S. *A Journey through the Hebrew Scriptures*. New York: Harcourt Brace, 1995.

—"'Second Wave' Social-Scientific Criticism." Pages 17–34 in *Tracking "The Tribes of Yahweh": On the Trail of a Classic*. Edited by Roland Boer. JSOTSup 351. Sheffield: Sheffield Academic Press, 2001.

Gadamer, Hans Georg. *Truth and Method*. Translated by Joel Weinsheimer and Donald G. Marshall. New York: Crossroad, 1989.

Garbini, Giovanni. *History and Ideology in Ancient Israel*. Translated by John Bowden. London: SCM Press.

—*Myth and History in the Bible*. Translated by Chiara Peri. JSOTSup 362. Sheffield: Sheffield Academic Press, 2003.

García Martínez, F., and J. Trebolle Barrera. *The People of the Dead Sea Scrolls*. Translated by W. G. E. Watson. Leiden: Brill, 1995.

García Martínez, F., and A. S. van der Woude. "A Groningen Hypothesis of the Qumran Origins and Early History." *RevQ* 14 (1990): 521–41.

Geiger, Abraham. *Urlchrift und Uebersetzungen der Bibel in Ihrer Abhängigkeit von der Innern Entwickelung des Judenthums*. Breslau: Julius Hainauer, 1857

Genovese, Eugene D. "A New Departure." Pages 6–8 in Fox-Genovese and Lasch-Quinn, eds., *Reconstructing History*.

Gese, Hartmut. *Der Verfassungsentwurf des Ezechiel (Kap. 40–48) traditionsgeschichtlich untersucht*. BHT 25. Tübingen: J. C. B. Mohr, 1957.

Gottwald, Norman K. *The Hebrew Bible: A Socio-Literary Introduction*. Philadelphia: Fortress, 1985.

Grabbe, Lester L. *Ezra–Nehemiah*. Old Testament Readings. London: Routledge, 1998.

—ed. *Good Kings and Bad Kings*. Library of Hebrew Bible/Old Testament Studies 393. European Seminar in Historical Methodology 5. New York: T. & T. Clark, 2005.

—"Josephus and the Reconstruction of the Judean Restoration." *JBL* 106 (1987): 231–46.

—*Judaic Religion in the Second Temple Period: Belief and Practice from the Exile to Yavneh*. London: Routledge, 2000.

—*Judaism from Cyrus to Hadrian*. Vol. 1, *The Persian and Greek Periods*. Minneapolis: Fortress, 1992.

—"The Kingdom of Judah." Pages 79–122 in Grabbe, ed., *Good Kings and Bad Kings*.

—*Priests, Prophets, Diviners and Sages: A Socio-Historical Study of Religious Specialists in Ancient Israel*. Valley Forge, Pa.: Trinity, 1995.

—"Reconstructing History from the Book of Ezra." Pages 98–107 in Davies, ed., *Second Temple Studies*, vol. 1.

—"Reflections on the Discussion." Pages 339–50 in Grabbe, ed., *Good Kings and Bad Kings*.

—Review of Iain Provan, V. Philips Long, and Tremper Longman III. *A Biblical History of Israel*. Louisville, Ky.: Westminster John Knox, 2003. *Review of Biblical Literature* (August 2004). Online: www.bookreviews.org.

—"Sup-urbs or Only Hyp-urbs? Prophets and Populations in Ancient Israel and Socio-Historical Method." Pages 95–123 in *"Every City Shall be Forsaken": Urbanism and Prophecy in Ancient Israel and the Near East*. Edited by Lester L. Grabbe and Robert D. Haak. JSOTSup 330. Sheffield: Sheffield Academic Press, 2001.

—"Were the Pre-Maccabean High Priests 'Zadokites'?" Pages 205–15 in *Reading from Right to Left: Essays on the Hebrew Bible in Honour of David J. A. Clines*. Edited by J. Cheryl Exum and H. G. M. Williamson. JSOTSup 373. Sheffield: Sheffield Academic Press, 2003.

—"What Was Ezra's Mission?" Pages 286–99 in Eskenazi and Richards, eds., *Second Temple Studies*, vol. 2.

Graetz, Heinrich. *History of the Jews: From the Earliest Period to the Death of Simon the Maccabee (135 B.C.E.)*, vol. 1. Philadelphia: The Jewish Publication Society of America, 1891.

—*History of the Jews: From the Reign of Hyrcanus (135 B. C. E.) to the Completion of the Babylonian Talmud (500 C. E.)*, vol. 2. Philadelphia: The Jewish Publication Society of America, 1893.

Gray, George Buchanan. *A Critical Introduction to the Old Testament*. New York: Scribner's, 1913.

—*Sacrifice in the Old Testament: Its Theory and Practice*. Oxford: Clarendon, 1971.

Greenberg, Moshe. "The Design and Themes of Ezekiel's Program of Restoration." *Int* 38 (1984): 181–208.

—"Ezekiel 16: A Panorama of Passions"Pages 143–50 in *Love and Death in the Ancient Near East: Essays in Honor of Marvin H. Pope*. Edited by John H. Marks and Robert M. Good. Guilford, Conn.: Four Quarters, 1987.

Gunneweg, Antonius, H. J. *Esra*. Kommentar zum Alten Testament 19. Gütersloh: Gütersloher Verlagshaus Mohn, 1985.

—*Leviten und Priester*. FRLANT 89. Gottingen: Vandenhoeck & Ruprecht, 1965.

Haas, Peter J. "The Maccabean Struggle to Define Judaism." Pages 49–65 in *New Perspectives on Ancient Judaism: Religion, Literature and Society in Ancient Israel, Formative Christianity and Judaism*. Edited by J. Neusner, P. Borgen, E.S. Fierichs, and R. Forsley. Atlanta: Scholars Press, 1990.

Hale, J. R., ed. *The Evolution of British Historiography: From Bacon to Namier*. New York: World Publishing, 1964.

Halpern, Baruch. *The First Historians: The Hebrew Bible and History*. San Francisco: Harper & Row, 1988.

—"Sectionalism and the Schism." *JBL* 93 (1974): 519–32.

Hals, Ronald M. *Ezekiel*. FOTL 19. Grand Rapids: Eerdmans, 1989.

Hanson, Paul D. *The Dawn of Apocalyptic: The Historical and Sociological Roots of Jewish Apocalyptic Eschatology,* Rev. ed. Minneapolis: Fortress, 1979.

—"Israelite Religion in the Early Postexilic Period." Pages 485–508 in Miller, Hanson, and McBride, eds., *Ancient Israelite Religion.*

—"The Matrix of Apocalyptic." *CHJ* 524–33.

—*The People Called: The Growth of Community in the Bible*. San Francisco: Harper & Row, 1986. Reprinted with a new Introduction. Louisville, Ky.: Westminster John Knox, 2001.

Haran, Menachem. "The Law-Code of Ezekiel XL–XLVIII and Its Relation to the Priestly School." *HUCA* 50 (1979): 45–71.

—"Priests and Priesthood." *EncJud* 1071–87.

—*Temples and Temple-Service in Ancient Israel: An Inquiry into the Character of Cult Phenomena and the Historical Setting of the Priestly School*. Oxford: Clarendon, 1978.

Harrington, Daniel J., and John Strugnell, "Qumran Cave 4 Texts: A New Publication." *JBL* 112 (1993): 491–99.

Hauer, Christian E., Jr. *The Priests of Qumran*. Ph.D. diss., Vanderbilt University, 1959.

—"Who Was Zadok?" *JBL* 82 (1963): 89–94.

Hayes, John H. "The History of the Study of Israelite and Judaean History." Pages 1–69 in Hayes and Miller, eds., *Israelite and Judaean History*.

Hayes, John H., and J. Maxwell Miller, eds. *Israelite and Judaean History*. London: SCM Press and Trinity, 1977.

Heidegger, Martin. *Sein und Zeit*. Tübingen: Neomarius, 1949.

Hempel, Charlotte. "The Earthly Essene Nucleus of 1QSA," *DSD* 3 (1996): 253–69.

Hengel, Martin. *Judaism and Hellenism: Studies in Their Encounter in Palestine During the Early Hellenistic Period*. Translated by John Bowden. 2 vols. Philadelphia: Fortress, 1974.

Hertzberg, Hans Wilhelm. *I & II Samuel*. OTL. Philadelphia: Westminster, 1964.

Himmelfarb, Gertrude. "Postmodernist History." Pages 71–93 in Fox-Genovese and Lasch-Quinn, eds., *Reconstructing History*.

Hölscher, Gustav. *Hesekiel, Der Dichter und das Buch*. BZAW 39. Giessen: Töpelmann, 1924.

Hoonacker, Albin van. "Ezekiel's Priests and Levites." *ExpTim* 12 (1900–1901): 494–98.

Howie, Carl Gordon. *The Date and Composition of Ezekiel*. JBL Monograph Series 4. Philadelphia: Society of Biblical Literature, 1950.

Irwin, William. *The Problem of Ezekiel: An Inductive Study*. Chicago: University of Chicago Press, 1943.

Jaffee, Martin S. *Early Judaism*. Upper Saddle River, N.J.: Prentice–Hall, 1997,

Japhet, Sara. *I & II Chronicles: A Commentary*. OTL. Louisville, Ky.: Westminster John Knox, 1993.

—"Composition and Chronology in the Book of Ezra-Nehemiah." Pages 189–216 in Eskenazi and Richards, eds., *Second Temple Studies*, vol. 2.

—"The Relationship between Chronicles and Ezra–Nehemiah." Pages 298–313 in *Congress Volume: Leuven, 1989*. VTSup 43. Leiden: Brill, 1991.

Judge, H. G. "Aaron, Zadok, and Abiathar." *JTS* n.s. 7 (1956): 70–74.

Kapelrud, Arvid S. *The Question of Authorship in the Ezra-Narrative: A Lexical Investigation*. Oslo: Universitetsforlaget, 1944.

Katz, J. "In Clarification of the Term 'Forerunners of Zionism.'" Pages 104–15 in *Jewish Emancipation and Self-Emancipation*. Philadelphia: The Jewish Publication Society of America. 1986.

Katzenstein, H. J. "Some Remarks on the Lists of the Chief Priests of the Temple of Solomon." *JBL* 81 (1962): 377–84.

Kaufmann, Yehezkel. *The Religion of Israel: From Its Beginnings to the Babylonian Exile*. Translated and abridged by Moshe Greenberg. Chicago: University of Chicago Press, 1960. Trans. of תולדות האמונה הישראלית: מימי קדם עד סוף בית שני. Tel Aviv: Bialik Institute-Dvir, 1937–56.

—*History of the Religion of Israel: From the Babylonian Captivity to the End of Prophecy*, vol. 4. New York: Ktav, 1977.

—*The Religion of Israel: From Its Beginnings to the Babylonian Exile*. Translated by Moshe Greenberg. Chicago: University of Chicago Press, 1960.

Kennett, R. H. "The Origin of the Aaronite Priesthood." *JTS* 6 (1905): 161–86.

Klein, R.W., "The High Priestly Genealogies: A New Reconstruction." Unpublished paper delivered at the 1999 annual meeting of the Society of Biblical Literature (Boston, 23 November 1999).

Knight, Douglas, A. "Foreword." Pages xv–xvi in *Prolegomena to the History of Israel*. By Julius Wellhausen. Atlanta: Scholars Press, 1994.

—ed., *Julius Wellhausen and His Prolegomena to the History of Israel*. Semeia 25. Chico, Calif.: Scholars Press, 1982.

—"The Pentateuch." Pages 263–96 in Knight and Tucker, eds., *The Hebrew Bible and Its Modern Interpreters*.

—"Whose Agony? Whose Ecstasy? The Politics of Deuteronomic Law." Pages 97–112 in *Shall Not the Judge of All the Earth Do What is Right? Studies on the Nature of God in Tribute to James L. Crenshaw*. Edited by David Penchansky and Paul L. Redditt. Winona Lake, Ind.: Eisenbrauns, 2000.

Knight, Douglas A., and Gene M. Tucker, eds. *The Hebrew Bible and Its Modern Interpreters*. Atlanta: Scholars Press, 1985.

Knoppers, Gary N. *I Chronicles 1–9: A New Translation with Introduction* and Commentary. AB 12. New York: Doubleday, 2003.

—*I Chronicles 10–29: A New Translation with Introduction and Commentary*. AB 12A. New York: Doubleday, 2004.

—"Hierodules, Priests, or Janitors? The Levites in Chrnoicles and the History of the Israelite Priesthood." *JBL* 118 (1999): 49–72.

—"The Relationship of the Priestly Genealogies to the History of the High Priesthood in Jerusalem." Pages 109–34 in *Judea and the Judeans in the Neo-Babylonian Period*. Edited by Oded Lipschitz and Joseph Blenkinsopp. Winona Lake, Ind.: Eisenbrauns, 2003.

Koch, Klaus. "Ezra and Meremoth: Remarks on the History of the High Priesthood." Pages 105–10 in *"Sha'arei Talmon": Studies in the Bible, Qumran, and the Ancient Near East Presented to Shemaryahu Talmon*. Edited by Michael Fishbane and Emanuel Tov with the assistance of Weston W. Fields. Winona Lake, Ind.: Eisenbrauns, 1992.

—"Ezra and the Origins of Judaism." *JSS* 19 (1974): 173–97.

Koester, Helmut. *Introduction to the New Testament*. Vol. 1, *History, Culture and Religion of the Hellenistic Age*. New York: de Gruyter, 1982. Trans. of Chapters 1–6 of *Einführung in das Neue Testament*. Berlin: de Gruyter, 1982.

Kohler, Kaufmann. *The Origins of the Synagogue and the Church*. Edited with a bibliography by H. G. Enelow; New York: MacMillan, 1929.

—"Sadducees." *JE* 630–33.

König, Eduard. "The Priests and the Levites in Ezekiel XLIV 7–15." *ExpTim* 12 (1900–1901): 300–303.

Kosters, William Hendrik. *Die Wiederherstellung Israels in der persischen Periode*. Heidelberg: Hornung, 1895.

Kraus, Hans-Joachim. *Worship in Israel: A Cultic History of the Old Testament*. Translated by Geoffrey Buswell. Richmond: John Knox, 1962.

Krauss, Samuel. "Zadok." *JE* 628–30.

Kuenen, Abraham. *The Religion of Israel to the Fall of the Jewish State*. Translated by Alfred Heath May. 2 vols. London: Williams & Norgate, 1874–75.

Kugler, Robert A. "A Note on 1QS 9:14: The Sons of Righeousness or the Sons of Zadok?" *DSD* 3 (1996): 315–20.

—"Priesthood at Qumran." Pages 93–116 in *The Dead Sea Scrolls after Fifty Years*, vol. 2. Edited by Peter W. Flint and James C. Vanderkam. Leiden: Brill, 1999.

Kuhn, Thomas S. *The Structure of Scientific Revolutions*. 3d ed. Chicago: University of Chicago Press, 1996.

Lambert, Wilfred G. "Ancestors, Authors, and Canonicity: Additions and Corrections." *JCS* 11 (1957): 112.

Lapsley, Jacqueline E. "Shame and Self-Knowledge: The Positive Role of Shame in Ezekiel's View of the Moral Self." Pages 143–73 in *Book of Ezekiel: Theological and Anthropological Perspectives*. Edited by Margaret S. Odell and John T. Strong. Atlanta: Society of Biblical Literature, 2000.

Lauterbach, Jacob Z. "Sadducees and Pharisees: A Study of Their Respective Attitudes Towards the Law." Pages 176–98 in *Studies in Jewish Literature Issues in Honor of Professor Kaufmann Kohler, Ph.D., on the Occasion of His Seventieth Birthday*. Berlin: G. Reimer, 1913.

Lehmann, R. H. "Ben Sira and the Qumran Literature." *Revue Qumran* 3 (1961): 103–16.

Lemche, Niels Peter. *The Israelites in History and Tradition*. Library of Ancient Israel. Louisville, Ky.: Westminster John Knox, 1998.

—"On the Problems of Reconstructing Pre-Hellenistic Israelite (Palestinian) History." *Journal of Hebrew Scriptures* 3 (2000). No pages. Online: http://www.arts.ualberta.ca/JHS/Articles/article_13.htm.

Lenski, Gerhard. "Rethinking Macrosociological Theory." *American Sociological Review* 53 (1988): 163–71.

—*Power and Privilege: A Theory of Social Stratification*. Paperback ed. Chapel Hill: University of North Carolina Press, 1984 (1966).

Levenson, Jon D. *Theology of the Program of Restoration of Ezekiel 40–48*. HSM 10. Missoula, Mont.: Scholars, 1976.

Leví, I. "Un écrit sadducéen antérieur à la destruction du temple." *REJ* 61–62 (1911): 161–205.

Levine, Baruch A. "Priests." *IDB* 467–75.

Lim. Timothy H., "The Wicked Priests of the Groningen Hypothesis." *JBL* 112 (1993): 415–25

Liver, Jacob. *Chapters in the History of Priests and Levites: Studies in the Lists of Chronicles and Ezra and Nehemiah*. Publications of the Perry Foundation for Biblical Research in the Hebrew University of Jerusalem. Jerusalem: Magnes, 1968.

—"The 'Sons of Zadok the Priest' in the Dead Sea Sect." *RevQ* 21 (1967): 3–30.

Liverani, Mario. *Israel's History and the History of Israel*. Translated by Chiara Peri and Philip R. Davies. BibleWorld. London: Equinox, 2005. Originally published as *Oltre la Bibbia: Storia Antica di Israele*. Roma-Bari: Gius, Laterza & Figli Spa, 2003.

Long, V. Philips. "The Future of Israel's Past: Personal Reflections." Pages 580–92 in *Israel's Past in Present Research: Essays on Ancient Israelite Historiography*. Edited by V. Philips Long. Winona Lake, Ind.: Eisenbrauns, 1999.

Mansoor, M. "Sadducees." *EncJud* 14:620–22.

Mantel, Hugo. "The Dichotomy of Judaism During the Second Temple." *HUCA* 44 (1974): 55–87.

Martínez, F. García, and J. Trebolle Barrera. *The People of the Dead Sea Scrolls*. Translated by W. G. E. Watson. Leiden: Brill, 1995.

Martínez. F. García, and A. S. van der Woude. "A Groningen Hypothesis of the Qumran Origins and Early History." *RevQ* 14 (1990): 521–41.

Mason, Stephen N. *Josephus and the New Testament*. Peabody, Mass.: Hendrickson, 1992.

—"Introduction." Pages 11–18 in *Understanding Josephus: Seven Perspectives*. Edited by Steve Mason. JSOTSup 32; Sheffield: JSOT Press, 1998.
—"Priesthood in Josephus and the 'Pharisaic Revolution.'" JBL 107 (1988): 657–61.
Matthews, Victor H., and James C. Moyer. *The Old Testament: Text and Context*. Peabody, Mass.: Hendrickson, 1997.
McCarter, P. Kyle, Jr. *II Samuel: A New Translation with Introduction, Notes and Commentary*. AB. Garden City, N.Y.: Doubleday, 1984.
McConville, J. G. *I & II Chronicles*. The Daily Study Bible. Philadelphia: Westminster, 1984.
—"Priests and Levites in Ezekiel: A Crux in the Interpretation of Israel's History." *TynBul* 34 (1983): 3–32.
McCullough, W. Stewart. *The History and Literature of the Palestinian Jews from Cyrus to Herod: 550 BC to 4 BC*. Toronto: University of Toronto Press, 1975.
McFadyen, J. E. *Introduction to the Old Testament*. New York: Armstrong, 1906.
McKeating, Henry. *Ezekiel*. OTG. Sheffield: Sheffield Academic Press, 1993.
McNutt, Paula. *Reconstructing of Society of Ancient Israel*. Library of Ancient Israel. London: SPCK. Louisville, Ky. Westminster John Knox, 1999.
Meek, Theophile James. "Aaronites and Zadokites." *AJSL* 45 (1929): 149–66.
Mein, Andrew. *Ezekiel and the Ethics of Exile*. Oxford Theological Monographs. Oxford: Oxford University Press, 2001.
Mendenhall, George E. "The Hebrew Conquest of Palestine." *BA* 25 (1962): 66–87.
Merrill, Eugene H. *Kingdom of Priests: A History of Old Testament Israel*. Grand Rapids: Baker, 1996.
Metso, Sarianna. "In Search of the *Sitz Im Leben* of the *Community Rule*," Pages 306–15 in *The Provo International Conference on the Dead Sea Scrolls: Technological Innovations, New Texts, and Reformuated Issues*. Edited by Donald W. Parry and Eugene Ulrich. STDJ. Leiden: Brill, 1999.
—*The Textual Development of the Qumran Community Rule*. Studies on the Texts of the Desert of Judah 21. Leiden: Brill. 1996.
Mettinger, Tryggve N. D. *Solomonic State Officials: A Study of the Civil Government Officials of the Israelite Monarchy*. ConBoT 5. New Testament Series. Lund: Gleerup, 1971.
Michaeli, Frank. *Les Livres des Chroniques, d'Esdras et de Néhémie*. CAT 16. Neuchâtel: Delachaux & Niestlé, 1967.
Milgrom, Jacob. *Leviticus 1–16: A New Translation with Introduction and Commentary*. AB 3. New York: Doubleday, 1991.
Milik, J. T. "Numérotation des feuilles des rouleaux dans le scriptorium de Qumran (Planches X et XI)." *Semeia* 27 (1977): 75–81.
—*Ten Years of Discovery in the Wilderness of Judaea*. SBT 26. London: SCM Press, 1959.
Millar, William R. *Priesthood in Ancient Israel*. Understanding Biblical Themes. St. Louis, Miss.: Chalice, 2001.
Miller, J. Maxwell. "Reading the Bible Historically: The Historian's Approach." Pages 11–28 in *To Each Its Own Meaning: An Introduction to Biblical Criticisms and Their Applications*. Edited by Stephen R. Haynes and Steven L. McKenzie. Louisville, Ky.: Westminster John Knox, 1993.
Miller, J. Maxwell, and John H. Hayes. *A History of Ancient Israel and Judah*. Philadelphia: Westminster, 1986.

Miller, John W. *The Origins of the Bible: Rethinking Canon History*. Theological Inquiries: Studies in Contemporary Biblical and Theological Problems. New York: Paulist, 1994.

Miller, Patrick D., Paul D. Hanson, and S. Dean McBride, eds. *Ancient Israelite Religion: Essays in Honor of Frank Moore Cross*. Philadelphia: Fortress, 1987.

Milman, Hanry Hart. *The History of the Jews from the Earliest Period Down to Modern Times*. 3 vols. New York: Crowell, 1881.

Min, Kyung-jin, *The Levitical Authorship of Ezra–Nehemiah*. JSOTSup 409. London: T&T Clark International, 2004.

Moehring, Horst R. "The *Acta Pro Judaeis* in the *Antiquities* of Flavius Josephus." Pages 124–58 in *Christianity, Judaism and Other Greco-Roman Cults: Studies for Morton Smith at Sixty*. Edited by Jacob Neusner. SJLA 12. Leiden: Brill, 1975.

Möhlenbrink, K. "Die levitischen überlieferungen des alten testaments." *ZAW* 52 (1934): 184–231.

Montgomery, James A. *The Books of Kings*. ITC. Edinburgh: T. & T. Clark, 1951.

Morgenstern, Julian. "A Chapter in the History of the High Priesthood." *AJSL* 55 (1938): 1–24, 183–97, 360–77.

Mosca, Gaetano. *The Ruling Class*. Translated by Hannah Kahn. New York: McGraw–Hill, 1939.

Myers, Jacob M. *I and II Esdras: Introduction, Translation and Commentary*. AB 42. Garden City, N.Y.: Doubleday, 1974.

—*I Chronicles: Introduction, Translation, and Notes*. AB 12. New York: Doubleday, 1965.

—*Ezra–Nehemiah*. AB 14. New York: Doubleday, 1965.

Nelson, Richard D. *Raising Up a Faithful Priest: Community and Priesthood in Biblical Theology*. Louisville, Ky.: Westminster John Knox, 1993.

Niditch, Susan. "Ezekiel 40–48 in a Visionary Context." *CBQ* 48 (1986): 208–24.

Nodet, Etienne. *A Search for the Origins of Judaism: From Joshua to the Mishnah*. Translated by Ed Crowley. JSOTSup 248. Sheffield: Sheffield Academic Press, 1997.

North, Francis Sparliing. "Aaron's Rise in Prestige." *ZAW* 66 (1954): 191–99.

North, Robert. "Theology of the Chronicler." *JBL* 82 (1963): 369–81.

Noth, Martin. *The Chronicler's History*. JSOTSup 50. Sheffield: JSOT Press, 1987.

—*The Deuteronomistic History*. JSOTSup15. Sheffield: Sheffield Academic Press, 1981. Trans. of pp. 1–110 in *Überlieferungsgeschichtliche Studien*. 2d ed. Tübingen: Niemeyer, 1957. Originally published as "Schriften der Königsberger Gelehrten Gesellschaft." *Geisteswissenschaftliche Klasse* 18 (1943): 43–266.

—*Geschichte Israels*. Göttingen: Vandenhoeck & Ruprecht, 1956.

—*The History of Israel*. 2d ed. New York: Harper & Brothers, 1960.

—*A History of Pentateuchal Traditions*. Translated with an Introduction by Bernhard W. Anderson. Scholars Press Reprints and Translations Series. Atlanta: Scholars Press, 1981. Reprint from Englewood: Prentice–Hall, 1972.

Nurmela, Risto, *The Levites: Their Emergence as a Second-Class Priesthood*, South Florida Studies in the History of Judaism 193.1 Atlanta: Scholars Press, 1998

O'Brien, Julia. *Priest and Levite in Malachi*. SBLDS 121. Atlanta: Scholars Press, 1990.

Odell, Margaret S. "The Inversion of Shame and Forgiveness in Ezekiel 16.59–63." *JSOT* 56 (1992): 101–12.

Oesterley, W. O. E., and Theodore H. Robinson. *Introduction to the Books of the Old Testament*. New York: Macmillan, 1934.

—*A History of Israel: From the Fall of Jerusalem, 586 B.C. To the Bar-Kokhba Revolt, A.D. 135*, vol. 2. Oxford: Clarendon, 1934–38.

Olyan, Saul M. "Ben Sira's Relationship to the Priesthood." *HTR* 80 (1987): 261–86.

—"Zadok's Origins and the Tribal Politics of David." *JBL* 101 (1982): 177–93.

Pakkala, Juha. *Ezra the Scribe: The Development of Ezra 7:10 and Nehemiah 8*. BZAW 347. Berlin: de Gruyter, 2004.

Pareto, Vilredo. *The Mind and Society*. Translated by A. Bongiorno and Arthur Livingstone. New York: Harcourt, Brace & World, 1935.

Patton, Corrine L. "'Should Our Sister Be Treated Like a Whore?' A Response to Feminist Critiques of Ezekiel 23." Pages 221–38 in *Book of Ezekiel*. Atlanta: Society of Biblical Literature, 2000.

Pedersen, Johannes. *Israel: Its Life and Culture*. 2 vols. Repr. South Florida Studies in the History of Judaism 29. Repr. Atlanta: Scholars, 1991.

Petersen, David L. "The Temple in Persian Period Prophetic Texts." Pages 125–45 in Davies, eds., *Second Temple Studies*, vol. 1.

Pfeiffer, Robert H. "Books of Ezra and Nehemiah." *IDB* 215–19.

—*History of New Testament Times with an Introduction to the Apocrypha*. New York: Harper, 1949.

—*Introduction to the Old Testament*. New York: Harper, 1941.

Pick, B. "The Jewish High Priests Subsequent to the Return from Babylon." *The Lutheran Church Review* 17 (1898): 127–42.

Polyani, Michael. *Personal Knowledge: Towards Post-Critical Philosophy*. New York: Harper & Row, Torchbooks, 1964.

Pope, Marvin H. "Mixed Marriage Metaphor in Ezekiel 16." Pages 384–99 in *Fortunate the Eyes That See: Essays in Honor of David Noel Freedman in Celebration of His Seventieth Birthday*. Edited by Astrid B. Beck et al. Grand Rapids: Eerdmans, 1995.

Provan, Iain, V. Philips Long, and Tremper Longman III. *A Biblical History of Israel*. Louisville, Ky.: Westminster John Knox, 2003.

Qimron, Elisha, and John Strugnell. *Qumran Cave 4: V: Miqṣat Maʿaśe ha-Torah*. DJD 10. Oxford: Clarendon, 1994.

Rad, G. von. *Old Testament Theology*. Vol. 1, *The Theology of Israel's Historical Traditions*. Translated by D.M.G. Stalker. New York: HarperCollins, 1962. Trans. of *Theologie des Alten Testamets*. Vol. 1, *Die Theologie der geschichtlichen Überlieferungen Israels*. Munich: Kaiser, 1957.

Ramsey, George W. "Zadok." *ABD* 4:1034–36.

Redford, Donald B. *Egypt, Canaan, and Israel in Ancient Times*. Princeton: Princeton University Press, 1992.

Redpath, H. A. *The Book of the Prophet Ezekiel*. London: Methune, 1907.

Rehm, M. D. "Levites and Priests." *ABD* 4:297–310.

Reif, Stefan C. "The Discovery of the Cambridge Genizah Fragments of Ben Sira: Scholars and Texts." Pages 1–22 in Beentjes, ed., *The Book of Ben Sira in Modern Research*.

Rendtorff, Rolf. "The Paradigm Is Changing: Hopes—and Fears." *BibInt* 1 (1992): 34–55.

—"What Happened to the Yahwist: Reflections After Thirty Years," *SBL Forum* 4 no. 5 (August 2006). No pages. Online: http://www.sbl-site.org/Article.aspx?ArticleId=553.

Ribuffo, Leo P. "Confession of an Accidental Historian." Pages 143–63 in Fox-Genovese and Lasch-Quinn, eds., *Reconstructing History.*

Robinson, H. Wheeler. *Two Hebrew Prophets: Studies in Hosea and Ezekiel.* London: Lutterworth, 1948.

Robinson, Theodore H. *A History of Israel: From the Exodus to the Fall of Jerusalem, 586 B.C.* 2 vols. Oxford: Clarendon, 1932.

Rofé, A. "The Beginnings of Sects in Post-Exilic Judaism." *Cathedra* 49 (1988): 13–22.

Rooke, Deborah W. *Zadok's Heirs: The Role and Development* of the High Priesthood in Ancient Israel. Oxford Theological Monographs. Oxford: Oxford University Press, 2000.

Rowley, H. H. "The Book of Ezekiel in Modern Study." *BJRL* 36 (1953): 146–90.

—*The Growth of the Old Testament.* London: Hutchinson University Library, 1950.

—*Worship in Ancient Israel: Its Forms and Meanings.* London: SPCK, 1967.

—"Zadok and Nehushtan." *JBL* 58 (1939): 113–41.

—*The Zadokite Fragments and the Dead Sea Scrolls.* New York: Macmillan, 1952.

Rudolph, W. *Chronikbücher.* HAT 1/21. Tübingen: Mohr, 1955.

—*Ezra und Nehemia.* HAT 1/20. Tübingen: Mohr, 1949.

Russell, D. S. *The Jews from Alexander to Herod.* The New Clarendon Bible: Old Testament 5. London: Oxford University Press, 1967.

Sabourin, Leopold. *Priesthood: A Comparative Study.* Studies in the History of Religions 25. Leiden: Brill, 1973.

Sacchi, Paolo. *The History of the Second Temple Period.* JSOTSup 285. Sheffield: Sheffield Academic Press, 2000.

Sandmel, Samuel. *The Hebrew Scriptures: An Introduction to Their Literature and Religious Ideas.* New York: Knopf, 1963.

—*Judaism and Christian Beginnings.* New York: Oxford University Press, 1978.

Sasson, Jack M. "A Genealogical 'Convention' in Biblical Chronography?" *ZAW* 90 (1978): 171–85.

Schearing, Linda S. "Jerusha." *ABD* 3:768.

Schüer, Emil. *A History of the Jewish People in the Time of Jesus Christ.* Edinburgh: T. & T. Clark, 1890.

Schechter, Solomon. *Documents of Jewish Sectaries: Fragments of a Zadokite Work.* Two vols. in one. The Library of Biblical Studies. New York: Ktav, 1910.

—"Introduction." Pages v–x in *The Wisdom of Ben Sira: Portions of the Book Ecclesiasticus from Hebrew Manuscripts in the Cairo Genizah Collection Presented to the University of Cambridge by the Editors.* Edited by S. Schecther and C. Taylor. Cambridge: Cambridge University Press, 1899.

Schiffman, Lawrence H. "The New Halakhic Letter (4QMMT) and the Origins of the Dead Sea Sect." *BA* 52 (1990): 64–73.

—*Reclaiming the Dead Sea Scrolls: Their True Meaning for Judaism and Christianity.* New York: Doubleday, 1994.

Schiffman, Lawrence H., and James C. VanderKam, eds. *Encyclopedia of the Dead Sea Scrolls*, vol. 1. New York: Oxford University Press, 2000.

—*From Text to Tradition: A History of Second Temple and Rabbinic Judaism.* Hoboken: Ktav, 1991.

Schwartz, Daniel R. "Law and Truth: On Qumran-Sadducean and Rabbinic Views of Law," Pages 229–40 in Dimant and Rappaport, eds., *The Dead Sea Scrolls.*

—"On Two Aspects of a Priestly View of Descent at Qumran." Pages 157–79 in *Archaeology and History in the Dead Sea Scrolls: The New York University*

Conference in Memory of Yigael Yadin. JSPSup 8. JSOT/ASOR Monographs 2. Sheffield: JSOT Press, 1990.

Scolnic, Benjamin E. *Chronology and Papponymy: A List of the Judean High Priests of the Persian Period*. The Hebrew Scriptures and Their World. Atlanta: Scholars Press, 1999.

Skehan, Patrick W., and Alexander A. Di Lella. *The Wisdom of Ben Sira: A New Translation with Notes; Introduction and Commentary*. AB 39. New York: Doubleday, 1987.

Smend, Rudolf. "Julius Wellhausen and His *Prolegomena to the History of Israel*." *Semeia* 25 (1983): 1–20.

Smith, Morton. *Palestinian Parties and Politics That Shaped the Old Testament*. New York: Columbia University Press, 1971.

Smith, W. F. "A Study of the Zadokite High Priesthood Within the Graeco-Roman Age: From Simeon the Just to the High Priests Appointed by Herod and Great." Ph.D. diss., Harvard University, 1961.

Smith, W. R., and A. Bertholet. "Priests." Pages 3837–47 in *Encyclopaedia Biblical: A Critical Dictionary of the Literary Political and Religious History the Archaeology Geography and Natural History of the Bible*. Edited by R. K. Cheyne and J. Sutherland Black. New York: Macmillan, 1902.

Soggin, J. Alberto. *A History of Ancient Israel*. Philadelphia: Westminster, 1984.

Sparks, Kenton L. *Ethnicity and Identity in Ancient Israel: Prolegomena to the Study of Ethnic Sentiments and their Expression in the Hebrew Bible*. Winona Lake, Ind.: Eisenbrauns, 1998.

Spinoza, Benedict de. *A Theologico-Political Treatise and a Political Treatise*. Translated by R. H. M. Elwes. New York: Dover Publications, 1951.

Stamm, J. J. "Hebräische Frauennamen." Pages 301–39 in *Hebräische Wortforschung. Festschrift zum 80. Geburstag von Walter Baumgartner*. Edited by Benedikt Hartmann et al. VTSup 16. Leiden: Brill, 1967.

Stanford, Michael. *An Introduction to the Philosophy of History*. Oxford: Blackwell, 1998.

Stegemann, Hartmut. "The Qumran Essenes—Local Members of the Main Jewish Union in Late Second Temple Times." Pages 83–166 in *The Madrid Qumran Congress: Proceedings of the International Congress on the Dead Sea Scrolls, Madrid 18–21 March, 1991*, vol. 1. Edited by Julio Trebolle Barrera and Luis Vegas Montaner. Leiden: Brill, 1992.

Stern, Ephraim. "Aspects of Jewish Society: The Priesthood and Other Classes." Pages 561–630 in *The Jewish People in the First Century: Historical Geography, Political History, Social, Cultural and Religious Life and Institutions*, vol. 2. Edited by S. Safrai and M. Stern. Amsterdam: Van Gorcum, 1976.

—"The Persian Empire and the Political and Social History of Palestine in the Persian Period." *CHJ* 70–87.

Stern, Menachem. "Priests and Priesthood: From the Beginning of the Hellenistic Era until the Destruction of the Temple." *EncJud* 1087–88.

Talmon, Shermaryahu. "The Emergence of Jewish Sectarianism in the Early Second Temple Period." Pages 587–616 in Miller, Hanson, and McBride, eds., *Ancient Israelite Religion*.

—"The Internal Diversification of Judaism in the Early Second Temple Period." Pages 16–43 in *Jewish Civilization in the Hellenistic-Roman Period*. Edited by Shermaryahu Talmon. Philadelphia: Trinity, 1991.

Tcherikover, Victor. *Hellenistic Civilization and the Jews*. Translated by S. Applebaum. Philadelphia: The Jewish Publication Society of America, The Magnes Press, 1959.

Thernstrom, Stephan. "Review Symposium: Gerhard E. Lenski, Power and Privilege: A Theory of Social Stratificaiton." *American Sociological Review* 31 (1966): 719–20.

Thompson, Thomas L. "Defining History and Ethnicity in the South Levant." Pages 166–78 in *Can a "History of Israel" Be Written?* Edited by Lester L. Grabbe. JSOTSup 245. Sheffield: Sheffield Academic Press. 1997.

—*Early History of the Israelite People: From the Written and Archaeological Sources*. Studies in the History of the Ancient Near East 4. Leiden: Brill, 1992.

—"Hidden Histories and the Problem of Ethnicity in Palestine." Pages 23–39 in *Western Scholarship and the History of Palestine*. Edited by Michael Prior. London: Melisende, 1998.

—*The Mythic Past: Biblical Archaeology and the Myth of Israel*. London: Basic Books, 1999.

Throntveit, Mark A. *When Kings Speak: Royal Speech and Royal Prayer in Chronicles*. SBLDS 93. Atlanta: Scholars Press, 1987.

Torrey, Charles Cutler. *The Composition and Historical Value of Ezra–Nehemiah*. BZAW 2. Giessen: Ricker, 1896.

—*Pseudo-Ezekiel and the Original Prophecy*. Yale Oriental Series: Researches 18. New Haven: Yale University Press, 1930.

Tuell, Steven. *The Law of the Temple in Ezekiel 40–48*. HSM 49. Atlanta: Scholars Press, 1992.

VanderKam, James. C. *From Joshua to Caiaphas: High Priests After the Exile*. Minneapolis: Fortress, 2004.

—"Jewish High Priests of the Persian Period: Is the List Complete?" Pages 67–91 in *Priesthood and Cult in Ancient Israel*. Edited by G. Anderson and S. Olyan. Sheffield: Sheffield Academic Press, 1991.

—"The People of the Dead Sea Scrolls: Essenes or Sadducees?." *BR* (April 1991): 42–47.

—"Zadok and the SPR HTWRH HTWM in Dam. Doc. V, 2–5." *RevQ* 11 (1984): 561–70.

Van Seters, John. *In Search of History: Historiography in the Ancient World and the Origins of Biblical History*. New Haven: Yale University Press, 1983.

van Dijk-Hemmes, Fokkelien. "The Metaphorization of Woman in Prophetic Speech: An Analysis of Ezekiel 23." Pages 167–76 in *On Gendering Texts: Female and Male Voices in the Hebrew Bible*. Edited by Athalya Brenner and F. van Dijk-Hemmes. BibInt Series 1. Leiden: Brill, 1993.

Vermes, Geza. *The Dead Sea Scrolls in English*. 4th ed. London: Penguin, 1995.

—*The Dead Sea Scrolls: Qumran in Perspective*. London: Collins, 1977.

—*Discovery in the Judean Desert*. New York: Desclee, 1956.

—"The Leadership of the Qumran Community: Sons of Zadok–Priests–Congregation." Pages 375–84 in *Geschichte–Tradition–Reflexion: Festschrift für Martin Hengel zum 70. Geburtstag*. Edited by Hubert Cancik, Hermann Lichtenberger, and Peter Schäfer. Tübingen: J. C. B. Mohr, 1996.

—"Preliminary Remarks on Unpublished Fragments of the Community Rule Form Qumran Cave 4." *JJS* 42 (1991): 250–55.

Wallerstein, Immanuel. *The Modern World-System*, vol. 1. New York: Academic Press, 1974.

Weber, Max. *Ancient Judaism.* Translated and edited by Hans H. Gerth and Don Martindale. New York: Free Press/Macmillan, 1982.

Weems, Renita J. *Battered Love: Marriage, Sex, and Violence in the Hebrew Prophets.* OBT. Minneapolis: Fortress, 1995.

Weingreen, Jacob, *From Bible to Mishna: The Continuity of* Tradition (Manchester: Manchester University Press, 1976.

Welch, A. C. *The Work of the Chronicler.* London: Oxford University Press, 1939.

Wellhausen, Julius. *Prolegomena to the History of Ancient Israel.* Edinburgh: A. & C. Black, 1885.

Wernberg-Møller, P. "צדק, צדיק and צודק in the Zadokite Fragments (CDC), the Manual of Discipline (DSD) and the Habakkuk-Commentary (DSH)." *VT* 3 (1953): 310–15.

Whitelam, Keith. *The Invention of Ancient Israel: The Silencing of Palestinian History.* London: Routledge, 1994.

Widengren, G. "The Persian Period." Pages 489–538 in Hayes and Miller, eds., *Israelite and Judaean History.*

Willi, Thomas. *Die Chronik als Auslegung: Untersuchungen zur literarischen Gestaltung der historischen Überlieferung Israels.* Göttingen, Vandenhoeck & Ruprecht, 1972.

—"Late Persian Judaism and Its Conception of an Integral Israel According to Chronicles." Pages 146–62 in Eskenazi and Richards, eds., *Second Temple Studies,* vol. 2.

Williamson, H. G. M. *1 and 2 Chronicles.* NCB. Grand Rapids: Eerdmans, 1982.

—*Ezra and Nehemiah.* OTG 13. Sheffield: JSOT Press, 1987.

—"The Origins of the Twenty-Four Priestly Courses." Pages 251–68 in *Studies in the Historical Books of the Old Testament.* Edited by J. A. Emerton. VTSup 30. Leiden: Brill, 1979.

Wilson, Robert R. *Genealogy and History in the Biblical World.* New Haven: Yale University Press, 1977.

—*Prophecy and Society in Ancient Israel.* Philadelphia: Fortress, 1980.

—"The Old Testament Genealogies in Recent Research." *JBL* 94 (1975): 169–89.

Winter, Paul. "Twenty-Six Priestly Courses." *VT* 6 (1956): 215–17.

Wright, Benjamin G. " 'Fear the Lord and Honor the Priest': Ben Sira as Defender of the Jerusalem Priesthood." Pages 189–222 in Beentjes, ed., *The Book of Ben Sira in Modern Research.*

Yee, Gale A. *Poor Banished Children of Eve: Women as Evil in the Hebrew Bible.* Minneapolis: Fortress, 2004.

Zimmerli, Walther. *Ezekiel 2: A Commentary on the Book of the Prophet Ezekiel Chapters 25–48.* Translated by James D. Martin. Hermeneia—A Critical and Historical Commentary on the Bible. Philadelphia: Fortress, 1983.

INDEXES

INDEX OF REFERENCES

INDEX OF AUTHORS